Chas Addams

Happily Ever After

Chas Addams™

Happily Ever After

SIMON & SCHUSTER

New York   London   Toronto   Sydney

Many of the cartoons in this book were previously published
in other books and periodicals. See page 163 for acknowledgments.

Photograph on page vii © 1980, Lane Stewart.
Photograph on page viii © 1980, R. Thurber

Simon & Schuster
Rockefeller Center
1230 Avenue of the Americas
New York, NY 10020
Copyright © 2006 by Tee and Charles Addams Foundation.

For information about special discounts for bulk purchases,
please contact Simon & Schuster Special Sales at
1-800-456-6798 or business@simonandschuster.com.

Designed by Kim Llewellyn

Manufactured in the United States of America

1 3 5 7 9 10 8 6 4 2

Library of Congress Cataloging-in-Publication Data
Addams, Charles, 1912–1988
Happily ever after / Chas Addams.
p.   cm.
I. American wit and humor, Pictorial. 2. Love—Caricatures and cartoons.
3. Marriage—Caricatures and cartoons. I. Title.
NC1429.A25A4 2006
741.5'973—dc22
2005054663
ISBN-13: 978-1-4767-1120-1

Chas Addams

CHARLES SAMUEL ADDAMS (1912–1988) was the creator of the "Addams Family" cartoons, which first appeared in *The New Yorker* magazine in the 1930s. They became the inspiration for the popular television series, *The Addams Family*, debuting in 1964. Since then, sitcoms, animated television programs, and two motion pictures have been produced. Among his many achievements, he was honored with both the Yale Humor Award and a Special Edgar Award for "Cartoonist of the Macabre" by the Mystery Writers of America, Inc. in 1954. Although he coveted his longtime cubicle within the New Yorker offices, he divided much of the latter part of his life between a studio apartment in Manhattan and a cottage and converted stables in Westhampton Beach, while relishing visits with his abundance of close friends.

Charles Addams savored a prolific love life that was punctuated by a failed first marriage and a disastrous second one. Simultaneous to his bountiful dalliances, Addams was a lifelong collector of ancient armor

and weaponry and devices of execution and torture, part of his steadfast fascination with death and dying. Following a twenty-four year hiatus from the sanctity of marriage, he exchanged vows one last time in 1980, in characteristic Addams style, all dressed in black, when he wed Tee Matthews in her Water Mill, New York pet cemetery.

It should come as no surprise that he delighted in incorporating these diverse passions into a multitude of cartoons which focus on romantic torment and wedded mayhem. As both reporter and inventor, Addams introduced a stab of abnormality into the mundaneness of everyday life, giving equal motivation to the partners in their plots of each others demise, a recurring theme that appeared throughout his five decades in print.

This volume is a collection of Charles Addams's published and previously unpublished work dedicated to that treacherous revenge and that well deserved retribution of which most real-life partners in any relationship dare only dream.

—H. Kevin Miserocchi
October 2005

Tee and Charles Addams Foundation

In 1999 his late widow, Tee, founded the Tee and Charles Addams Foundation as a not-for-profit organization devoted to educating the public about the lifetime achievements in cartoon art that are the legacy of Charles Addams. In continuation of a tradition with Simon & Schuster started by Addams in 1950, which resulted in the publication of nine books of cartoons over thirty years, the Foundation reissued *The Charles Addams Mother Goose* as a deluxe edition in 2002 with the Books for Young Readers division. In October 2005, the publication of the *Chas Addams Half-Baked Cookbook* marked the beginning of a new association with the Adult Publishing Group of Simon & Schuster, Inc.

In the Beginning

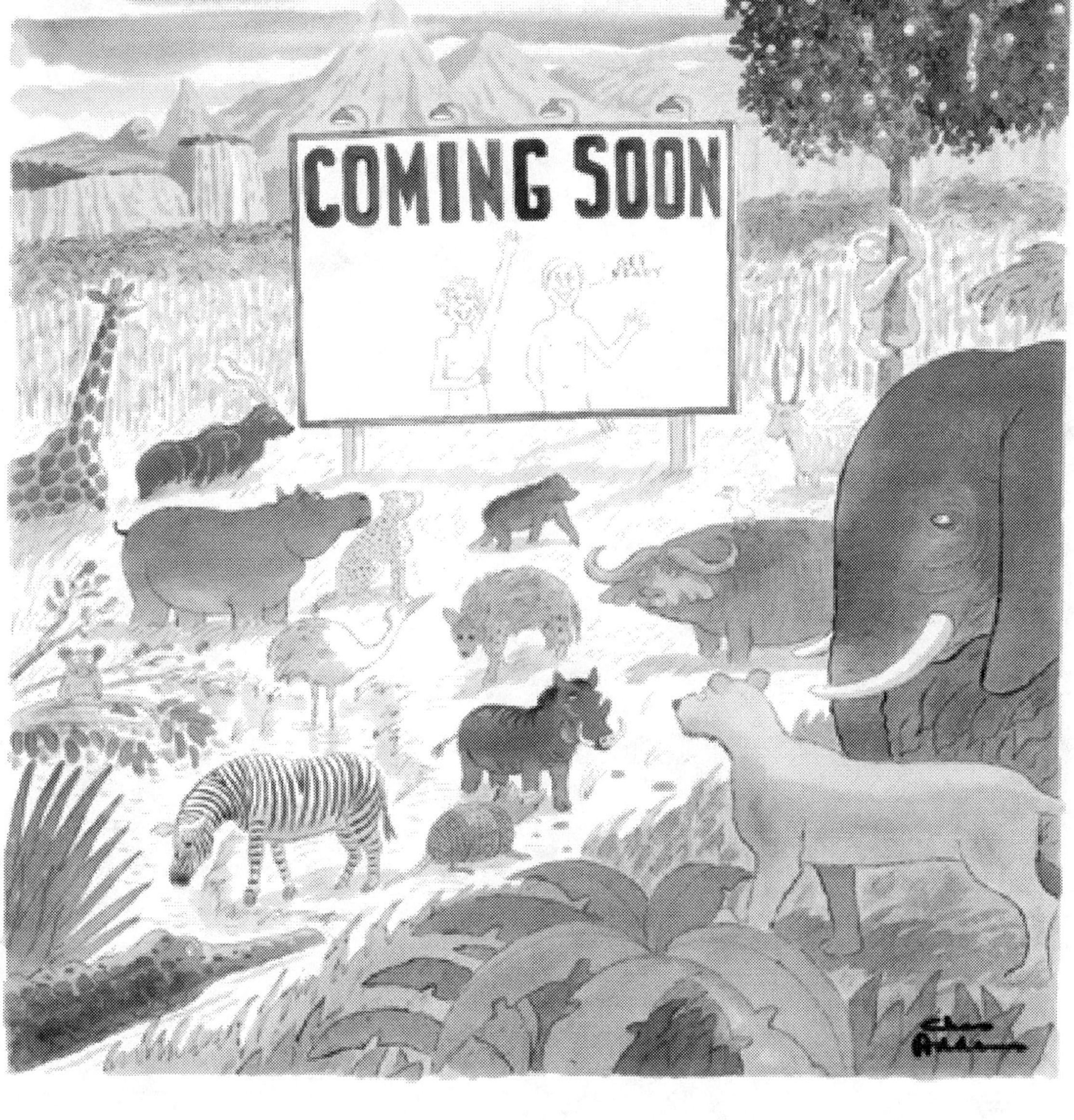
COMING SOON

On the FIFTH DAY

"Now, remember—act casual."

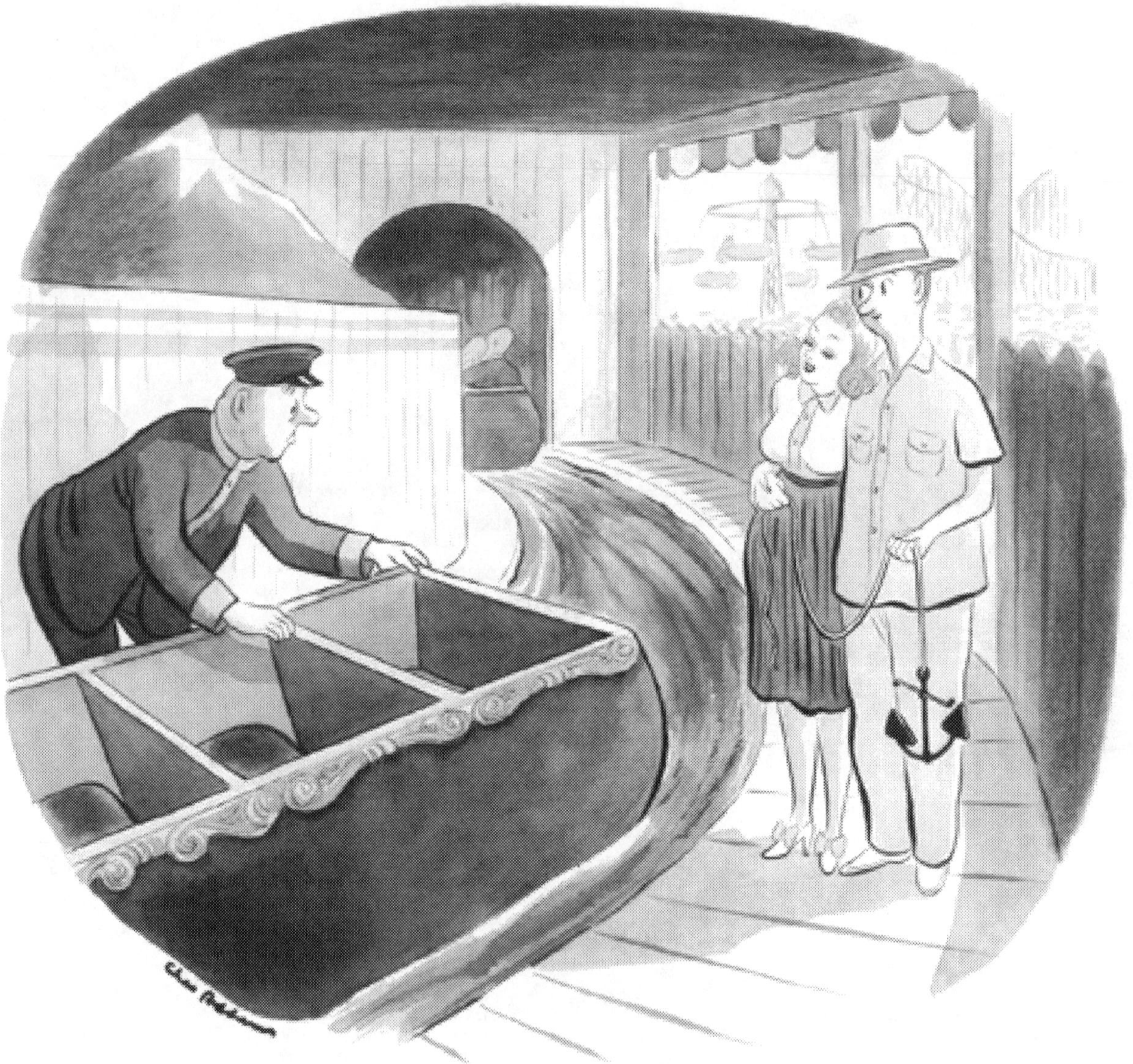

"She'll get him—it's just a question of time."

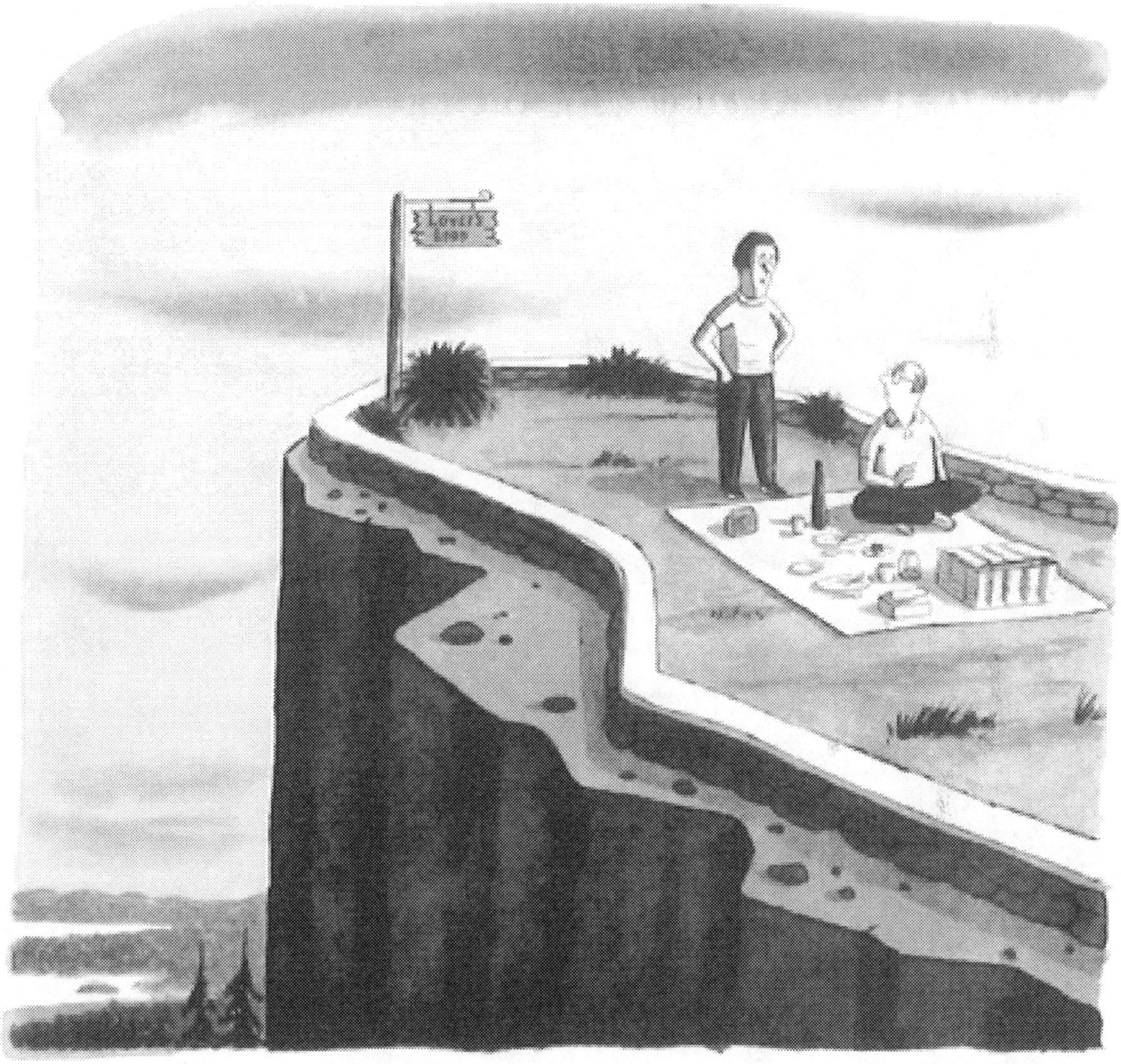

"Well, I'm ready if you are."

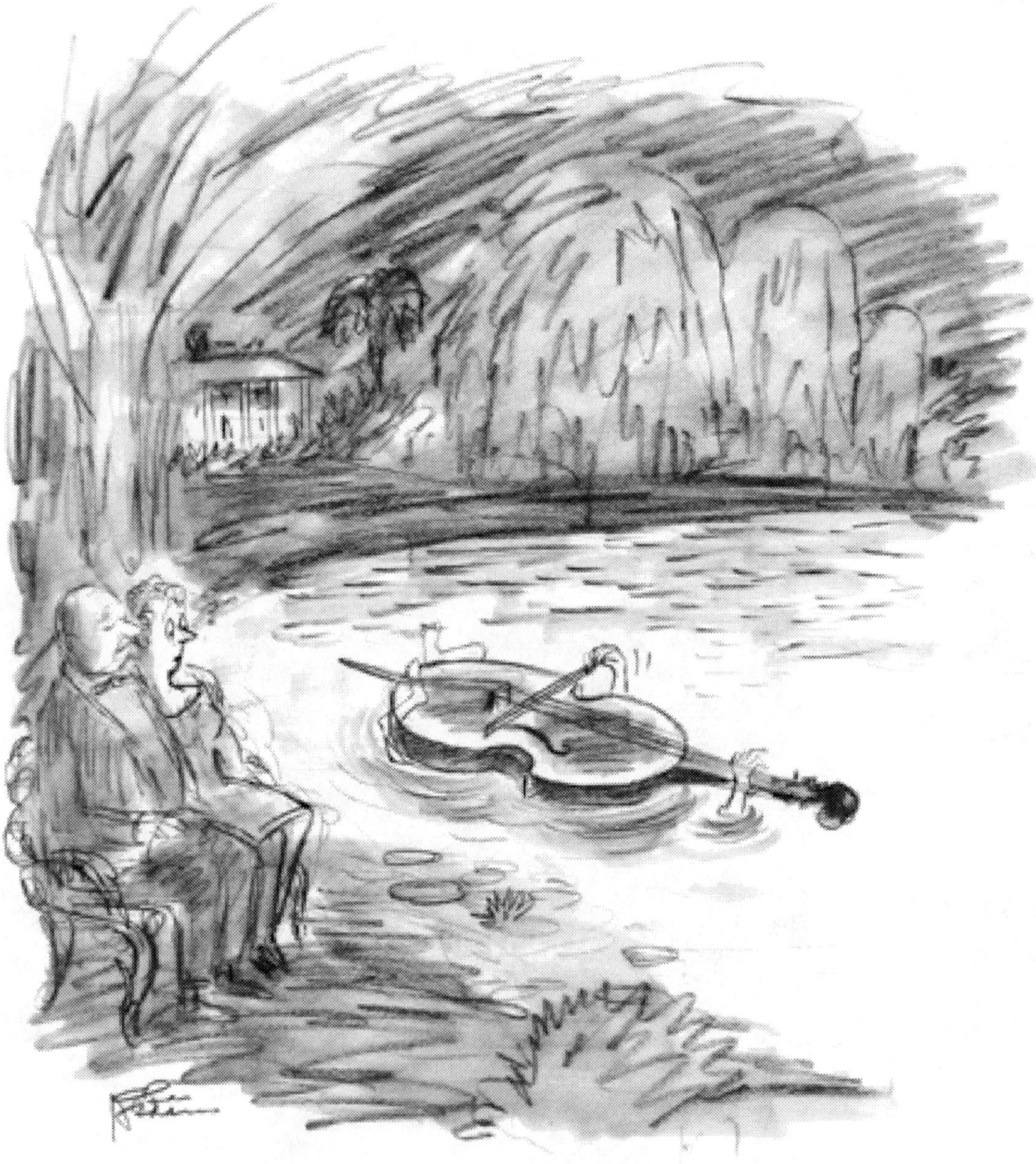

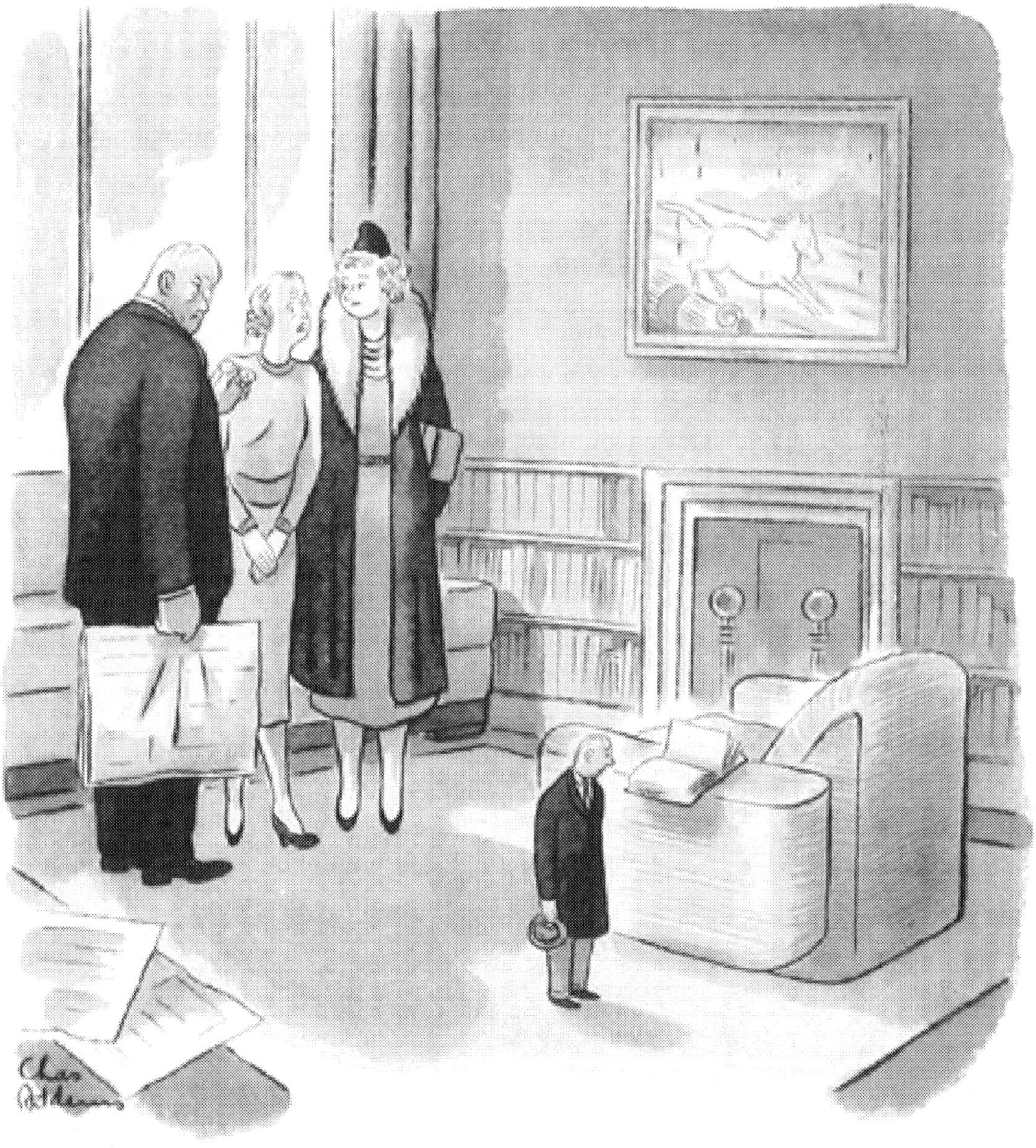

"Your father and I think he's very nice, dear, but he's awfully short, isn't he?"

"He still looks like a frog if you ask me."

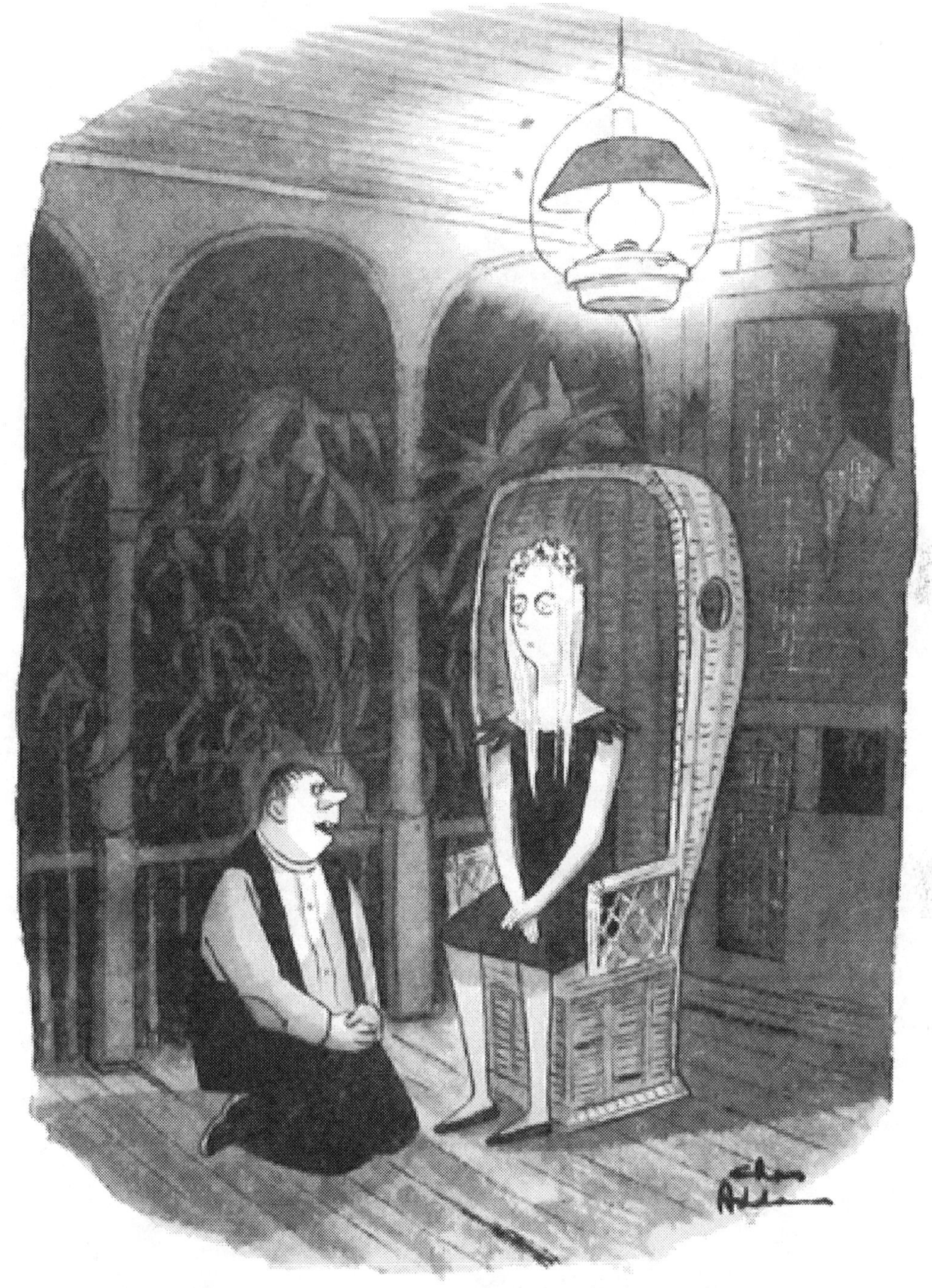

"There's enough hate in my heart for both of us."

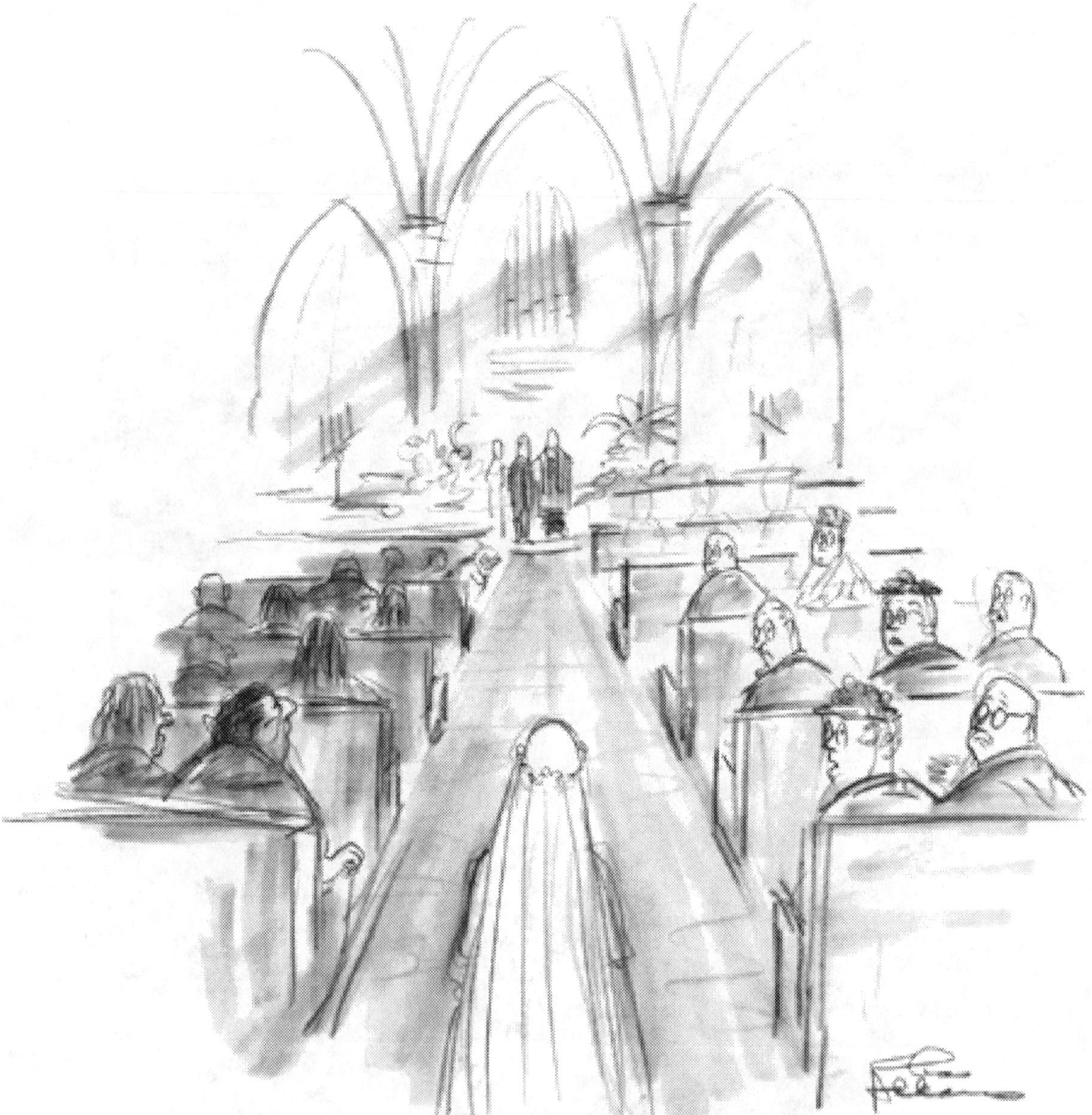

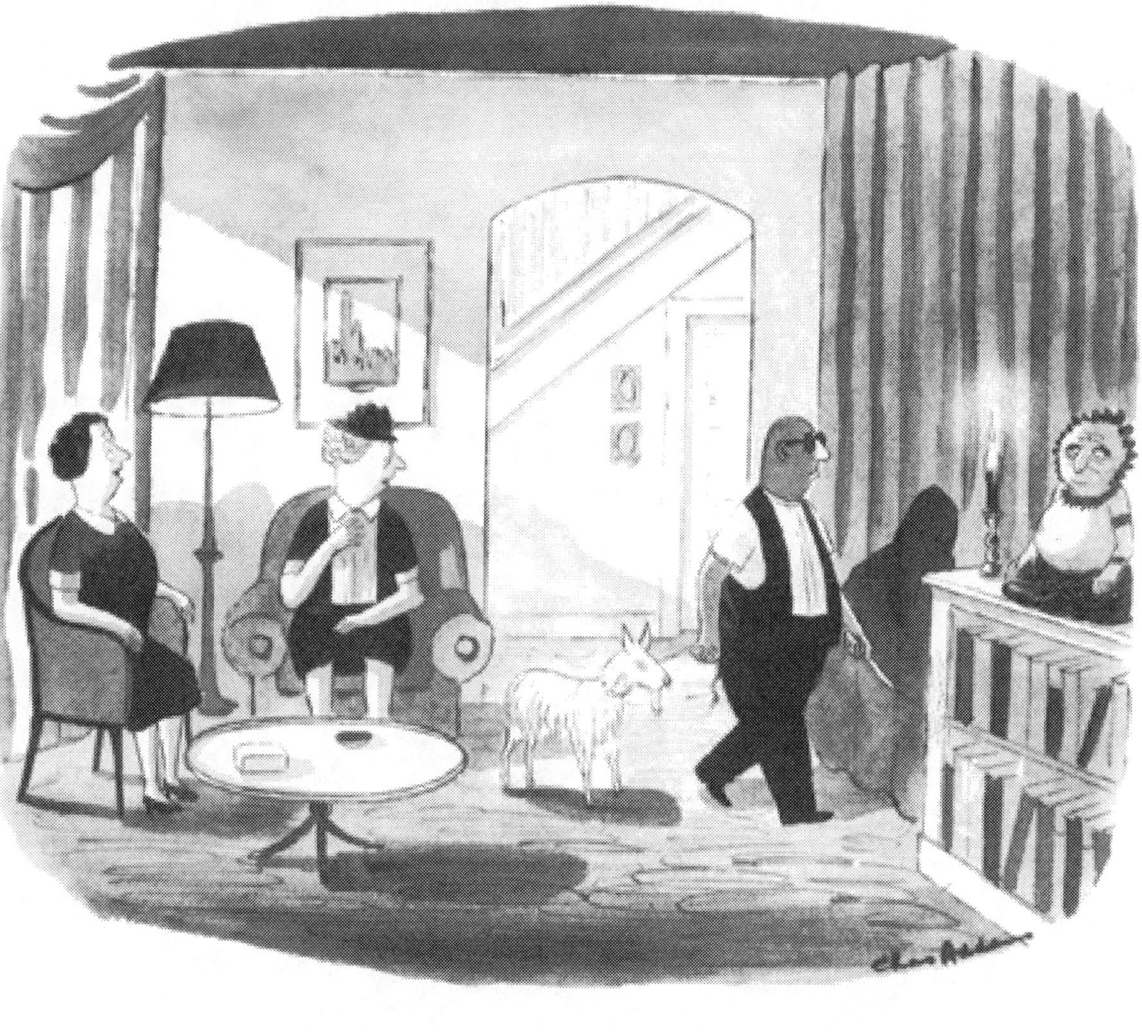

"Of course, my parents were furious when I married outside my religion."

"I'd love to marry you, Joe, but I'm already married to a flounder."

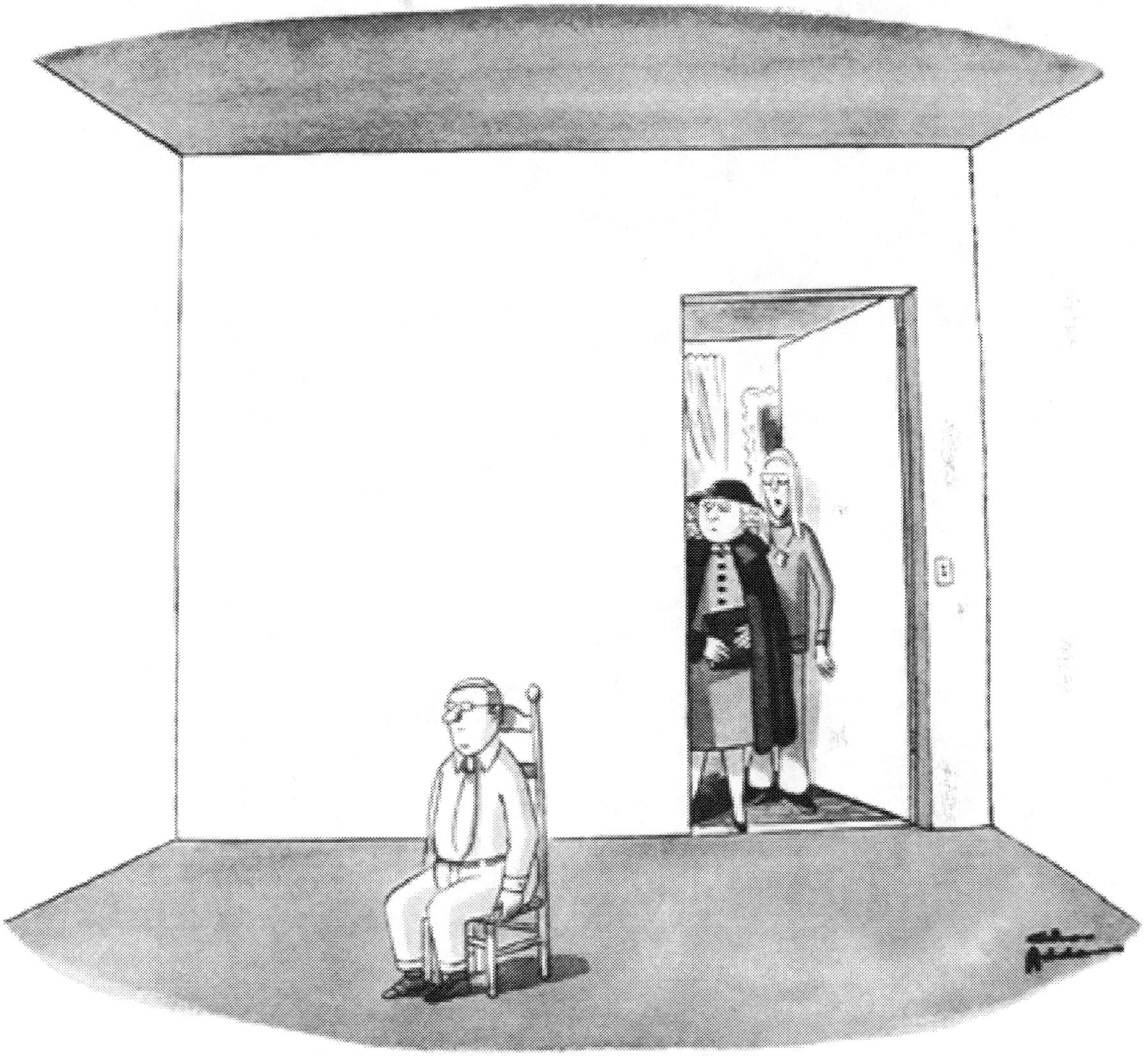

"This is Rodney's room."

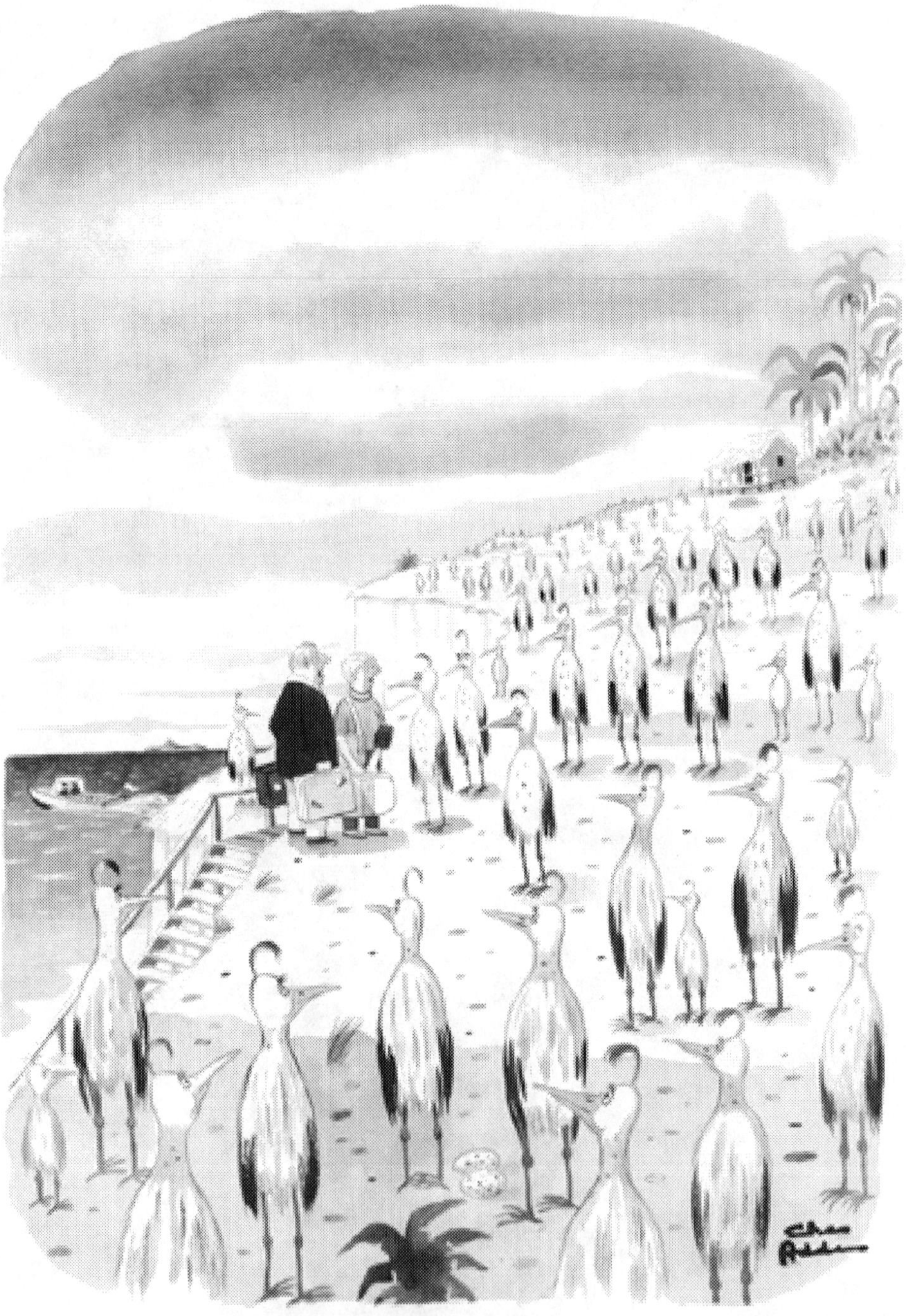

"Well, you wanted a place with more birds than people."

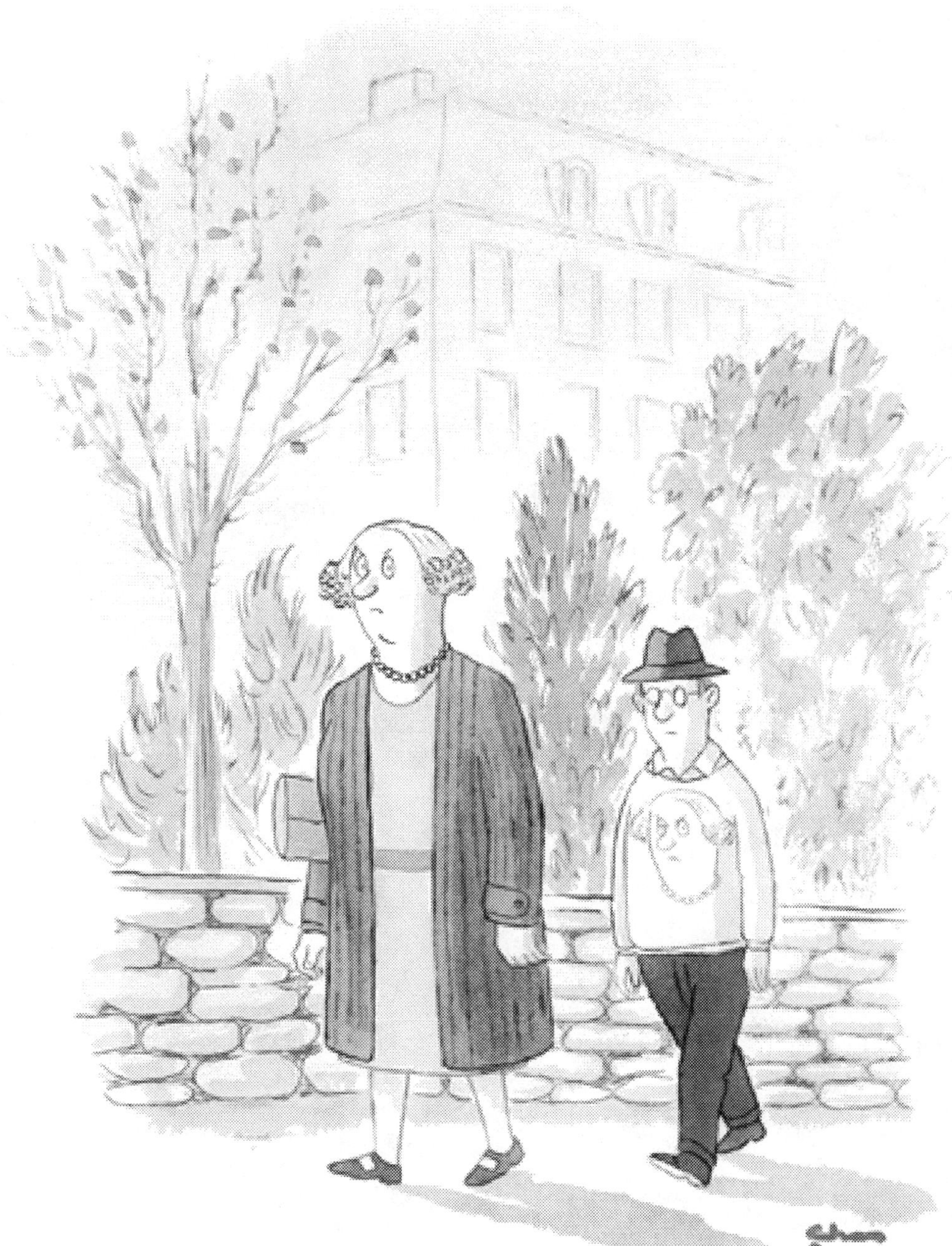

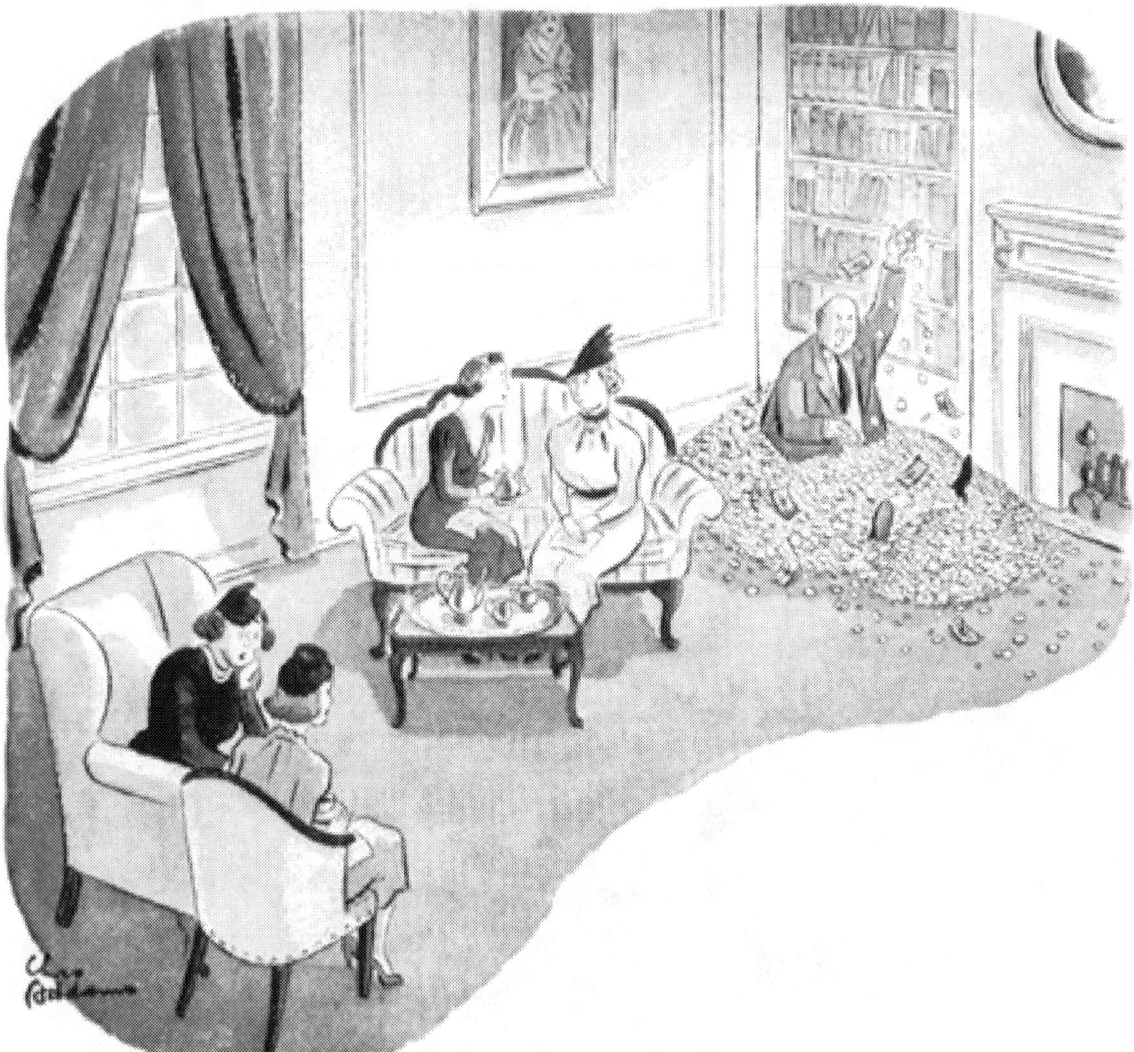

"He must have married her for her money."

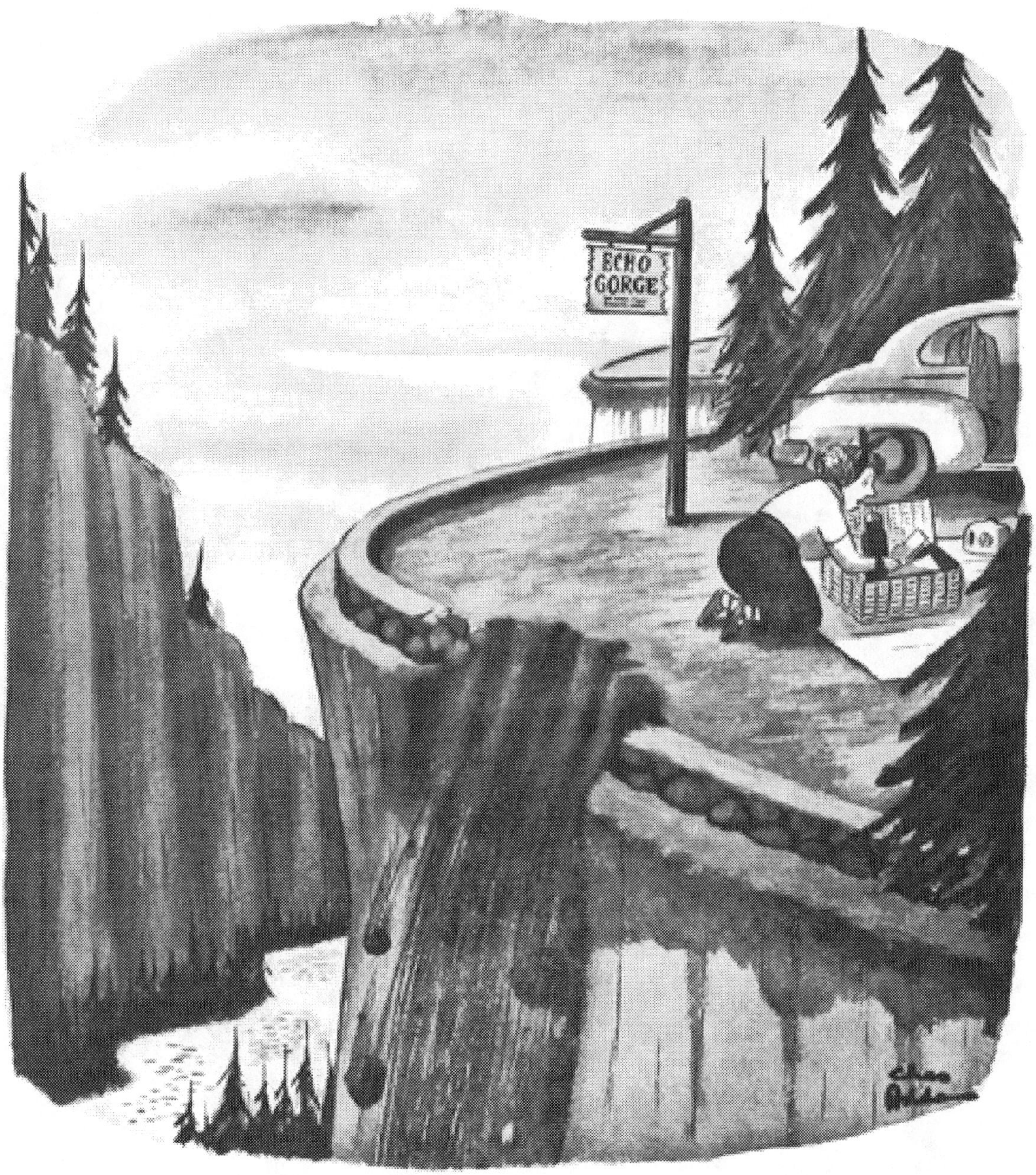
ECHO
GORGE

"For heaven's sake, Ed, holler something besides 'help.'
People might think we're really in trouble."

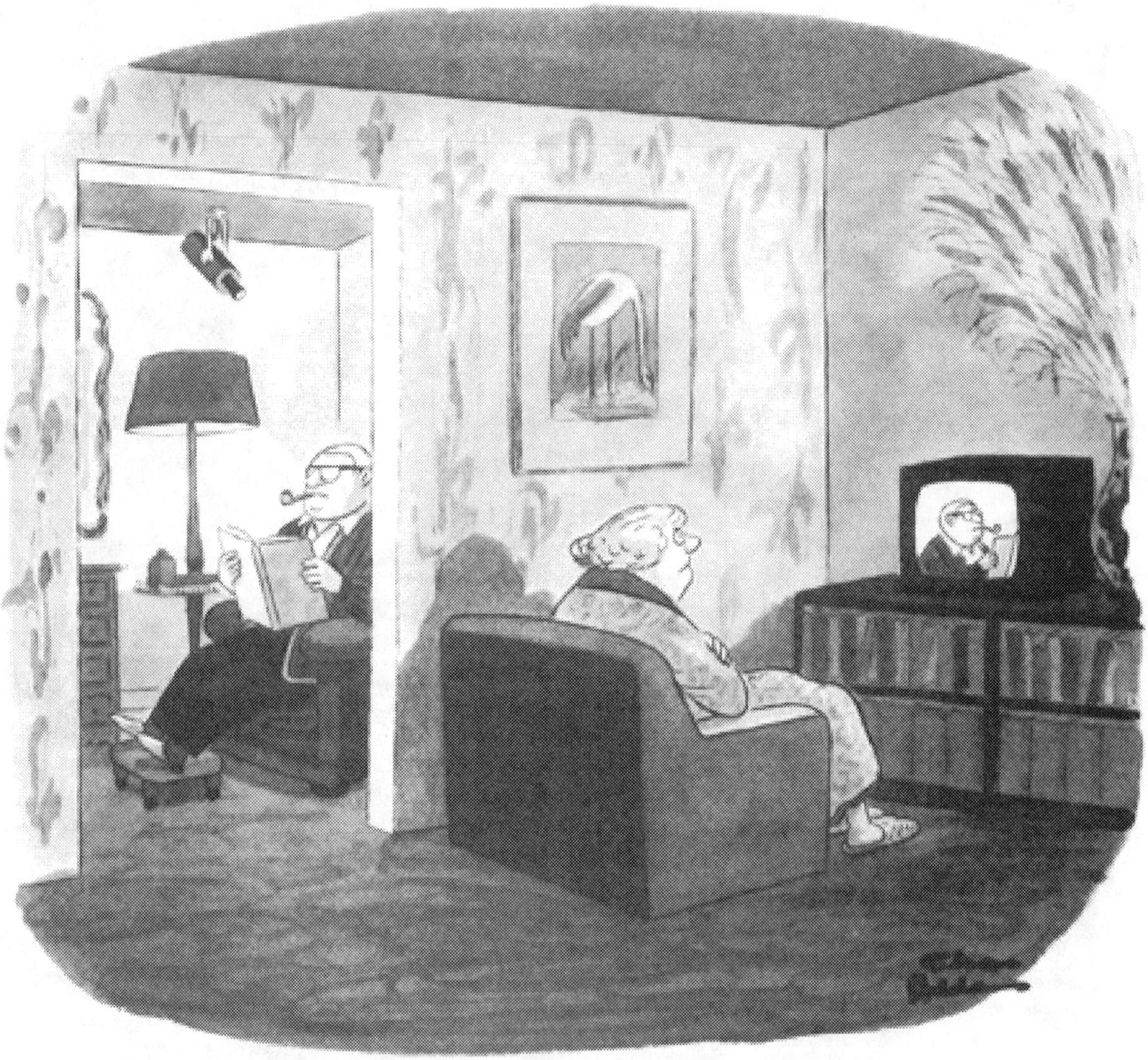

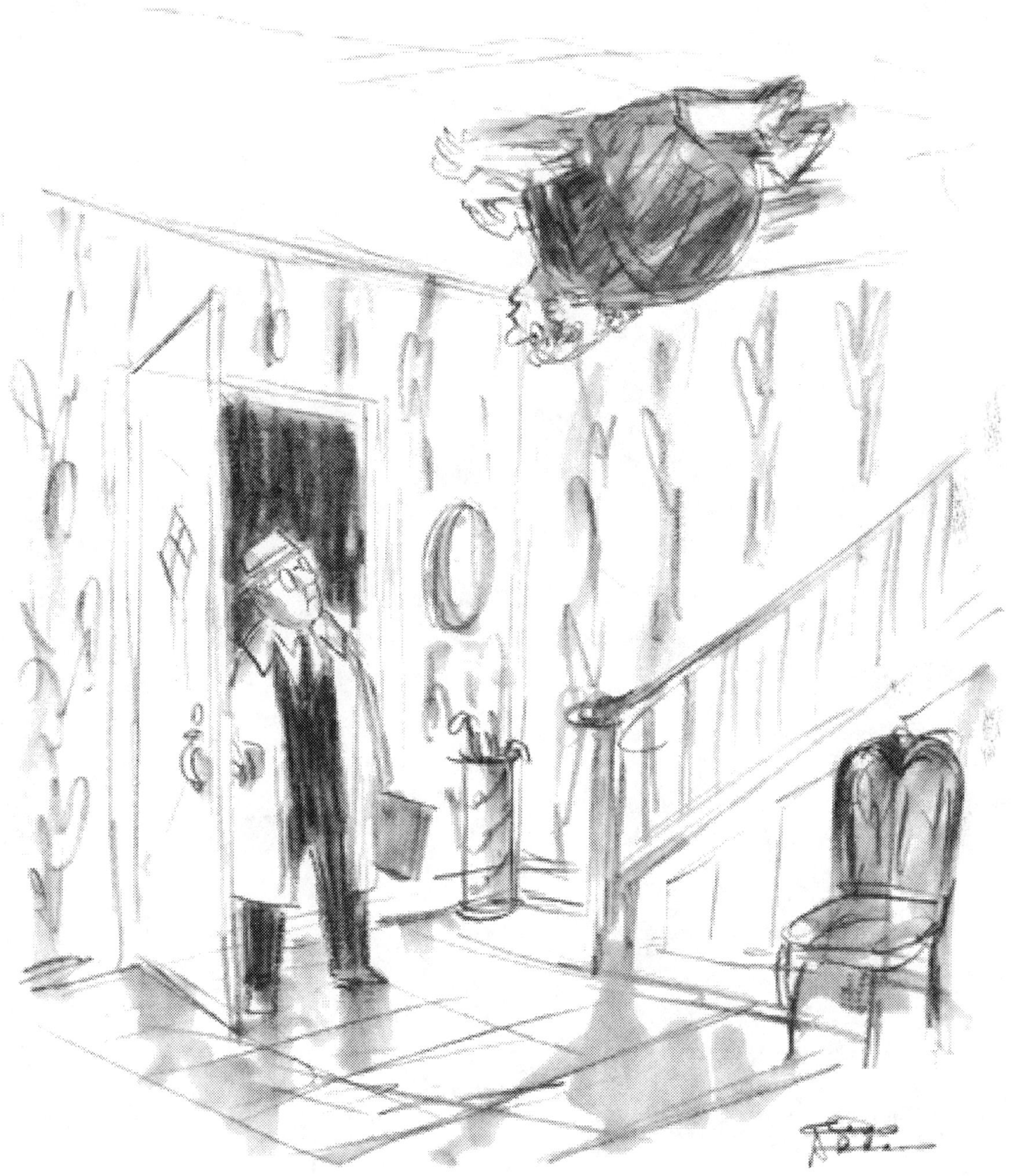

"Thank heavens you're home, Albert!"

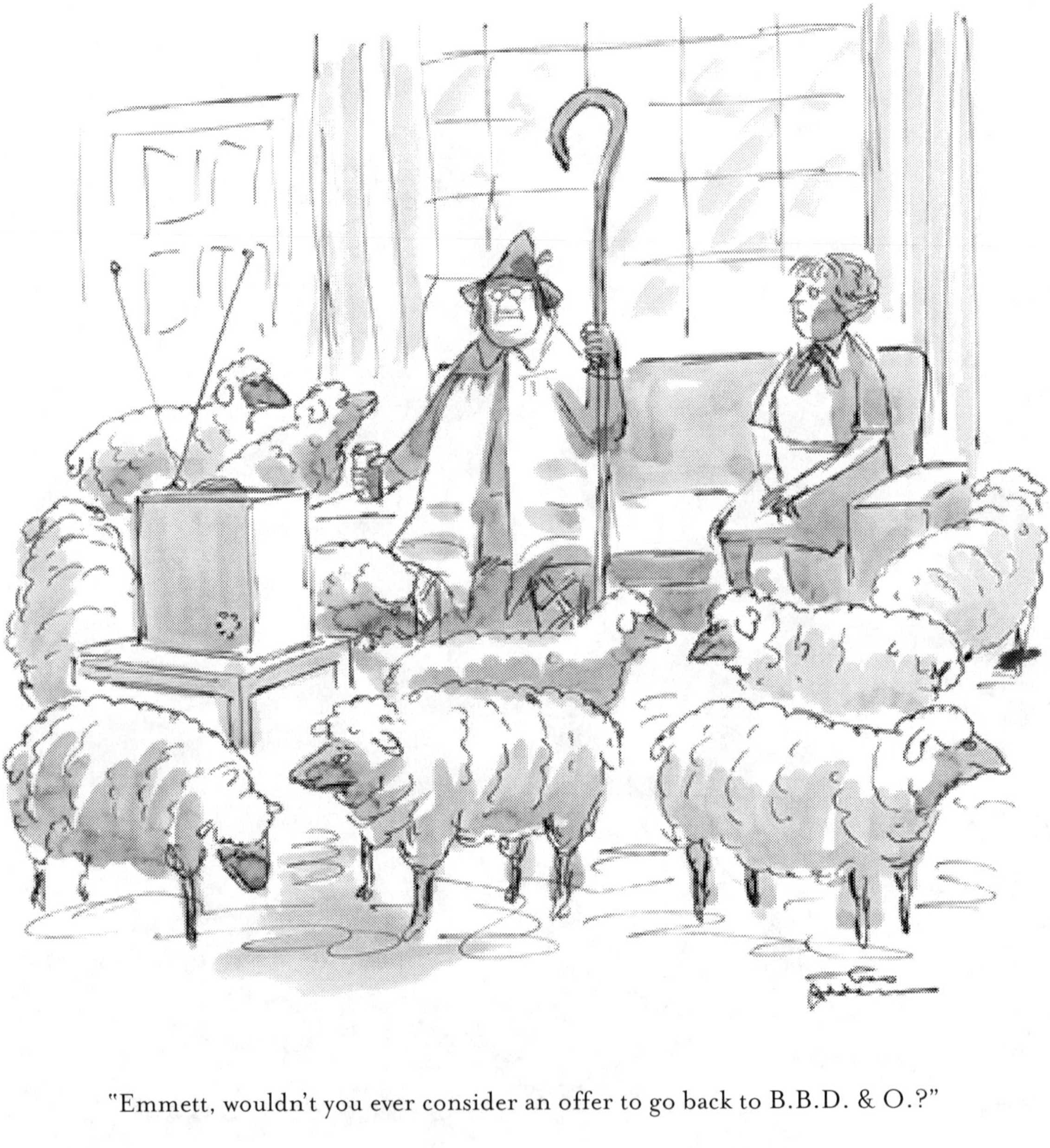

"Emmett, wouldn't you ever consider an offer to go back to B.B.D. & O.?"

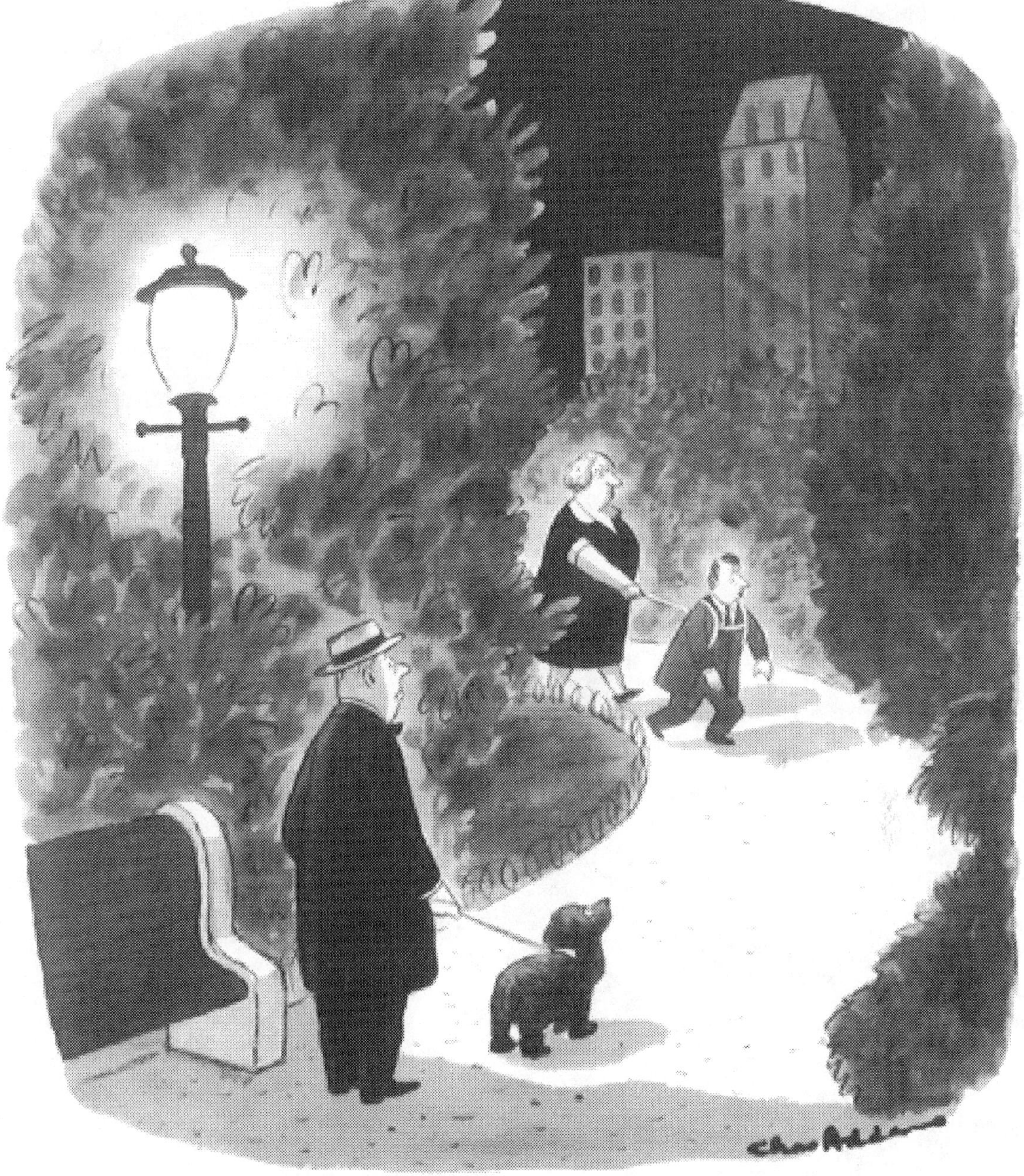

His Side

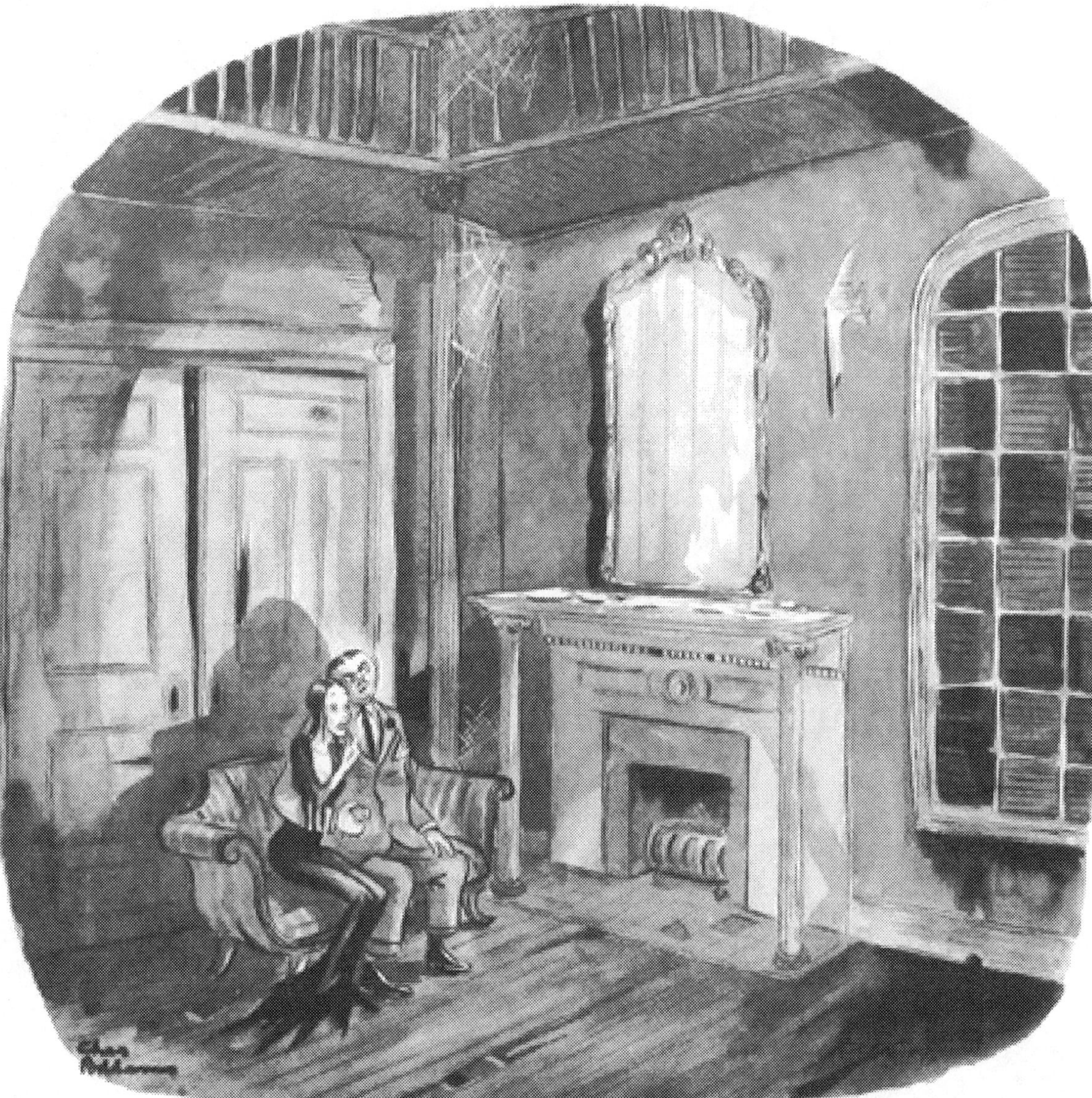

"Are you unhappy, darling?"
"Oh, yes, *yes*! Completely."

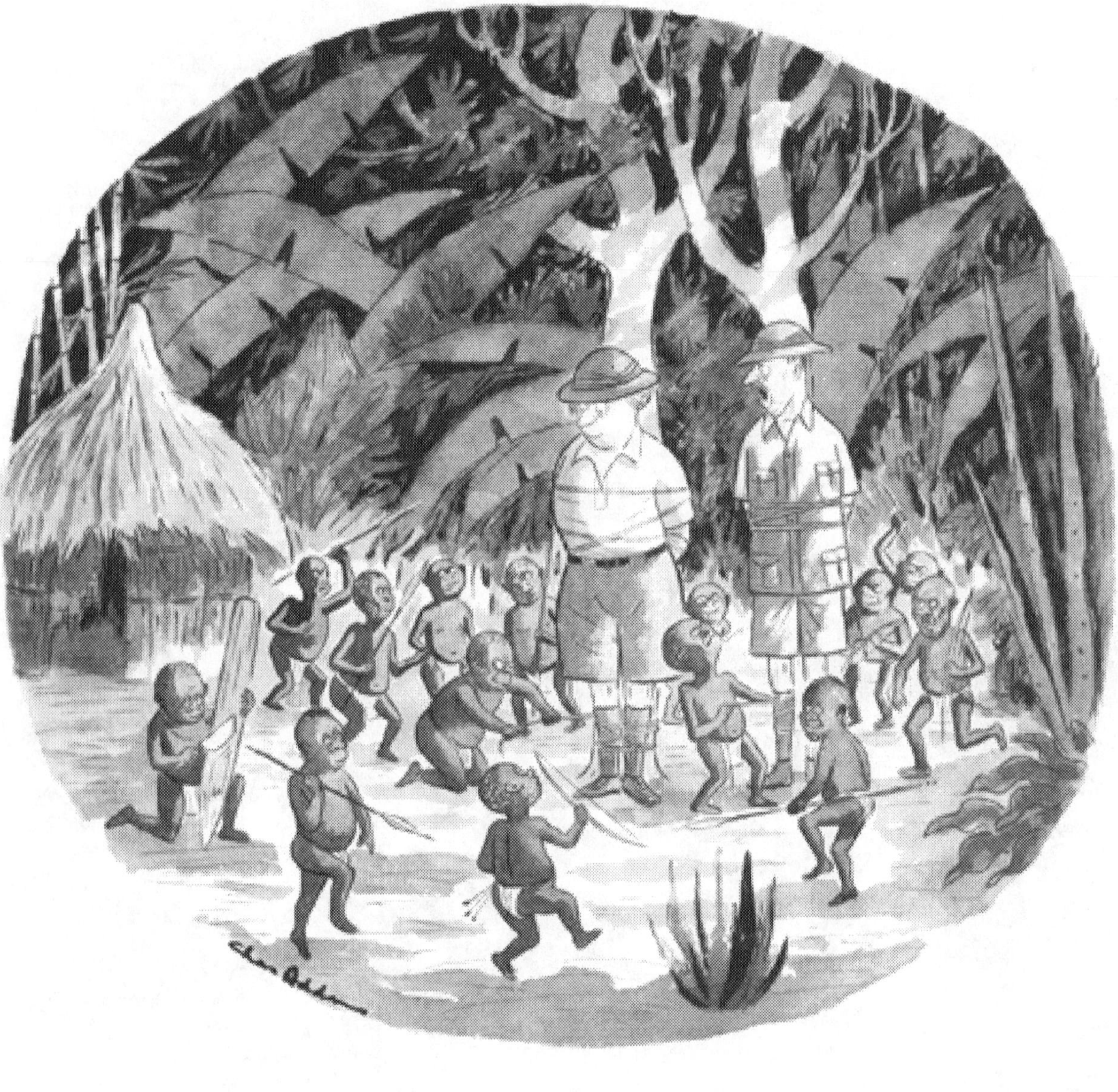

"Does it occur to you, Agatha, that this is hardly the occasion to use an expression like 'knee-high to a grasshopper'?"

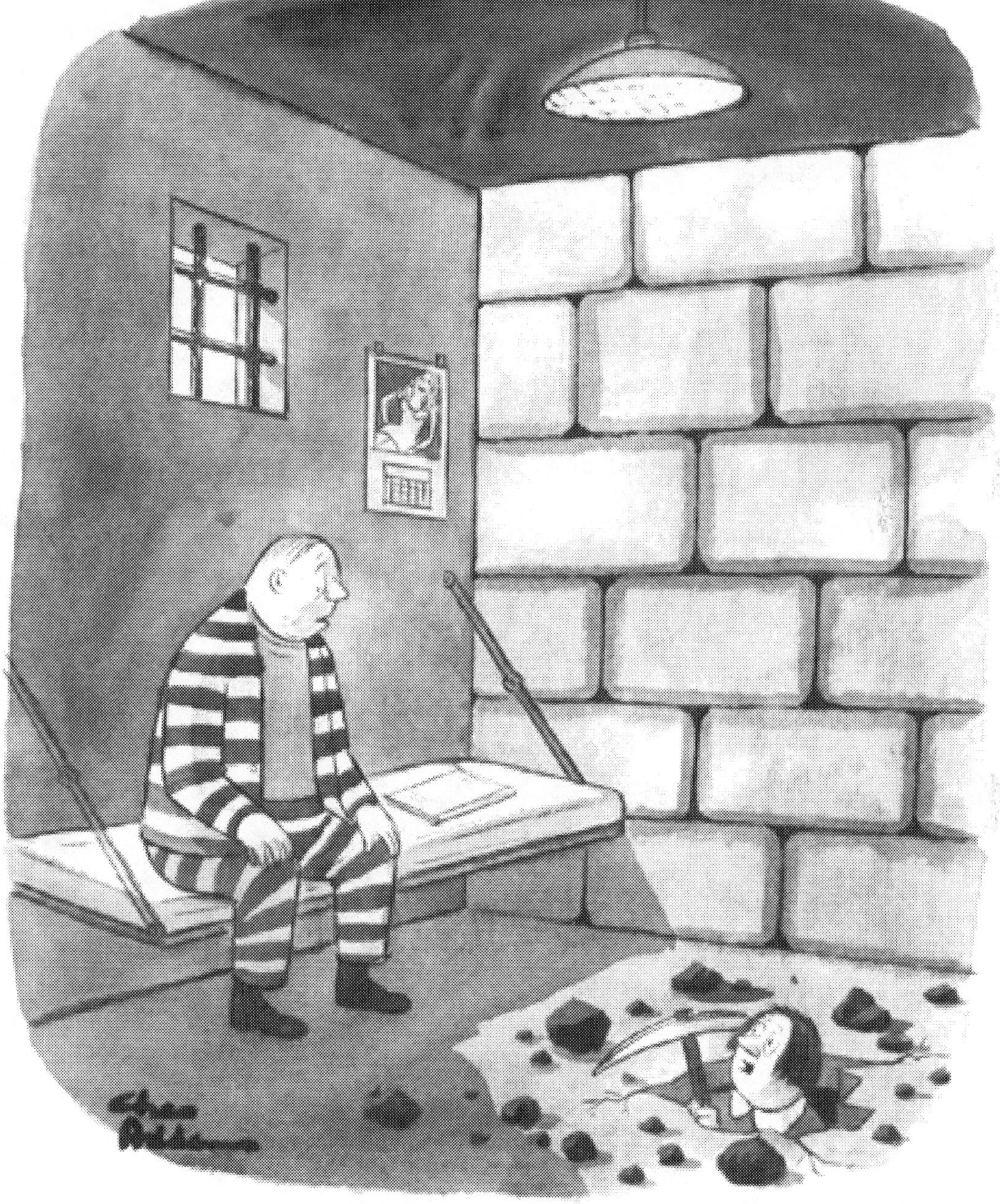

"I hope you're not angry, Ed. I just *had* to see you."

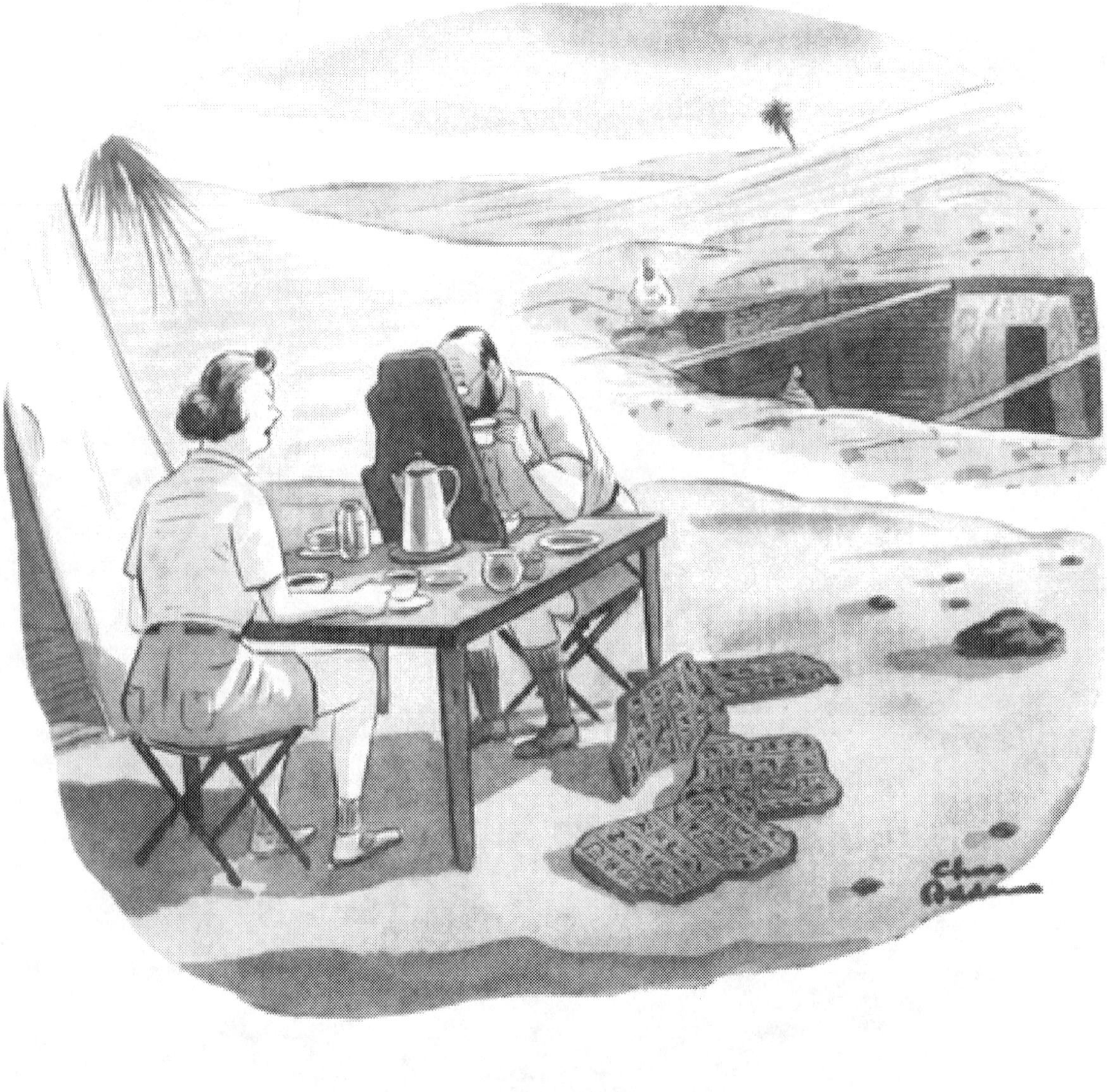
Chas Addams

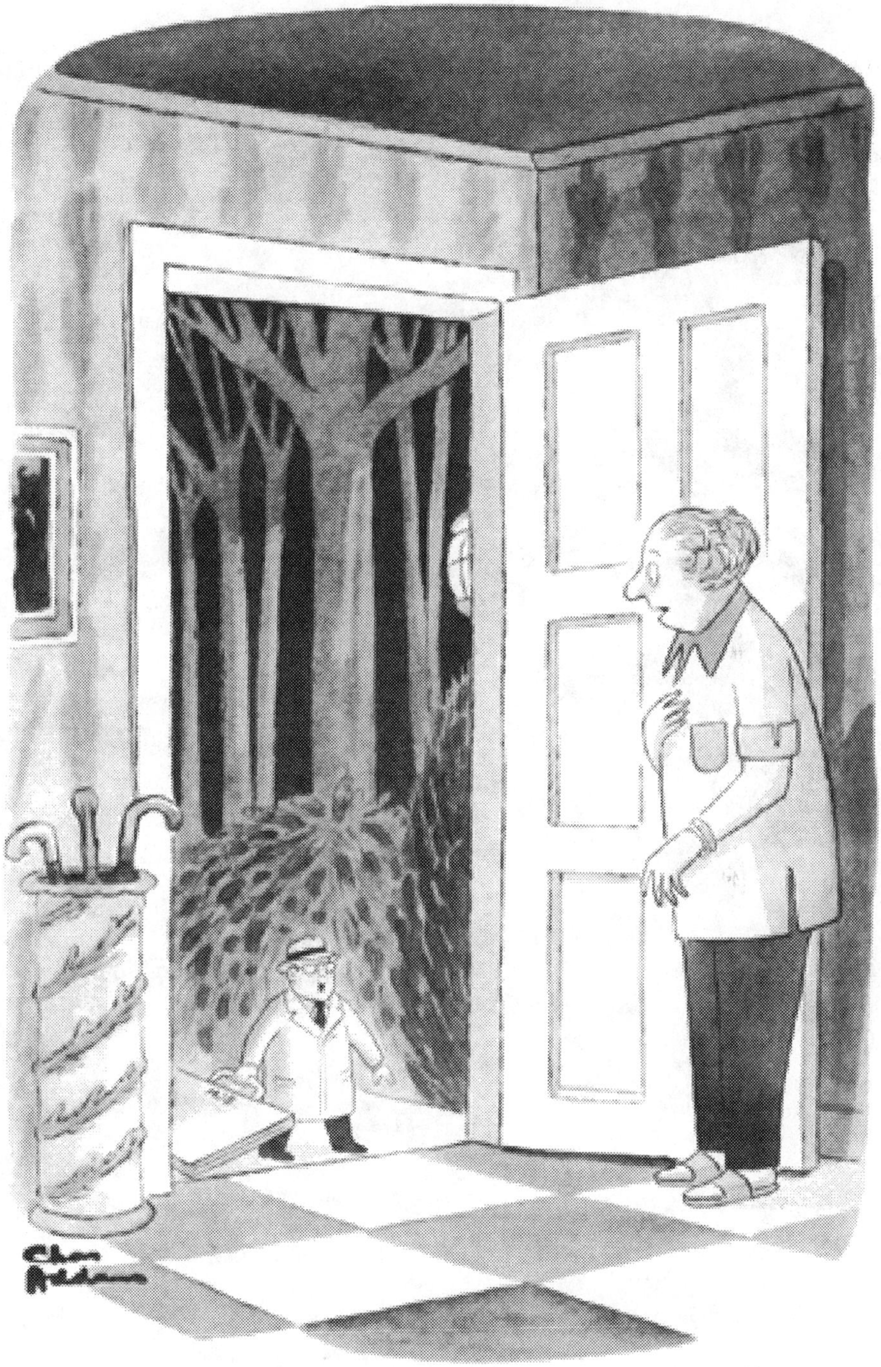

"First a drink, Margaret. Then we'll talk."

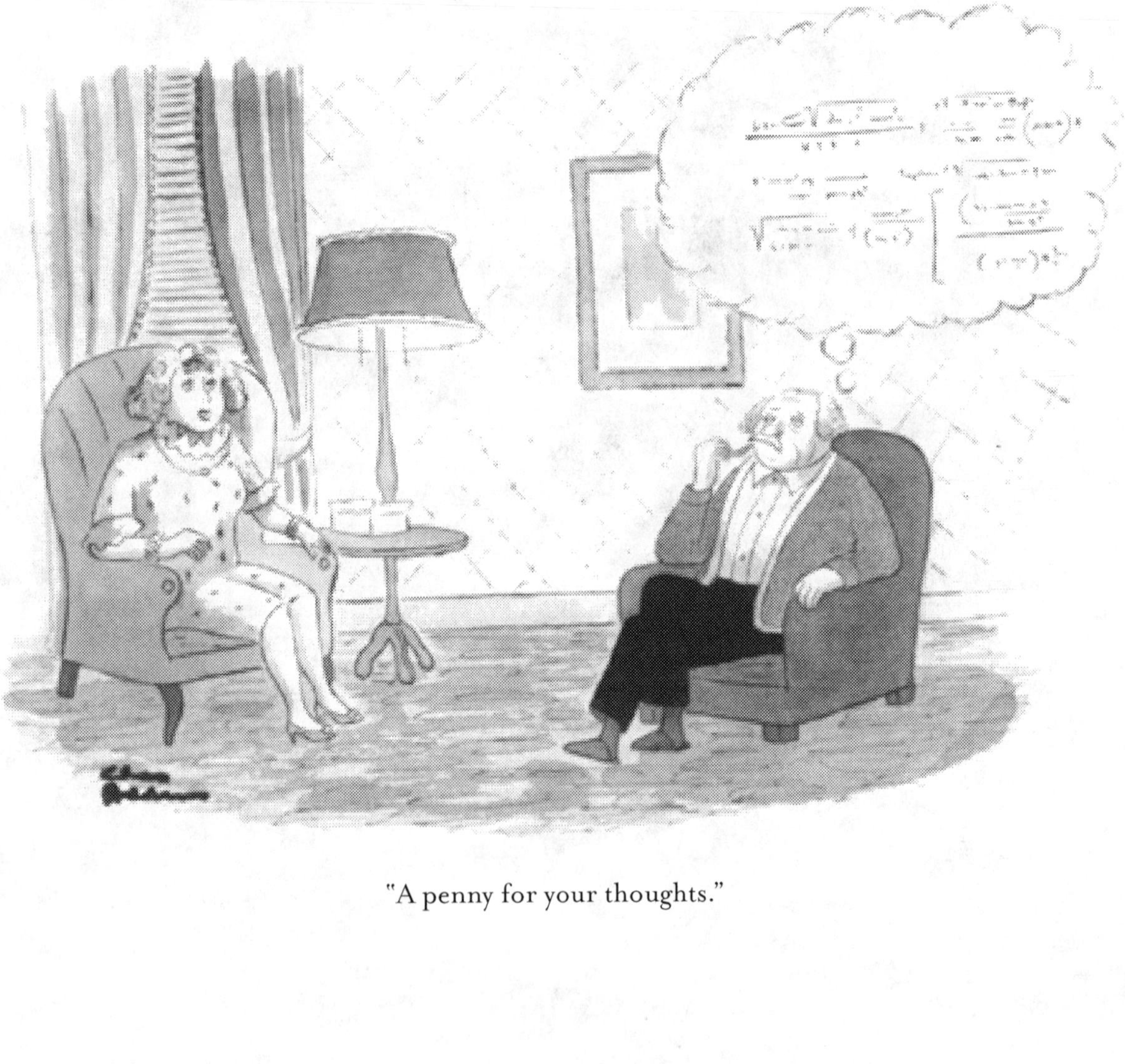

"A penny for your thoughts."

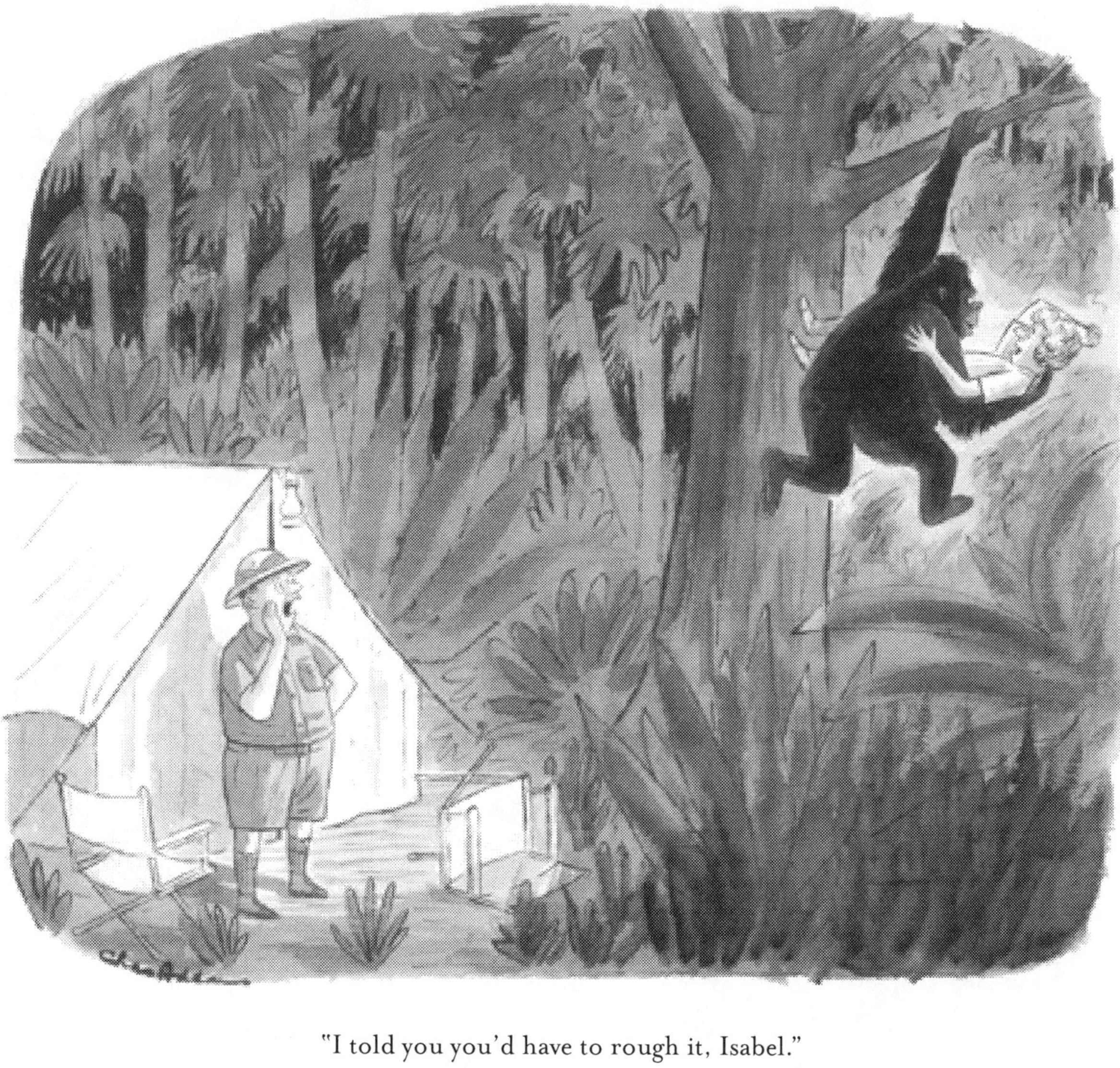

"I told you you'd have to rough it, Isabel."

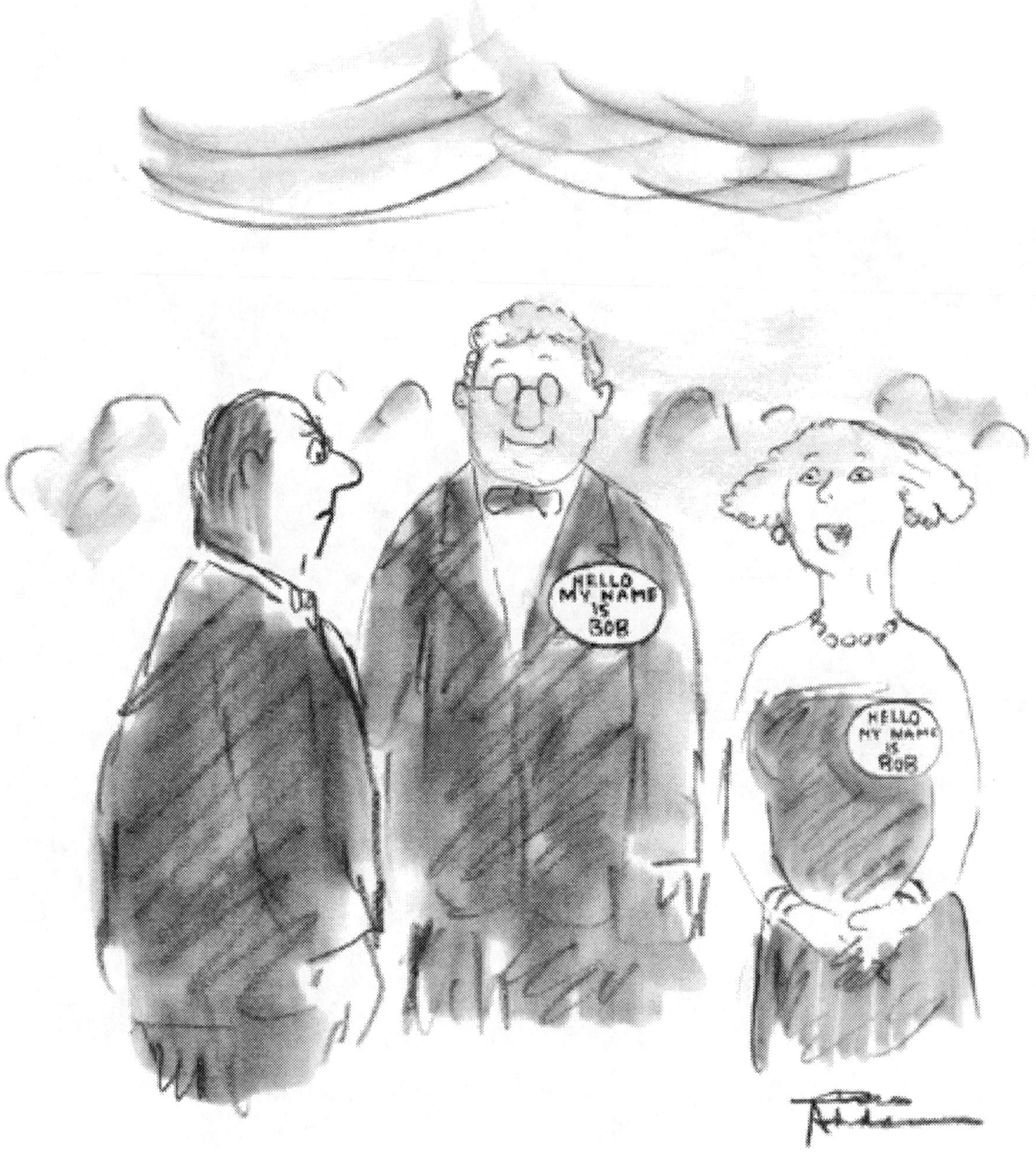
HELLO MY NAME IS BOB
HELLO MY NAME IS BOB

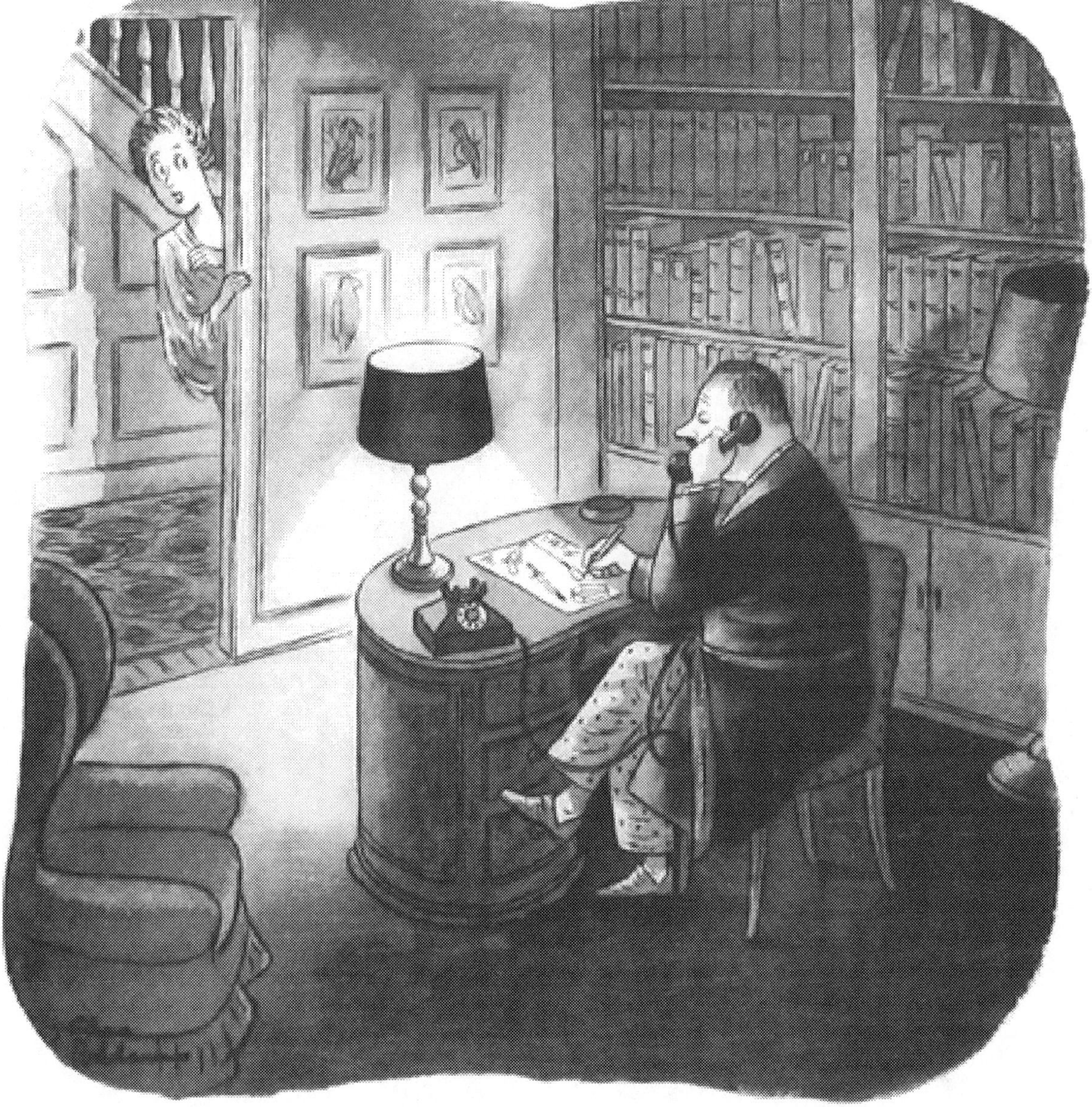

"Is that Mother, dear?"

"Hold it, Timon! The Queen wants a divorce."

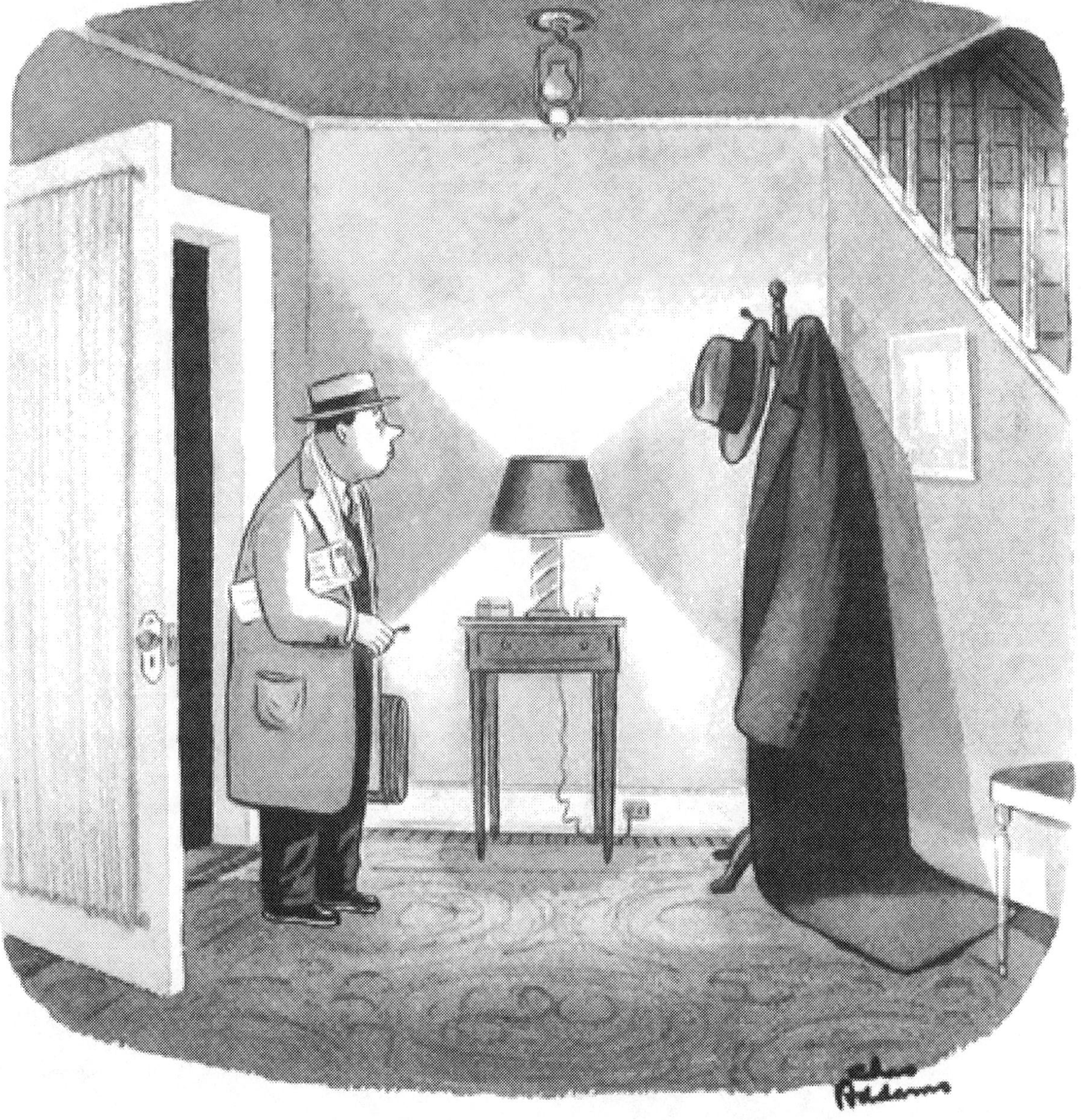
Chas Addams

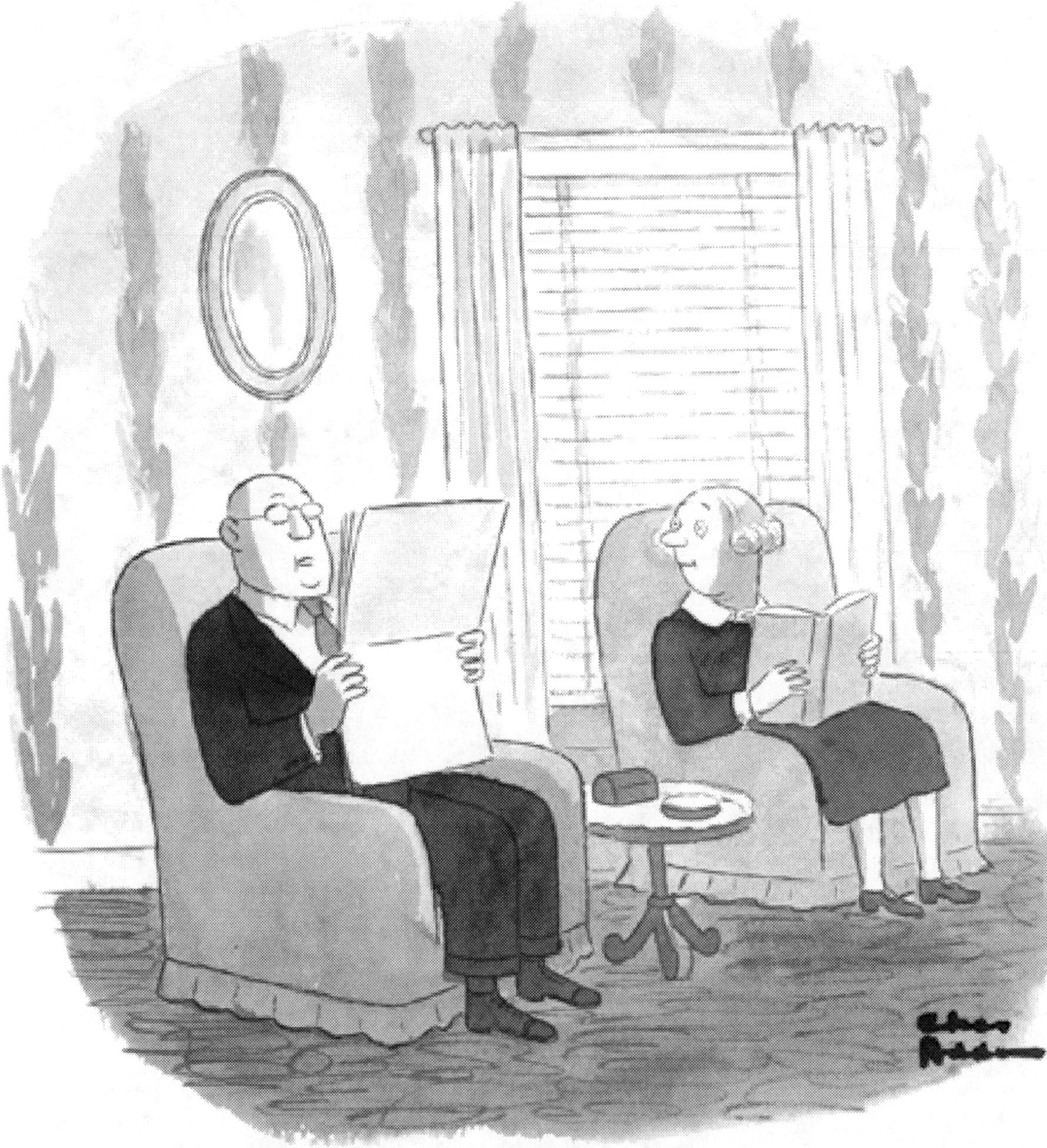

"No, Martha, I didn't say anything. Why should I say anything?"

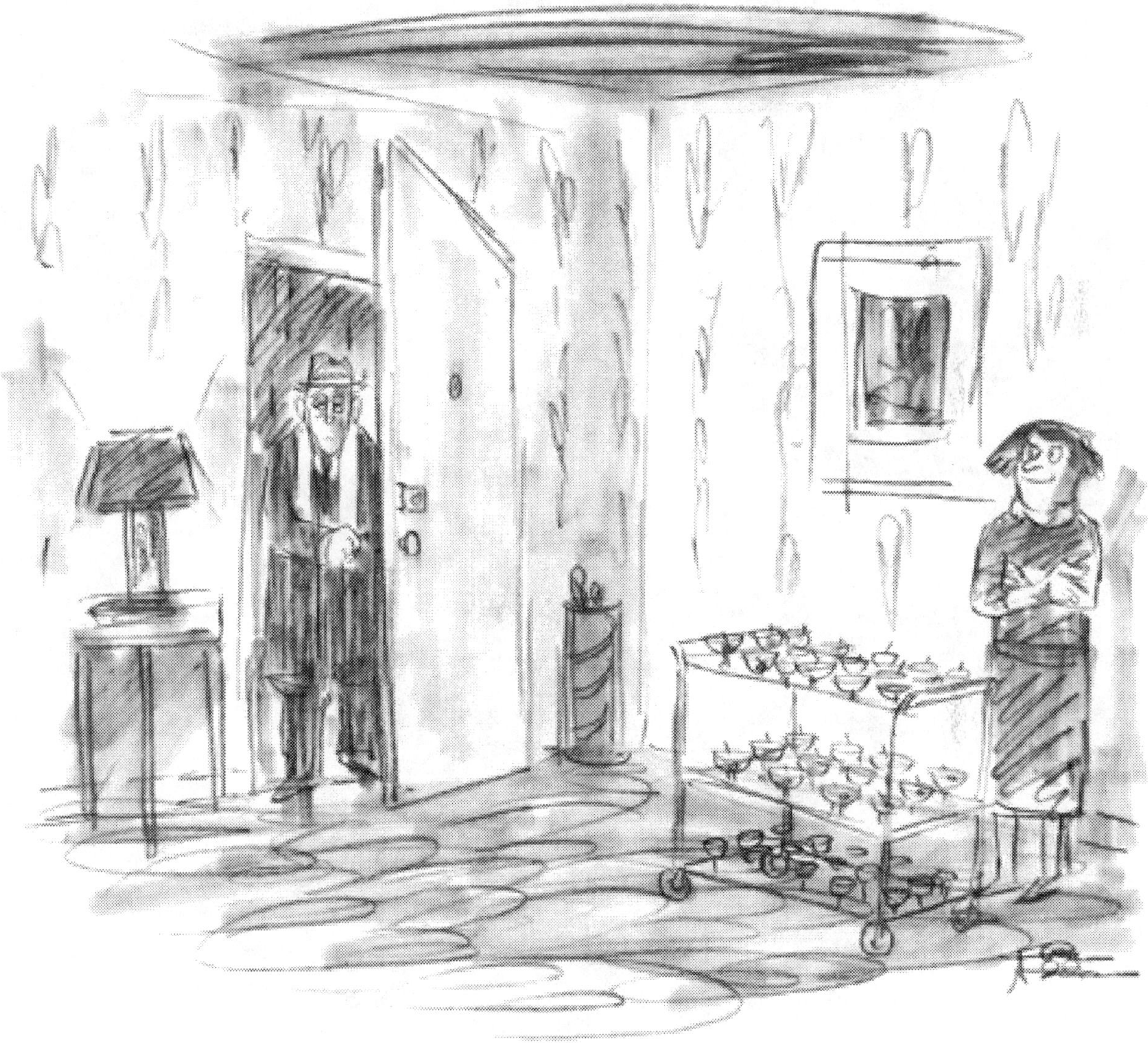

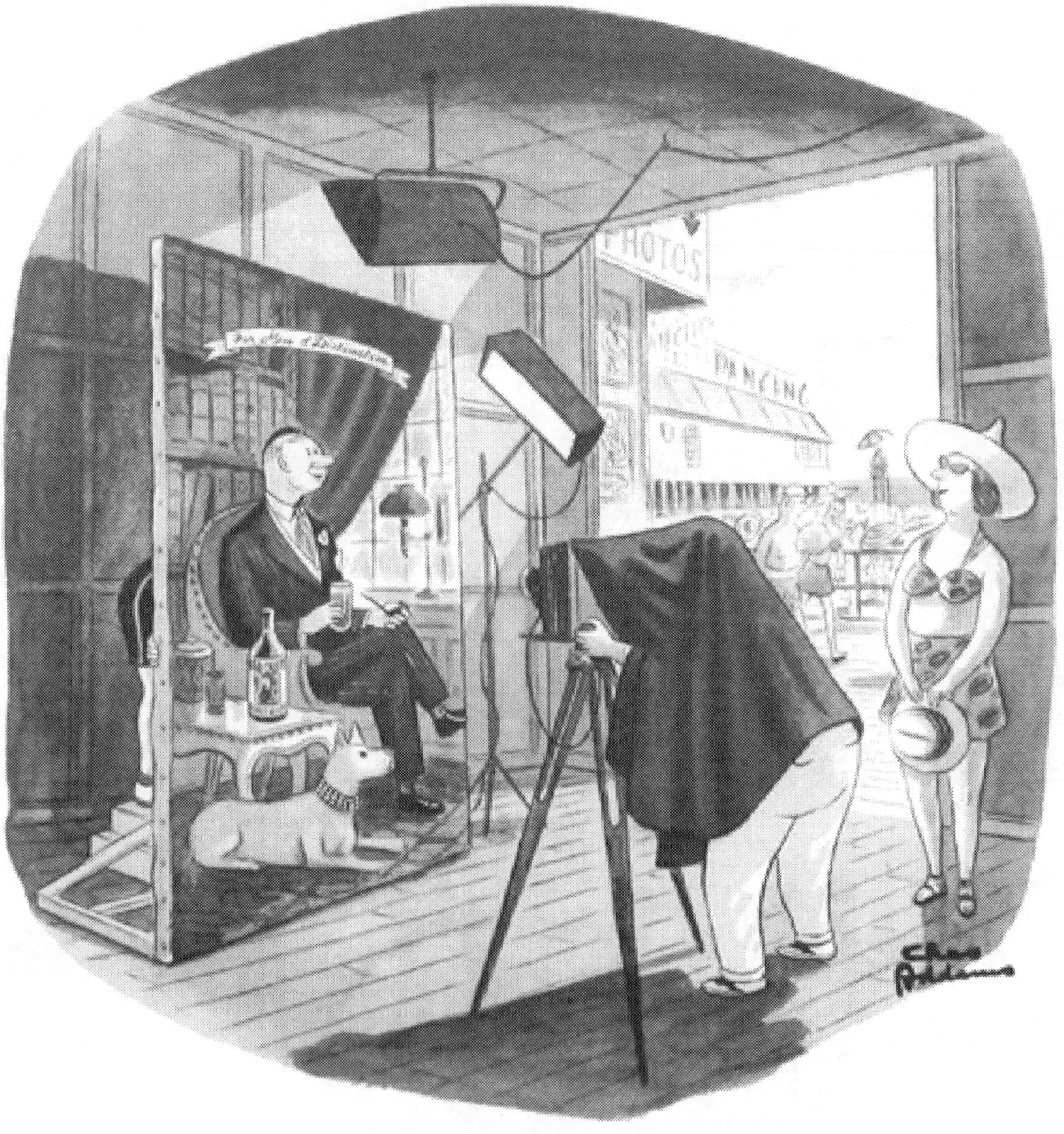
PHOTOS
DANCING
Chas Addams

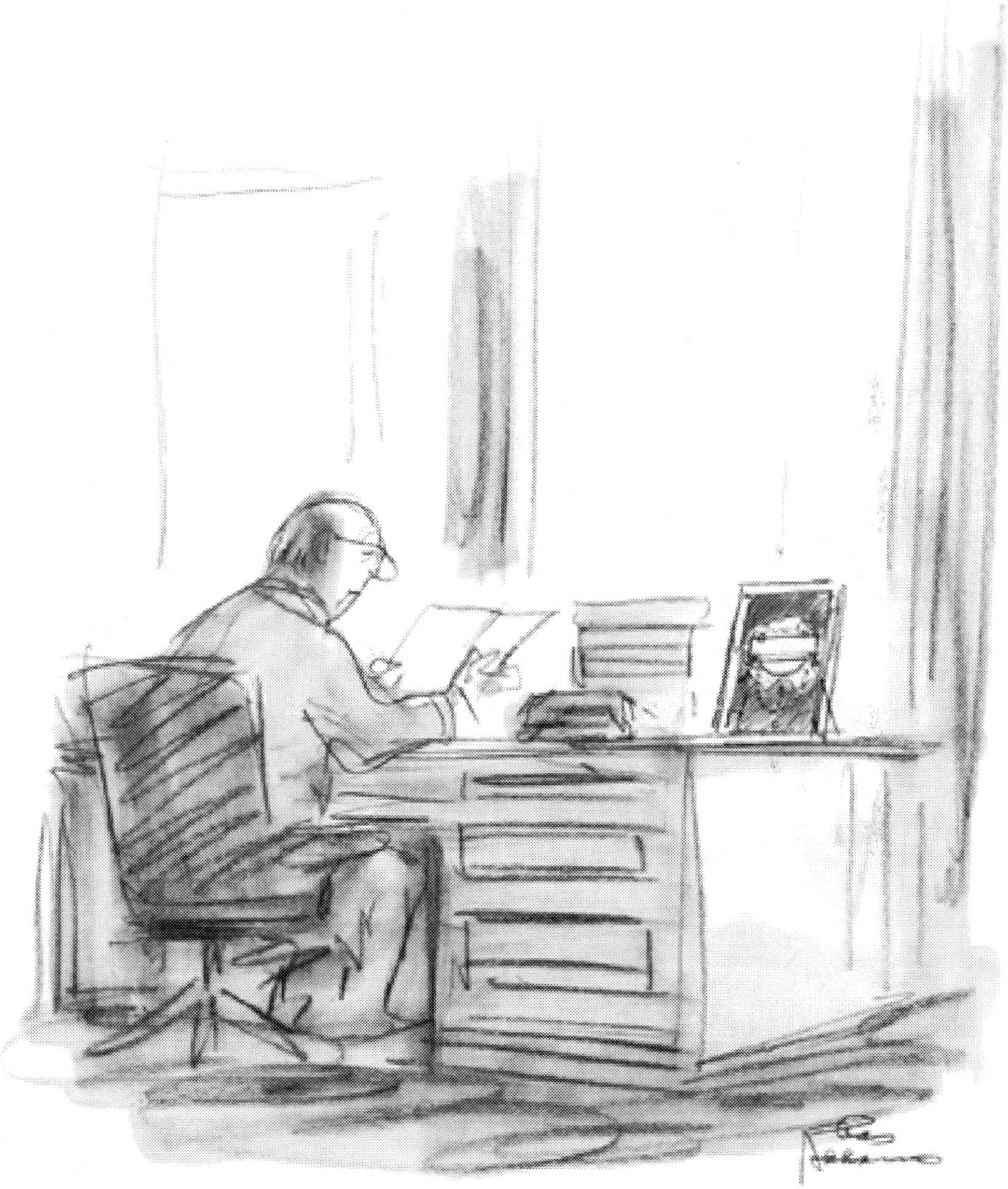

"Actually, the program is supposed to relieve prison crowding, but I'm just happy to have Roger home again."

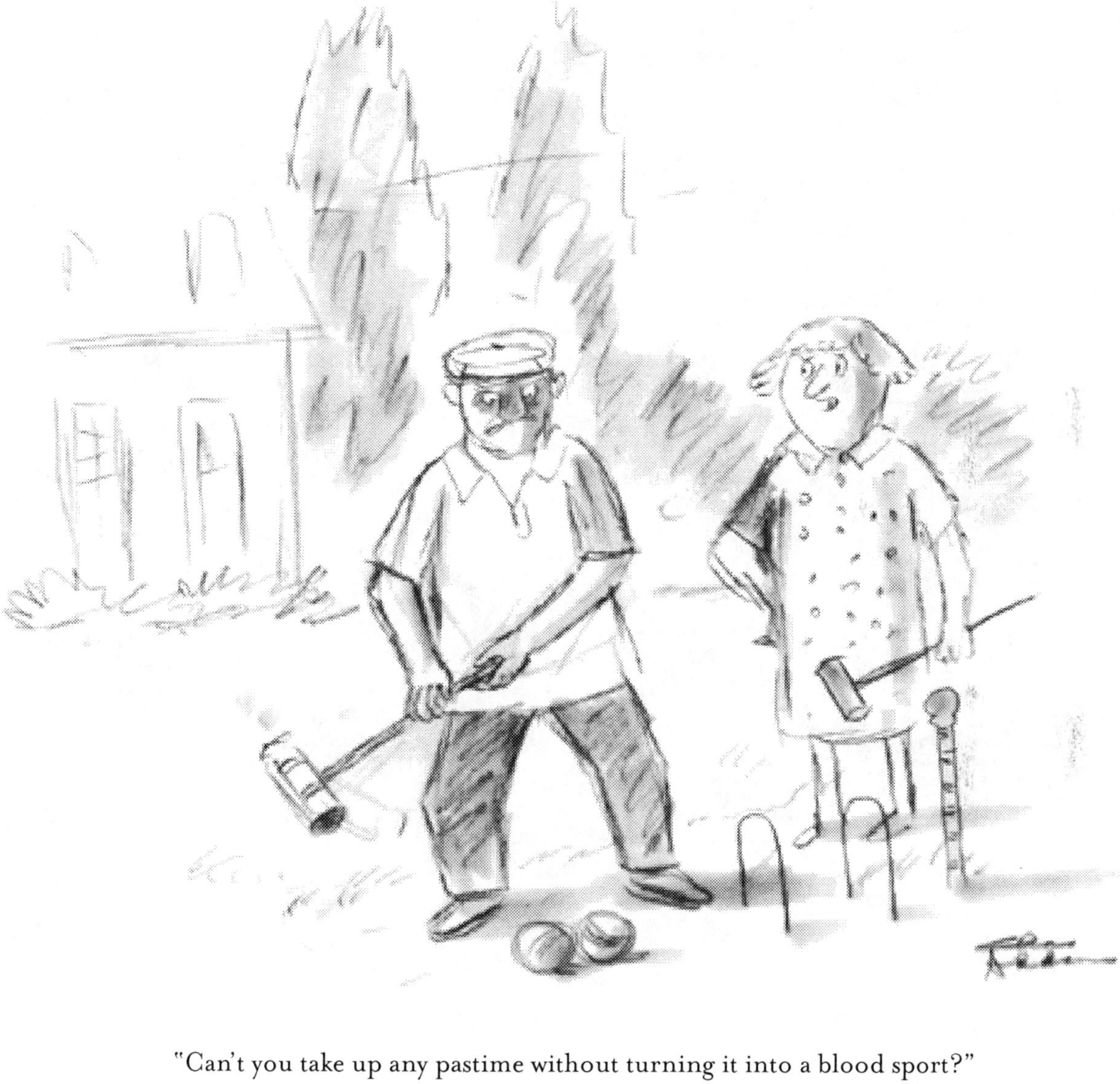

"Can't you take up any pastime without turning it into a blood sport?"

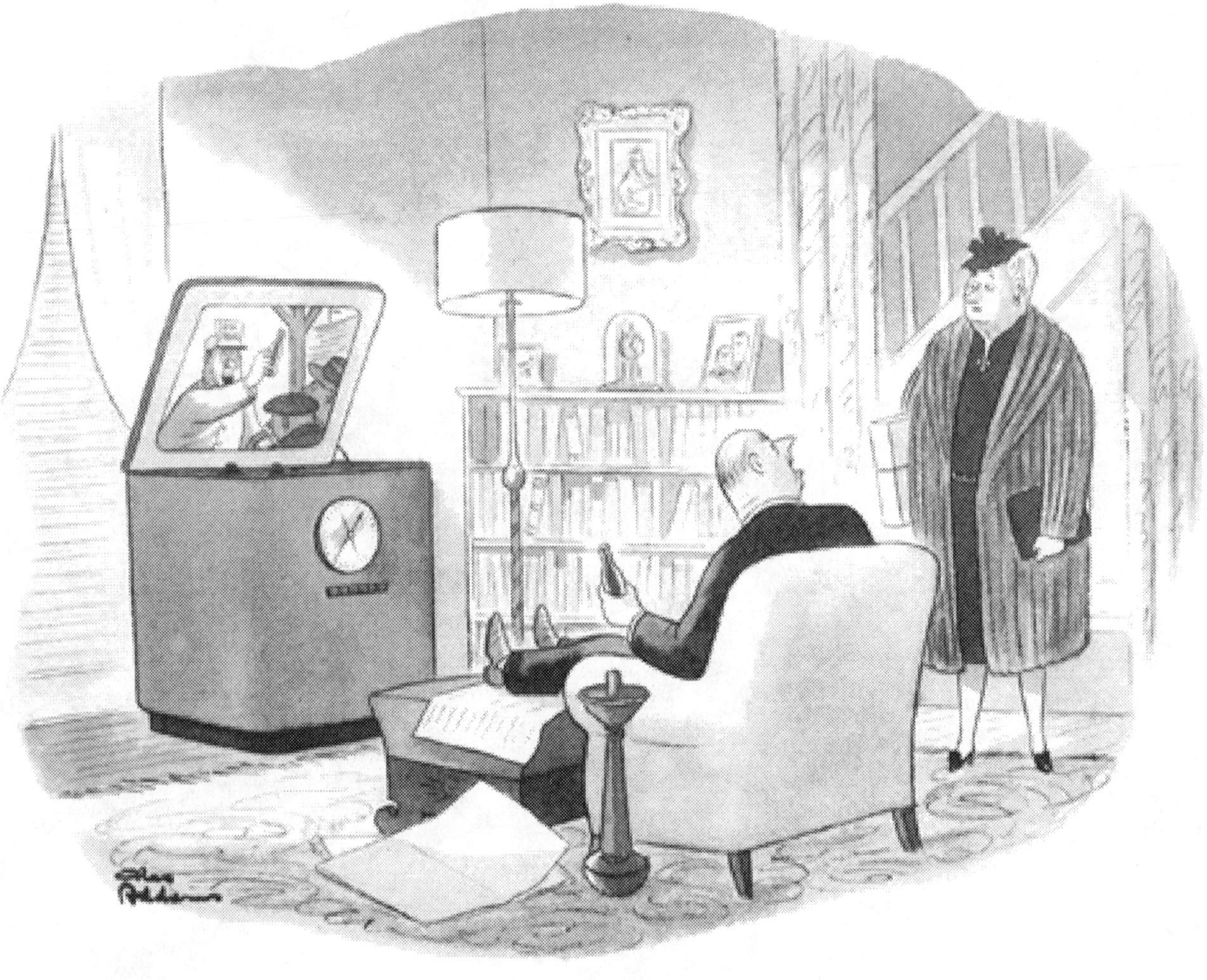

"I got it out of the refrigerator. Why?"

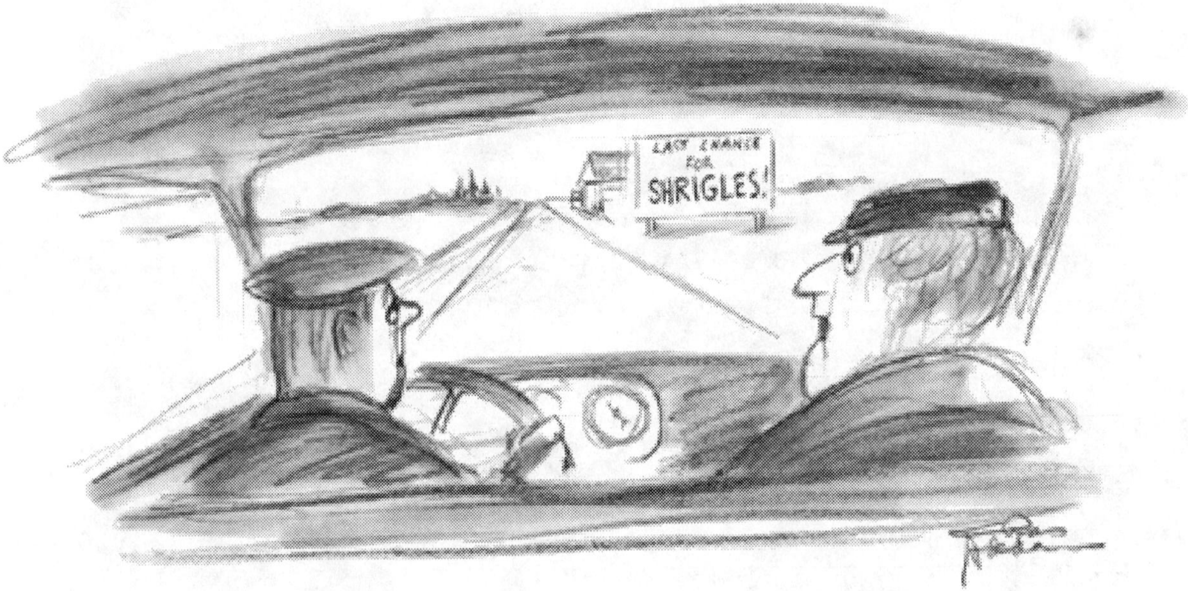
SHRIGLES!

"Never mind what they are, just stop and get some."

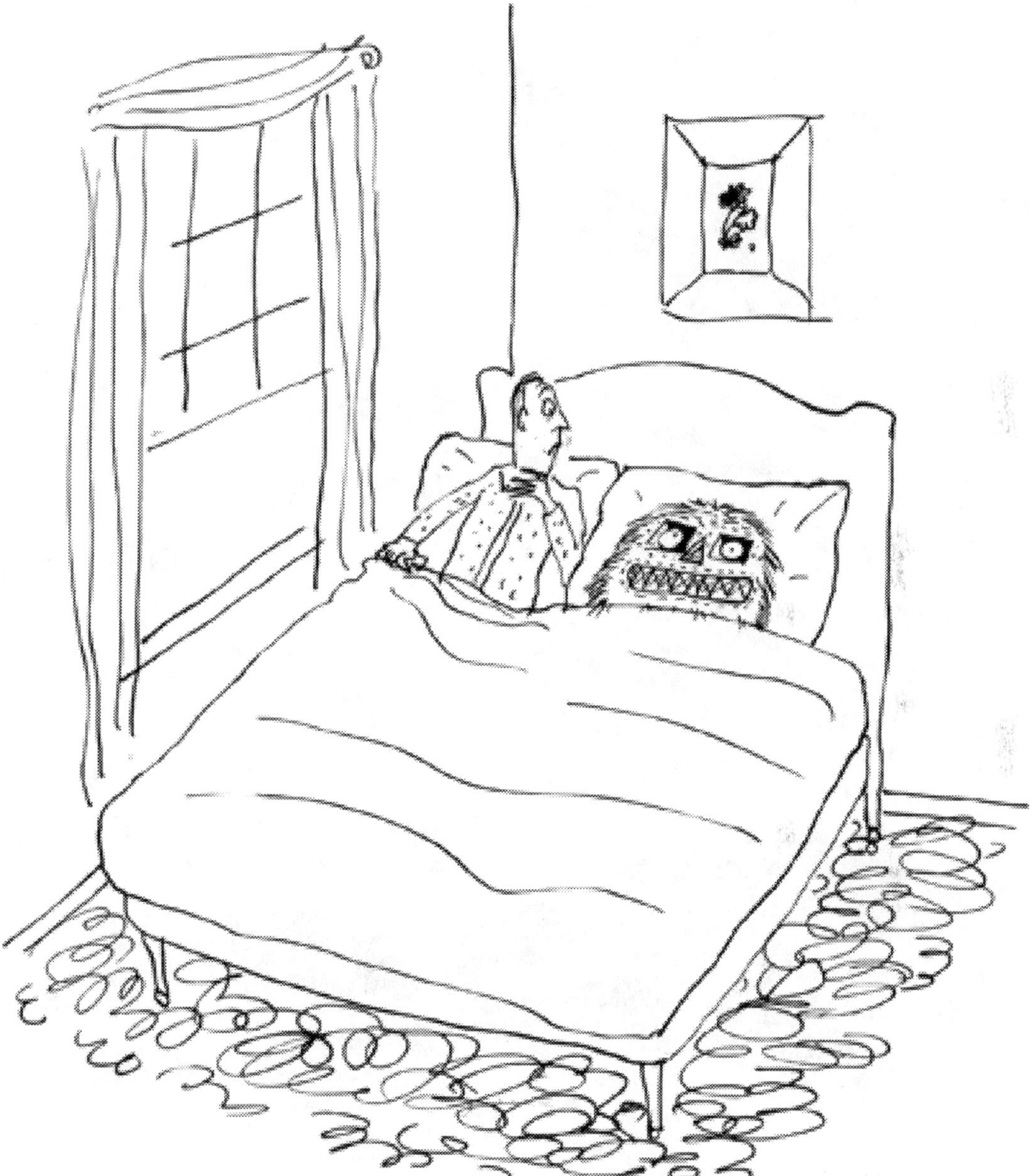

"I had the strangest dream last night."

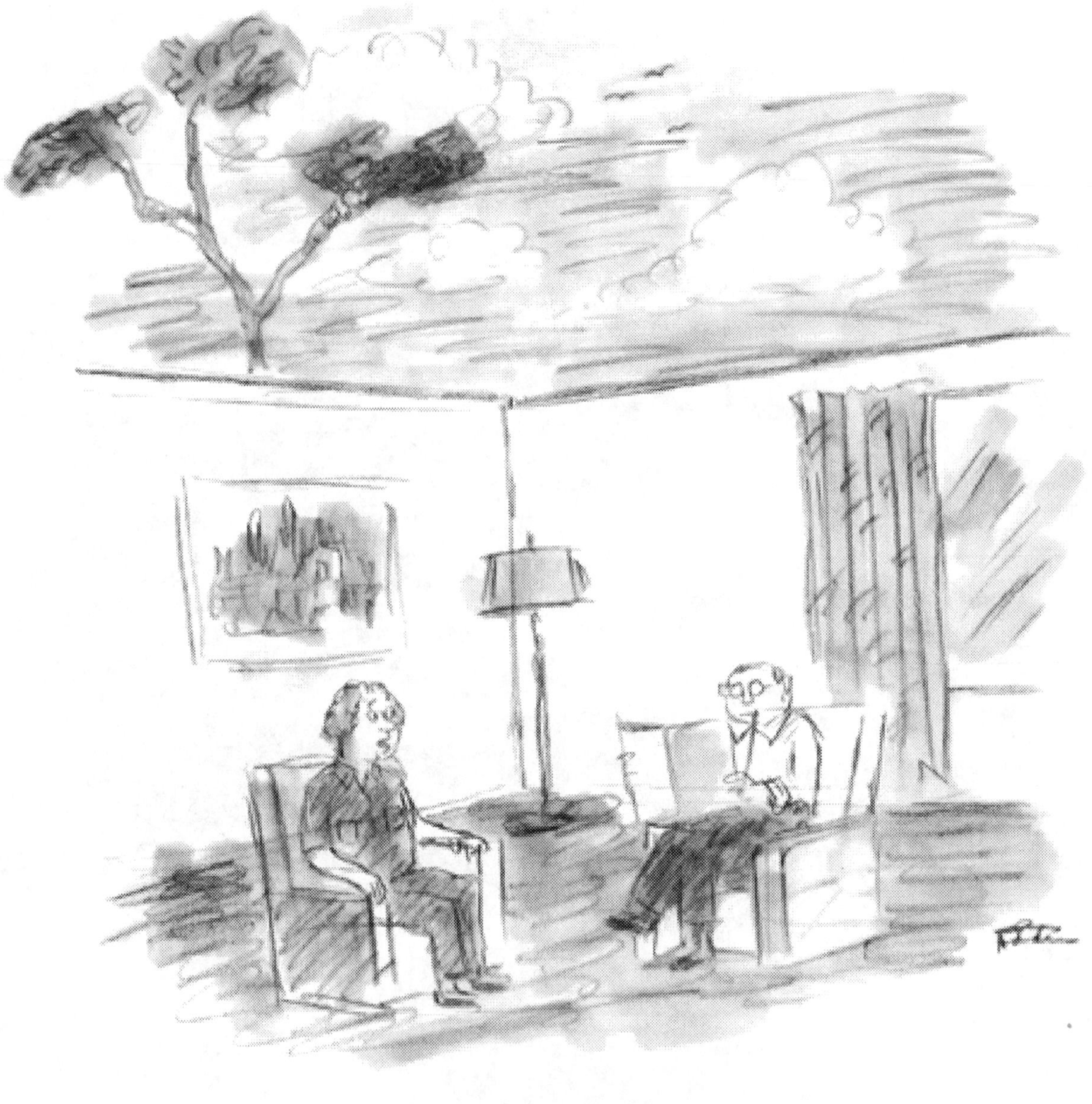

"Notice anything different?"

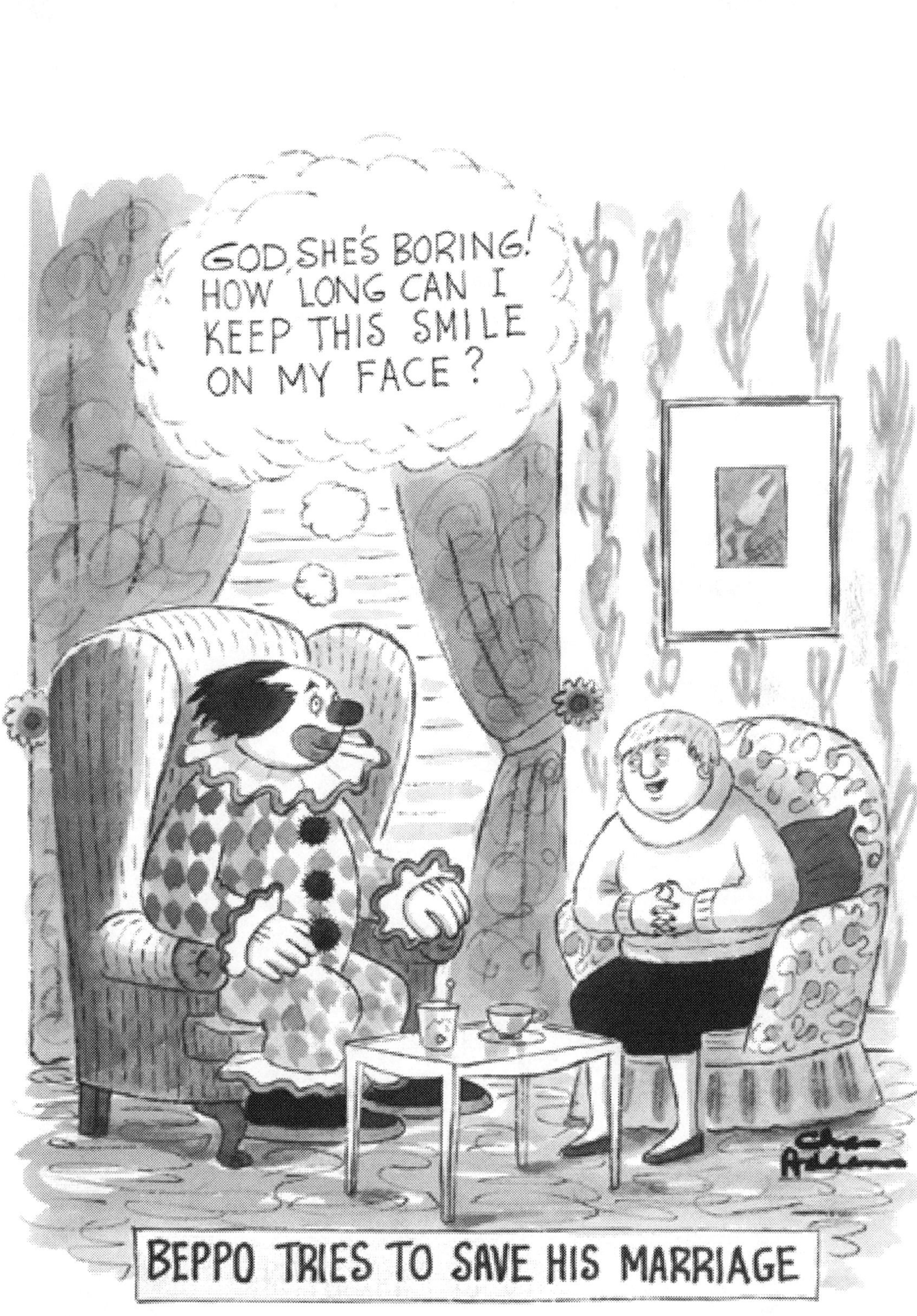
GOD, SHE'S BORING! HOW LONG CAN I KEEP THIS SMILE ON MY FACE?

BEPPO TRIES TO SAVE HIS MARRIAGE

"You've changed, Irma. You used to love Sousa marches."

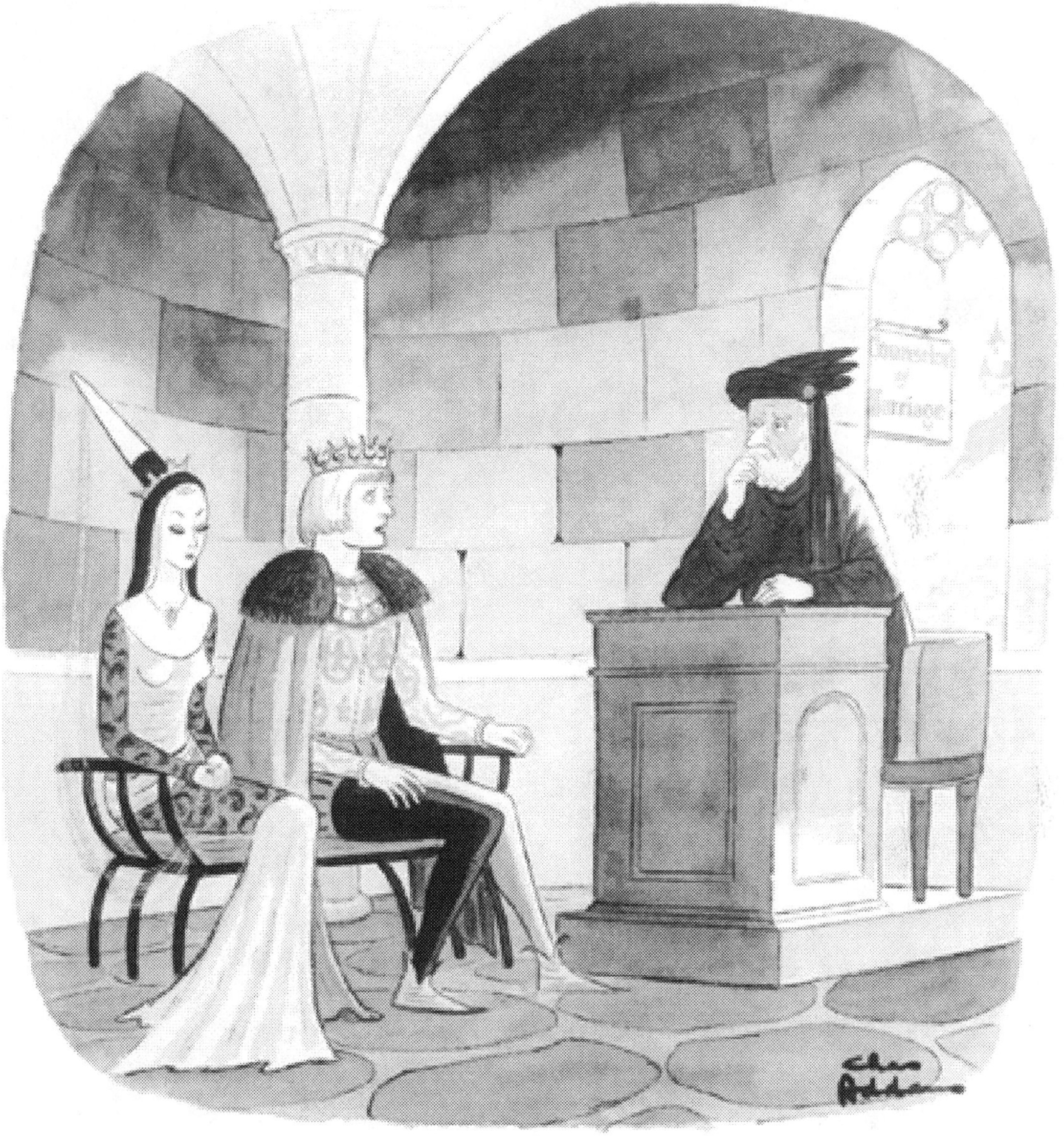

"We're not living happily ever after."

Her Side

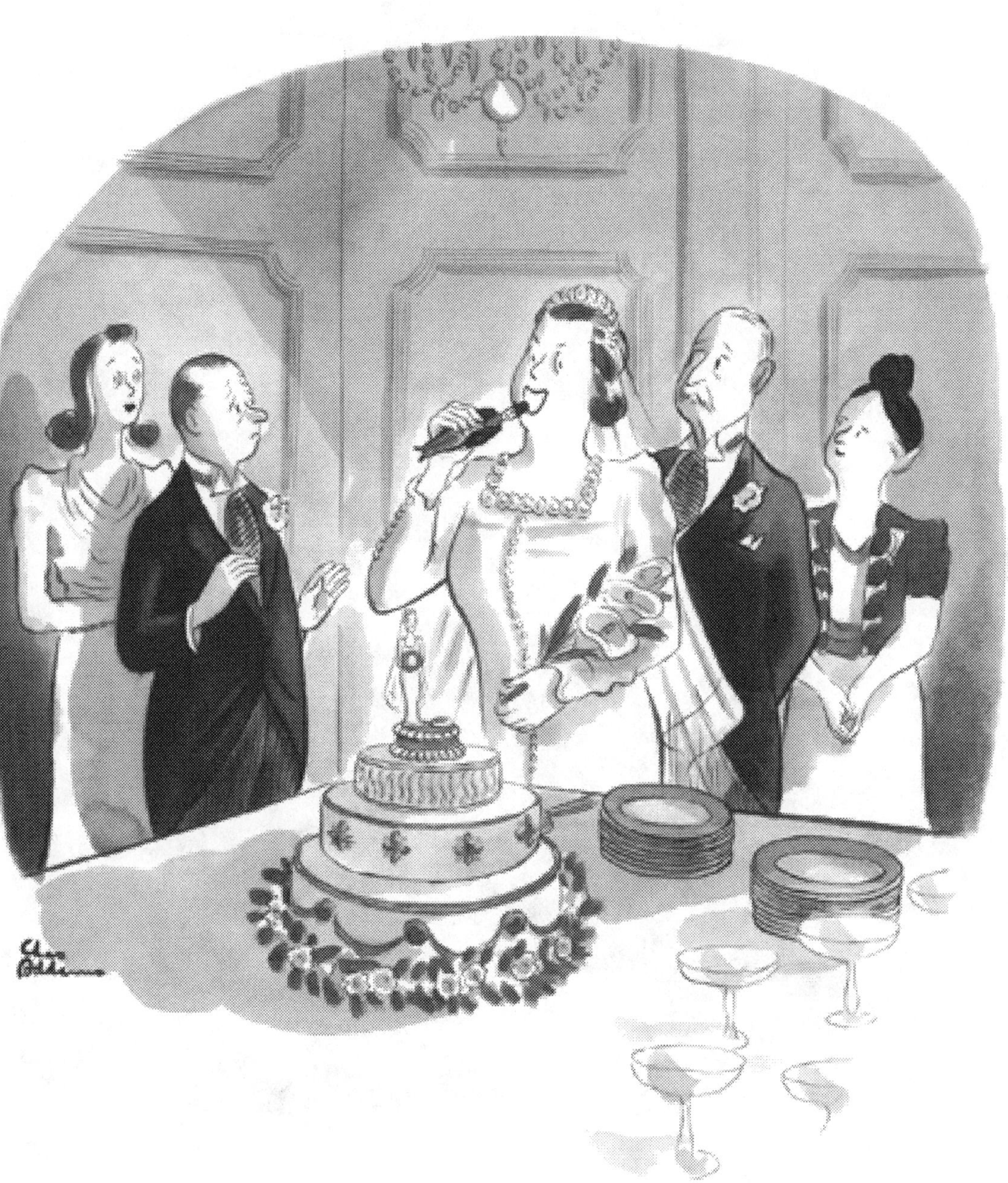

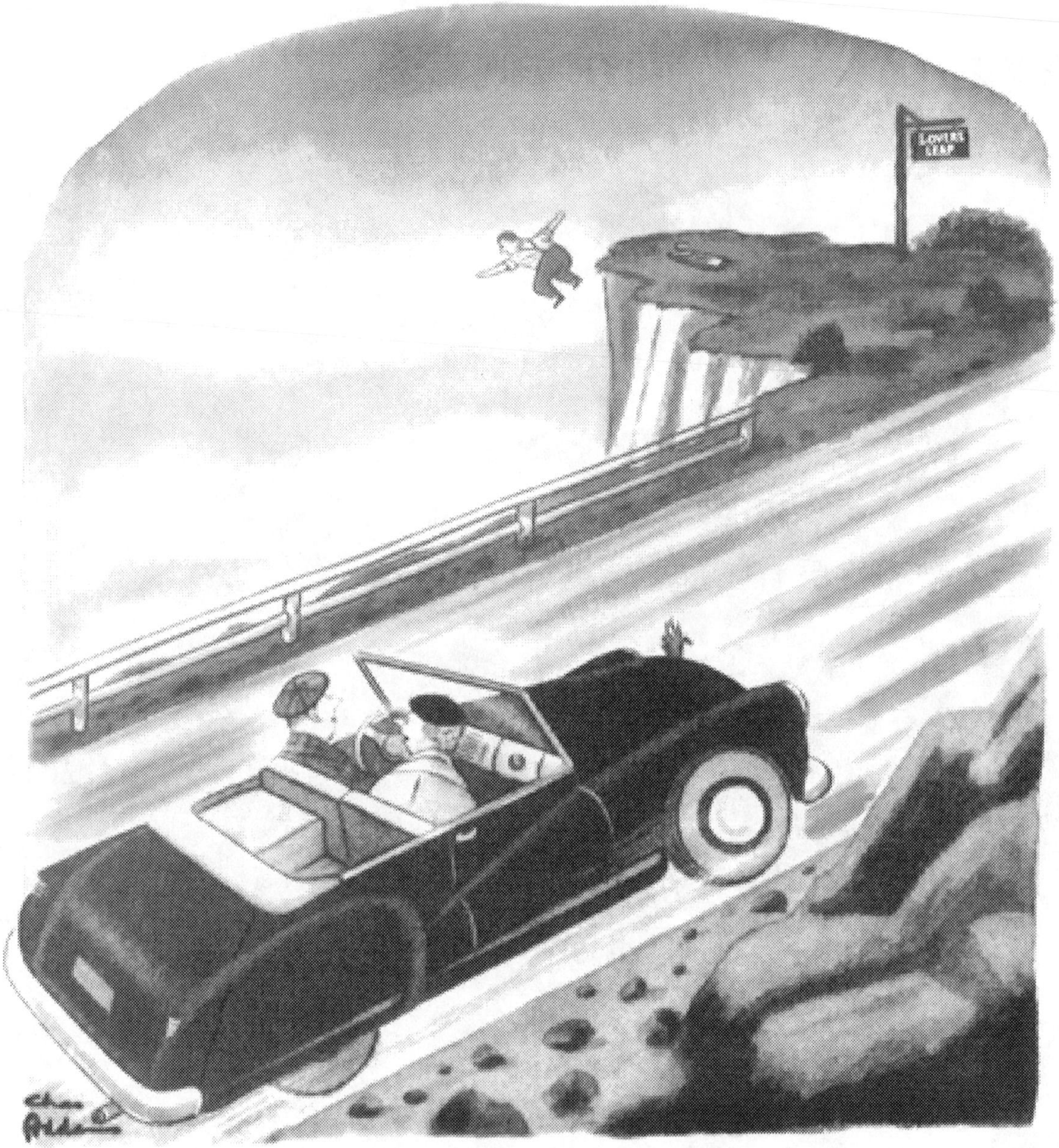

"You've never felt that way about me."

"Is there someone else, Narcissus?"

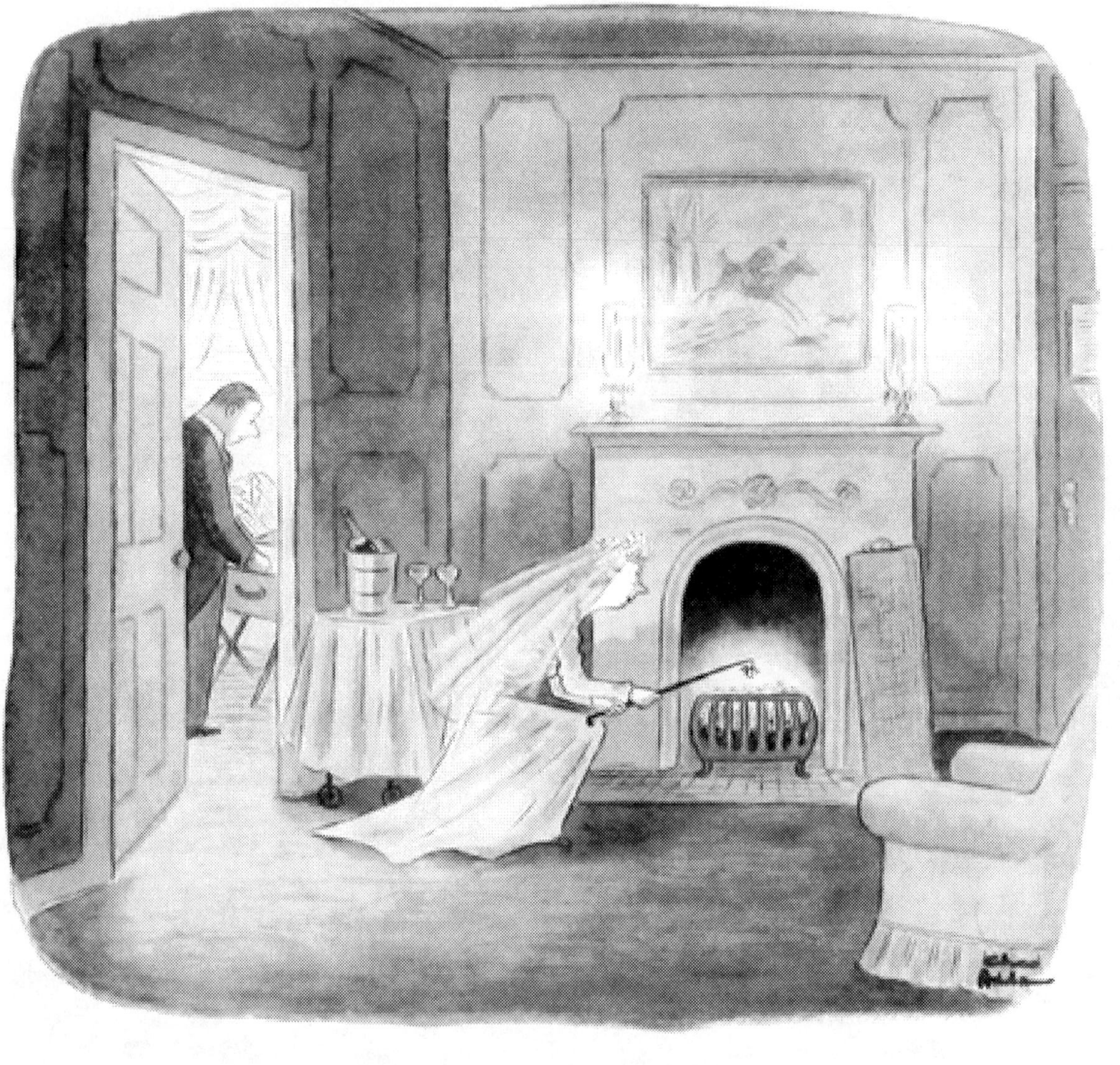

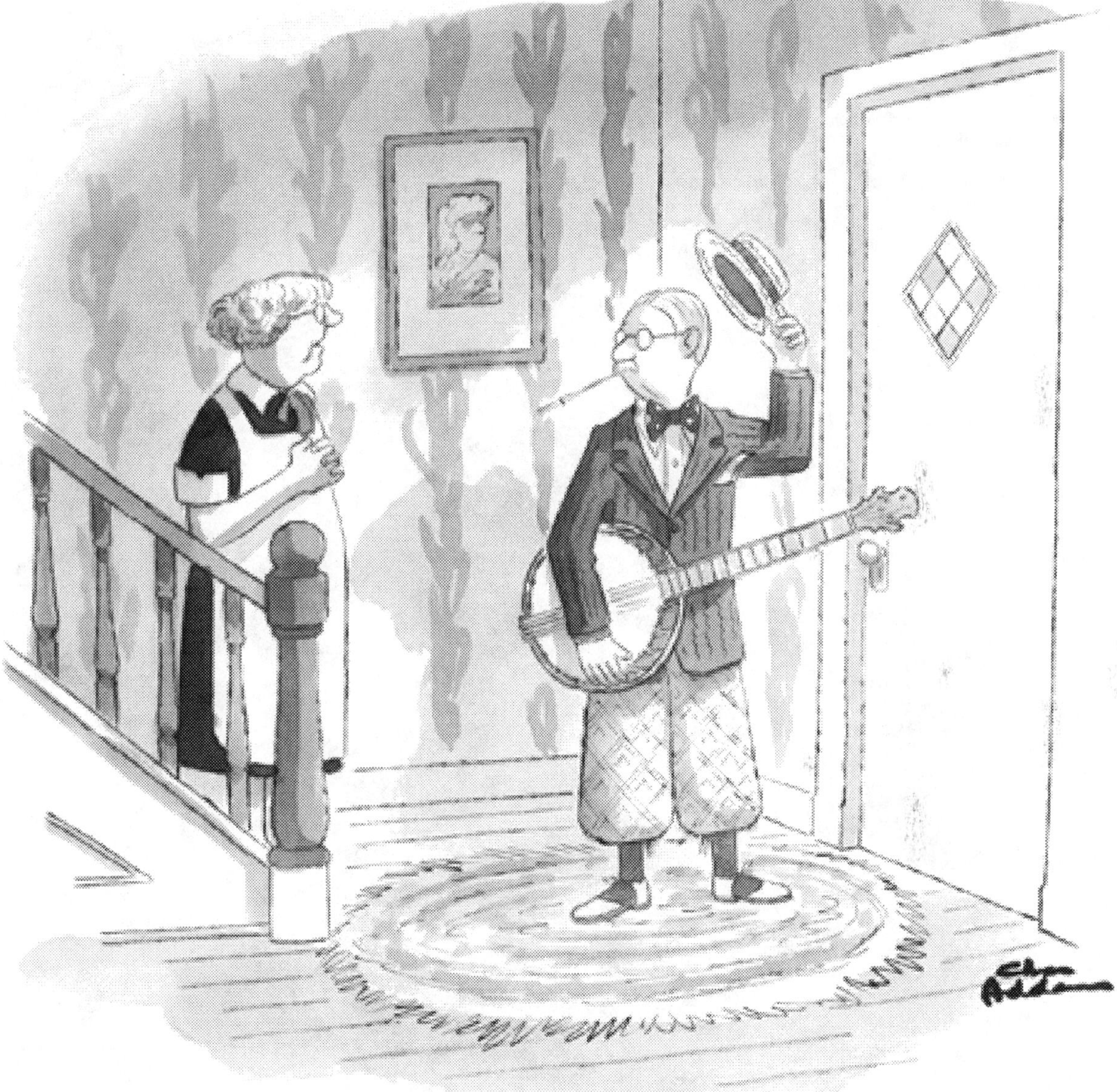

"You're seeing another woman, aren't you, Robert?"

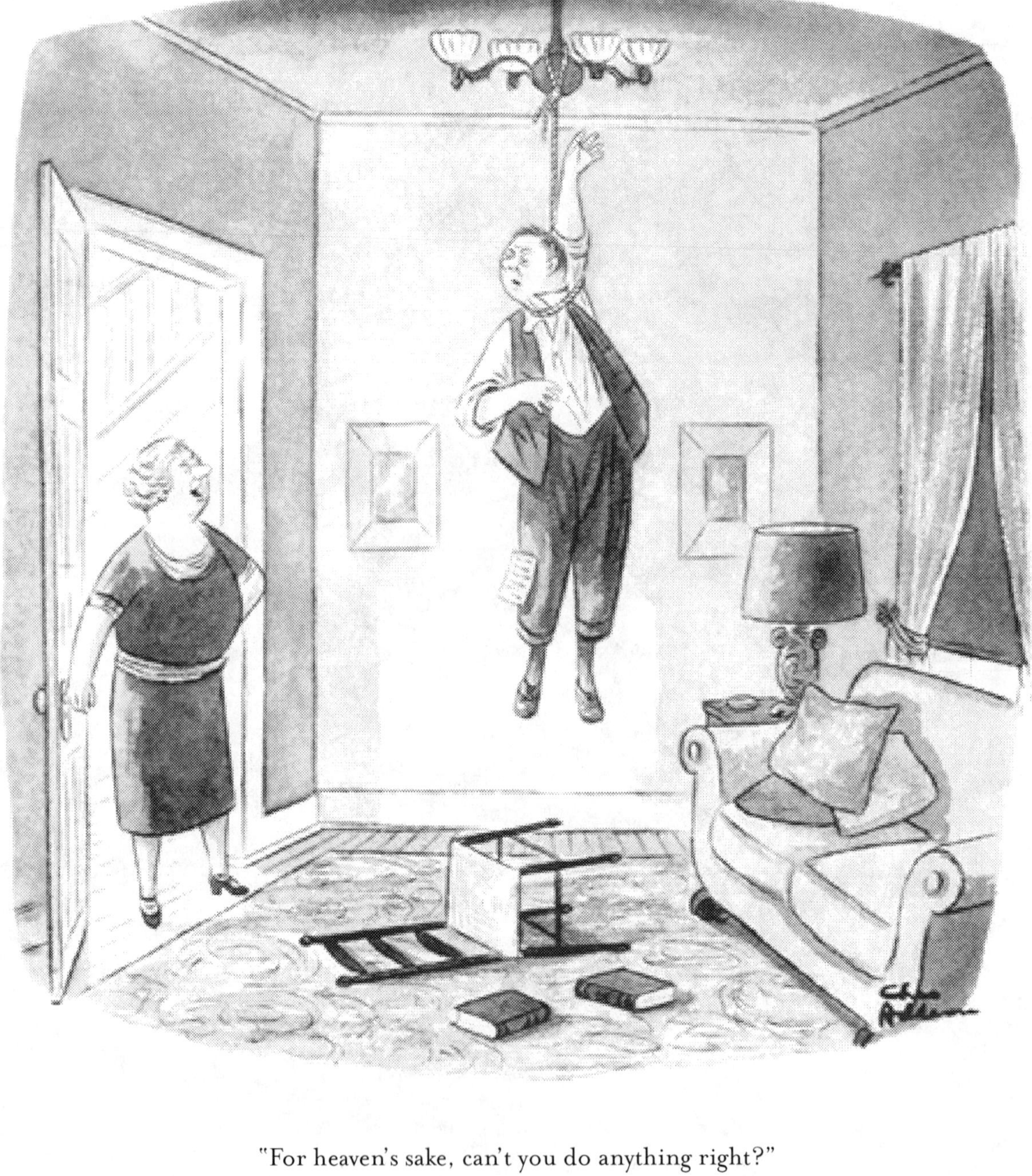

"For heaven's sake, can't you do anything right?"

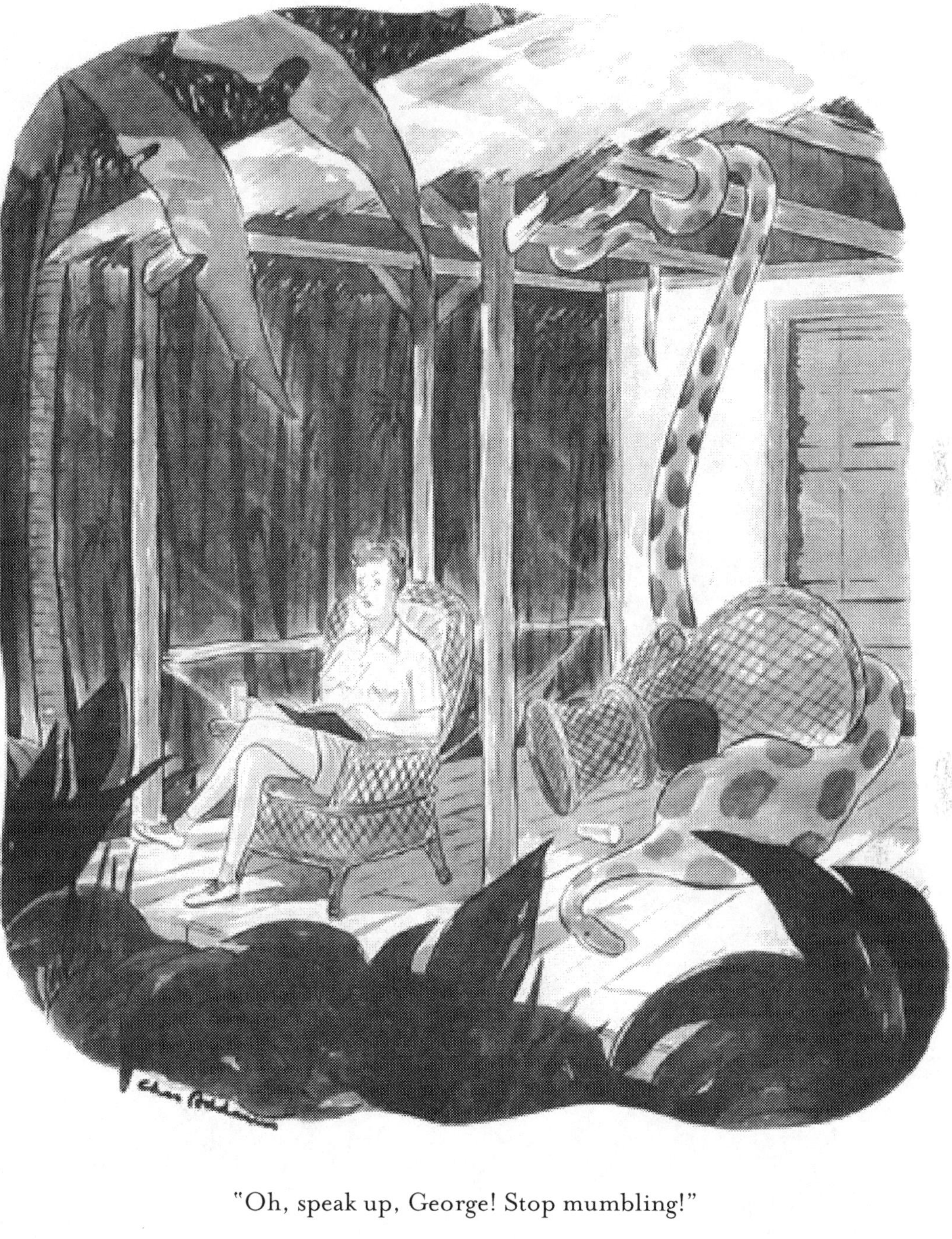

"Oh, speak up, George! Stop mumbling!"

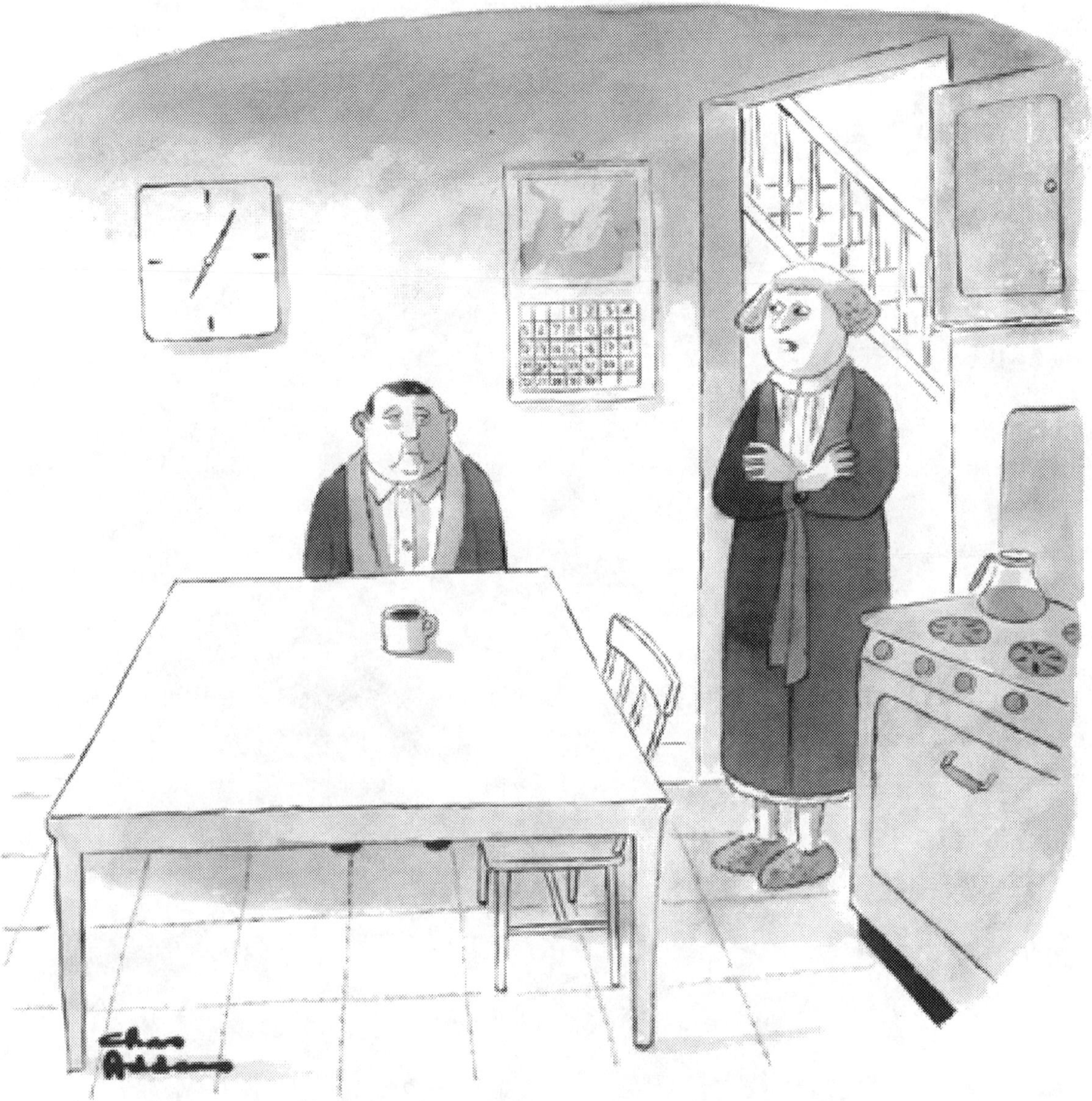

"In twenty-five words or less, how are you?"

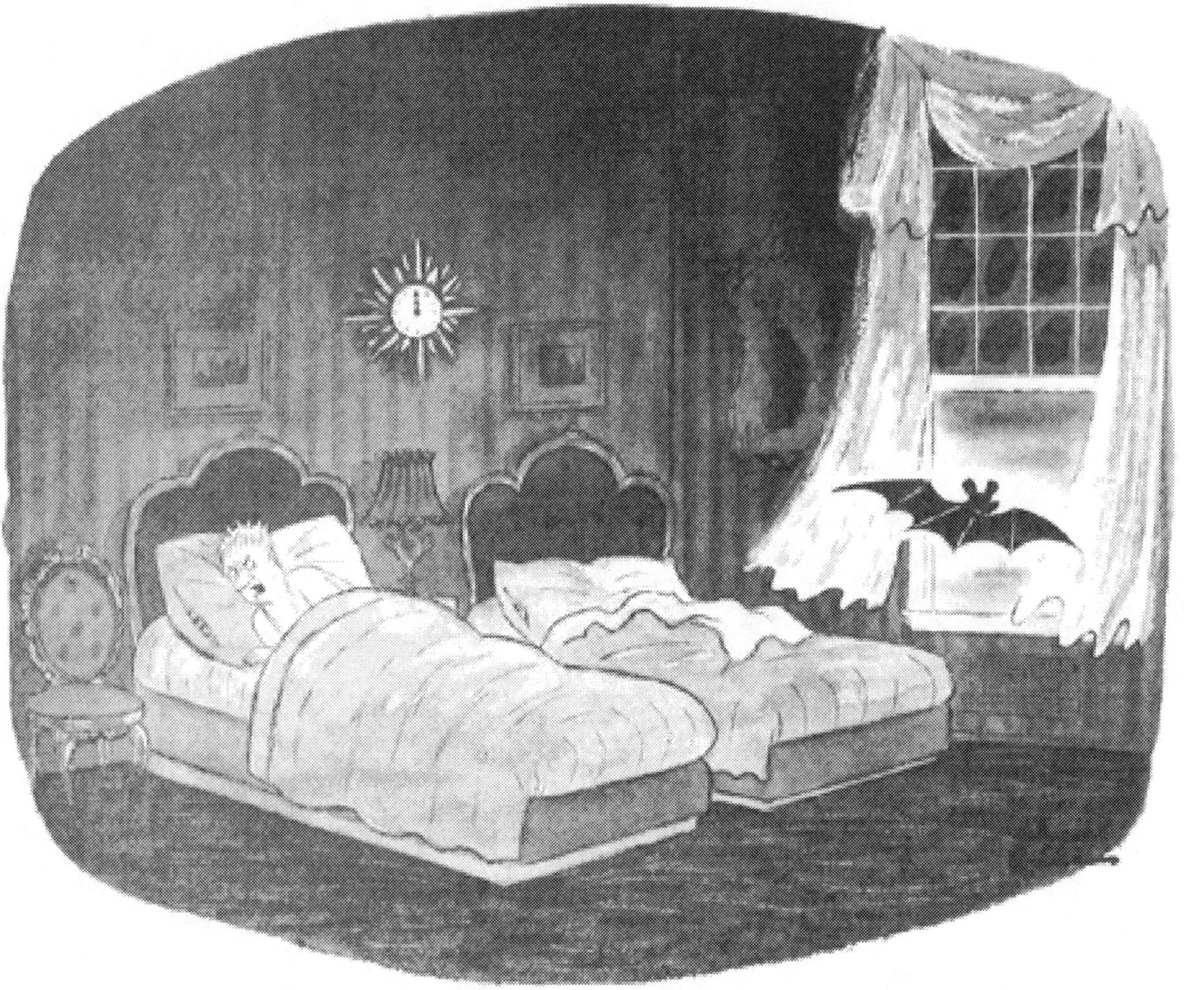

"... and don't think I don't know you're lying there wishing you were with someone else."

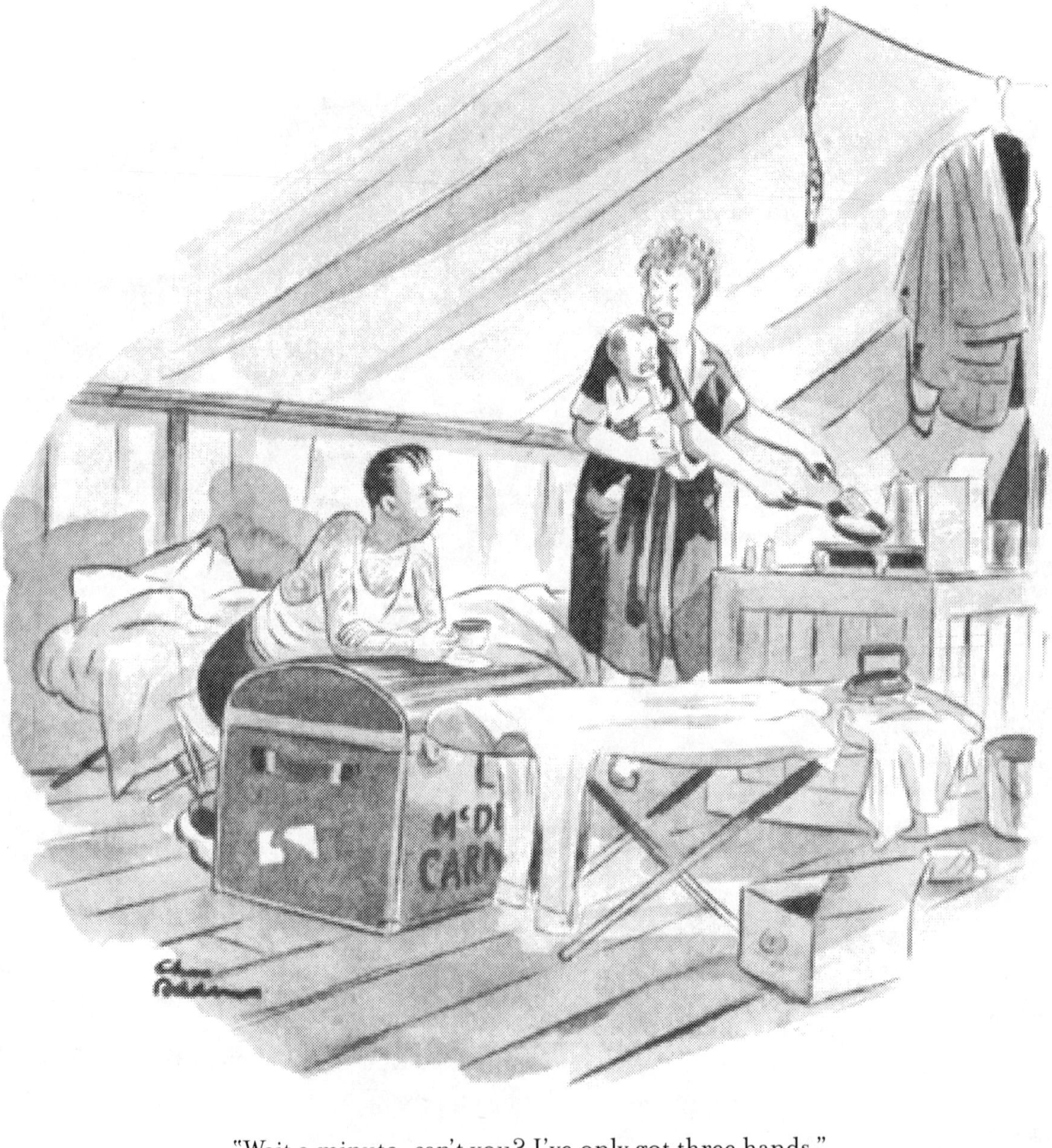

"Wait a minute, can't you? I've only got three hands."

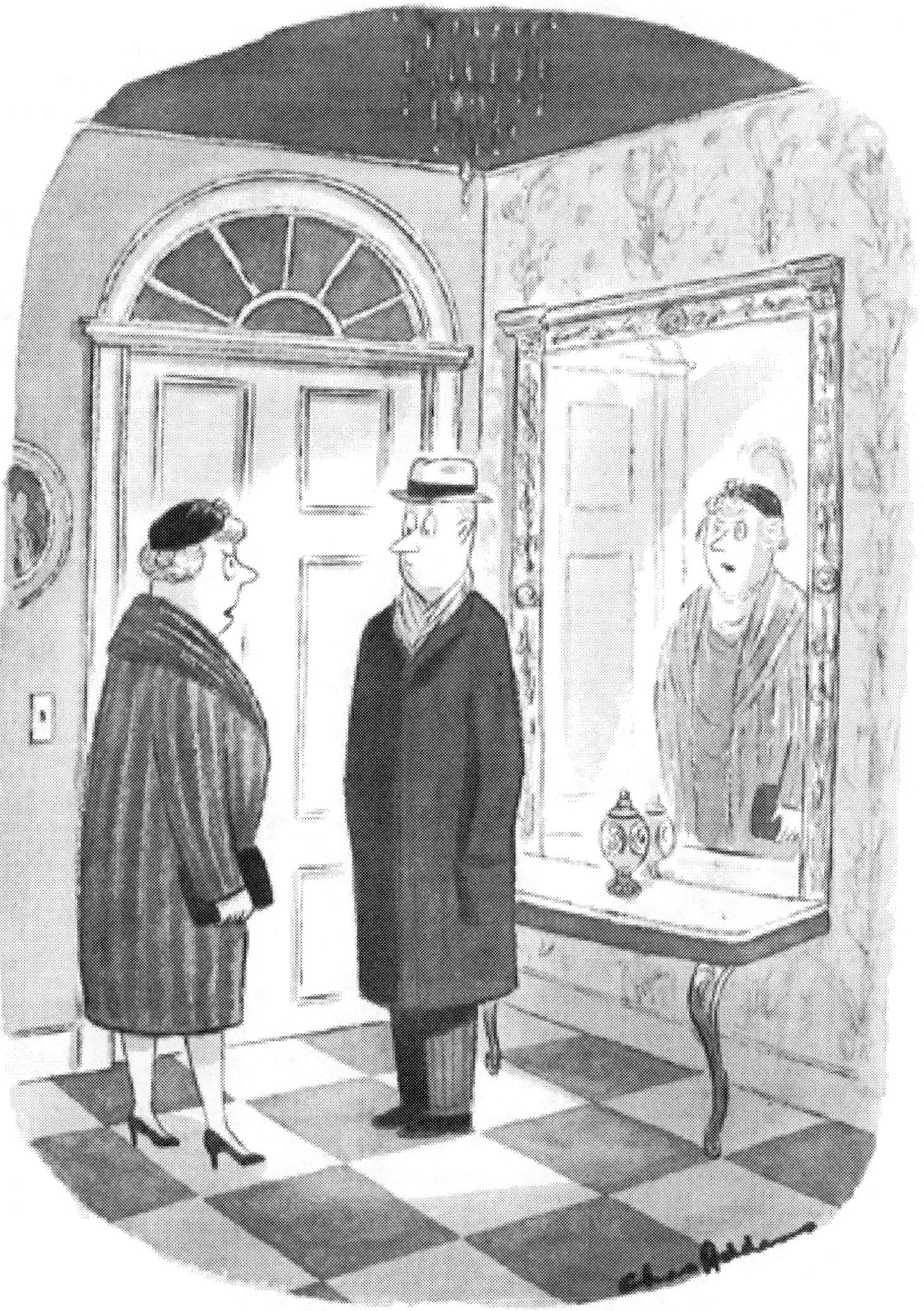

"Is something wrong, Robert? You've been acting so strange lately."

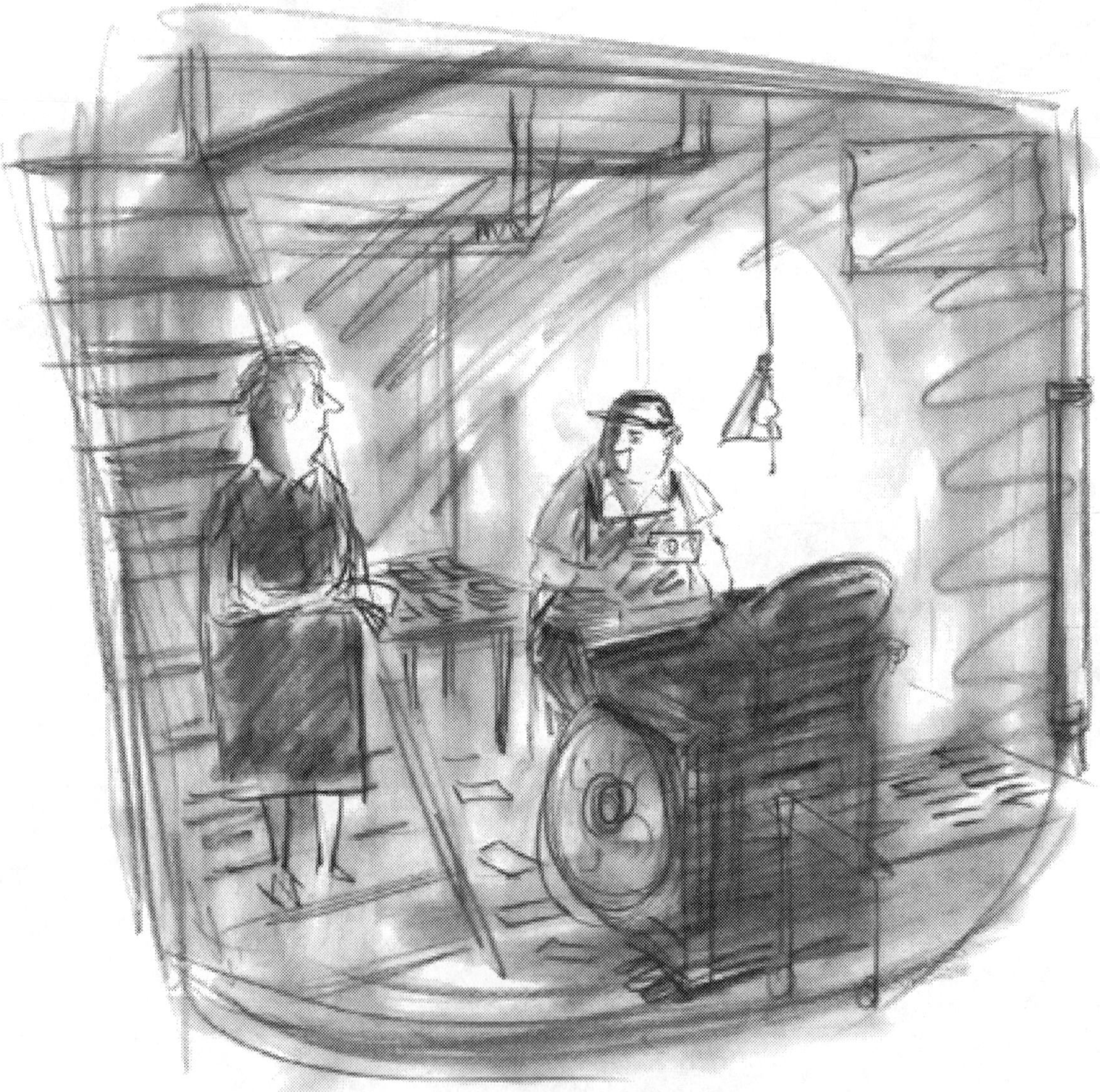

"It just doesn't look right. I'm the only one in my crowd without a credit card."

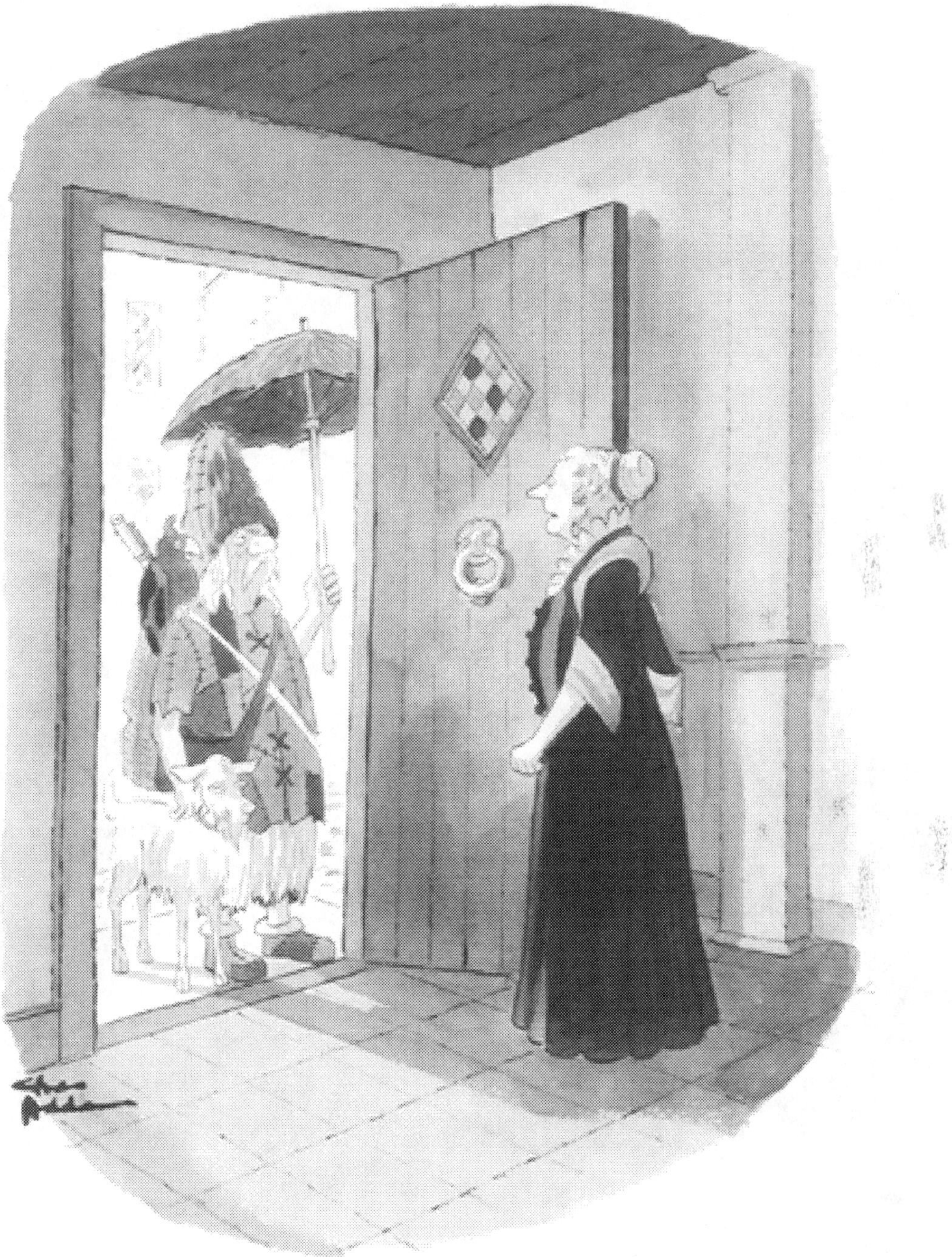

"This had better be good, Robinson."

"You know something? You're very tough to shop for."

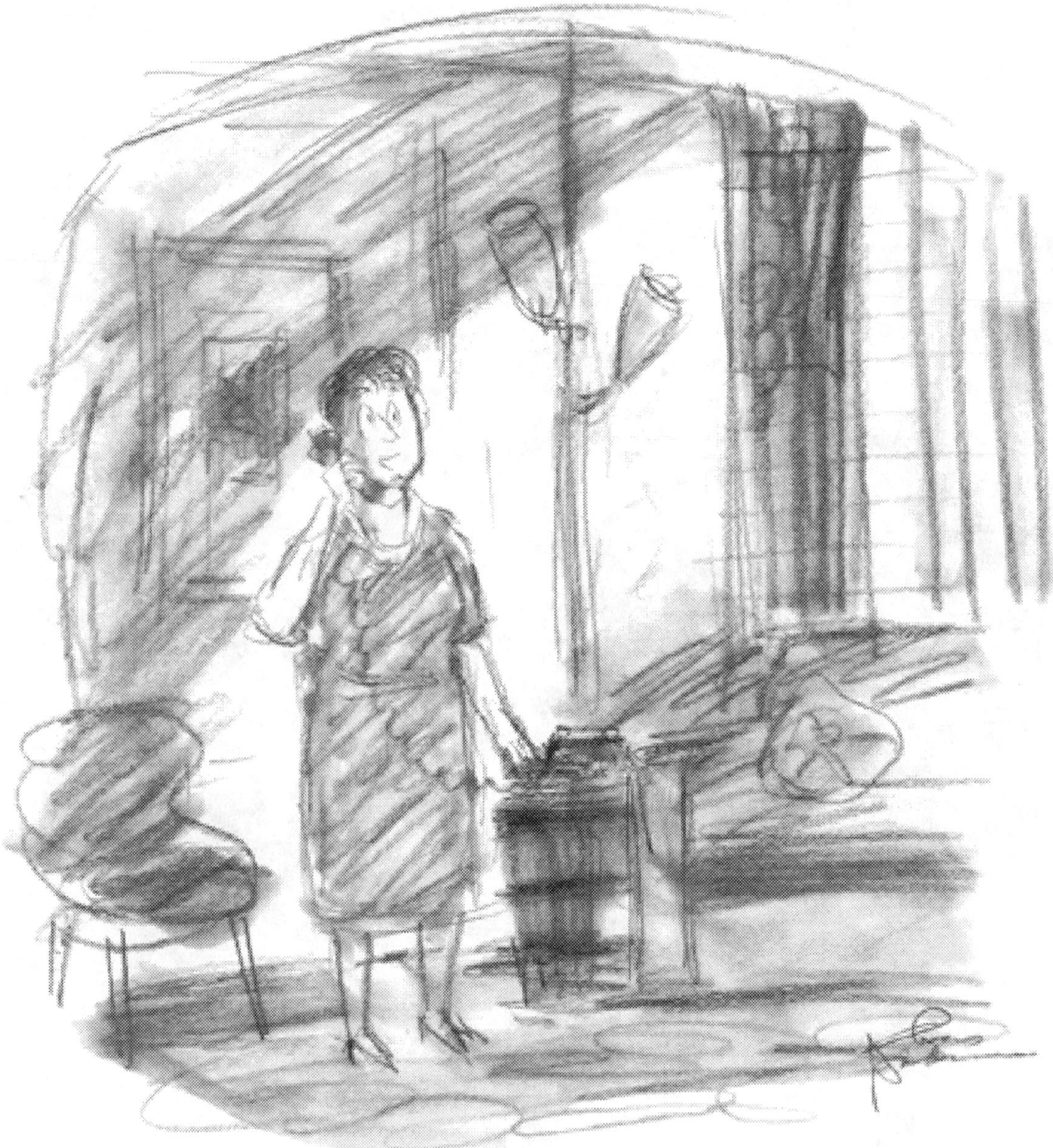

"I can't make it Tuesday, Helen. I have a session with the AA, an hour with my analyst, another chat with the marriage counselor, and then the check-in with my parole officer, but on Wednesday I'm free as a bird."

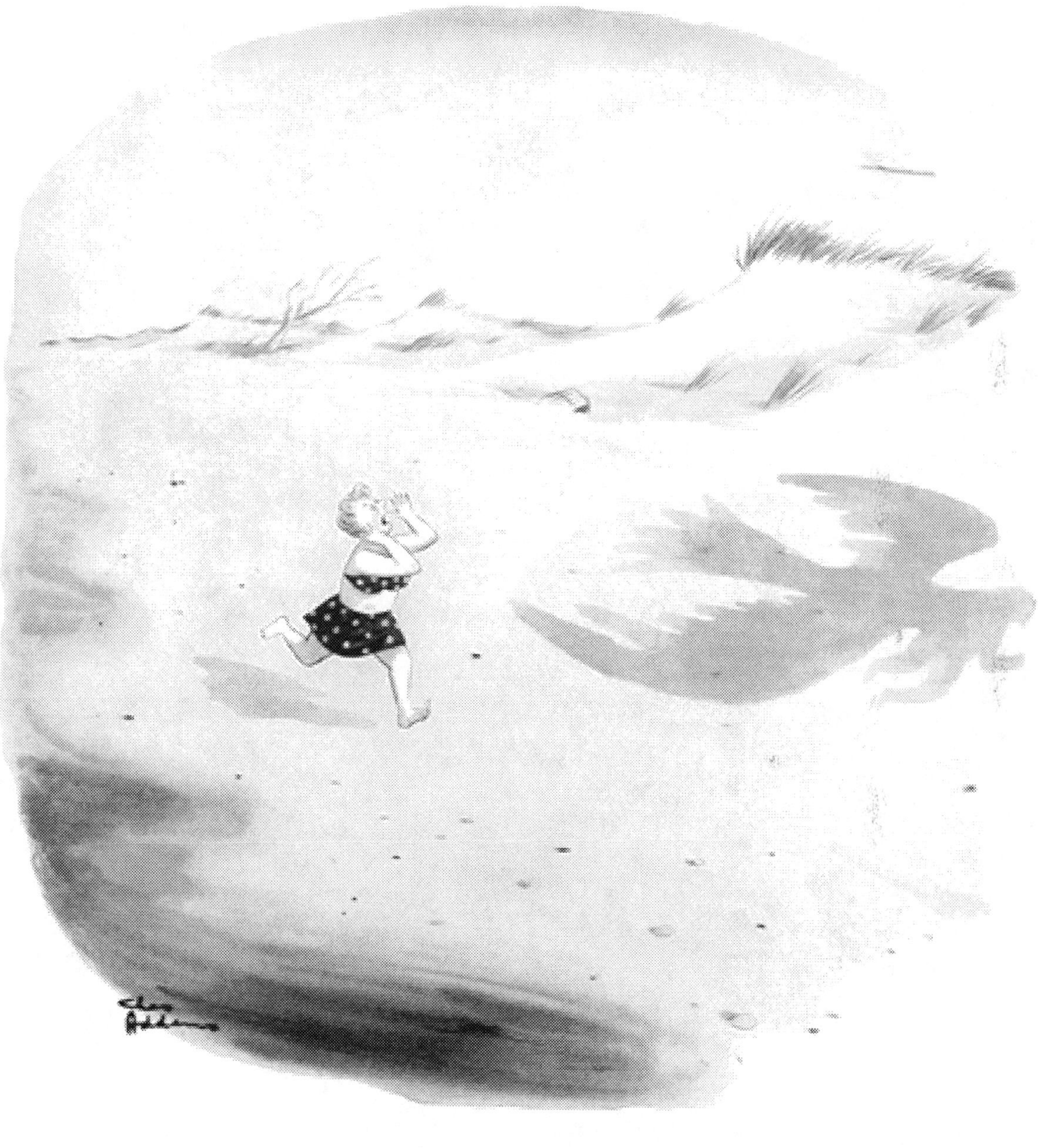

"George! George! Drop the keys!"

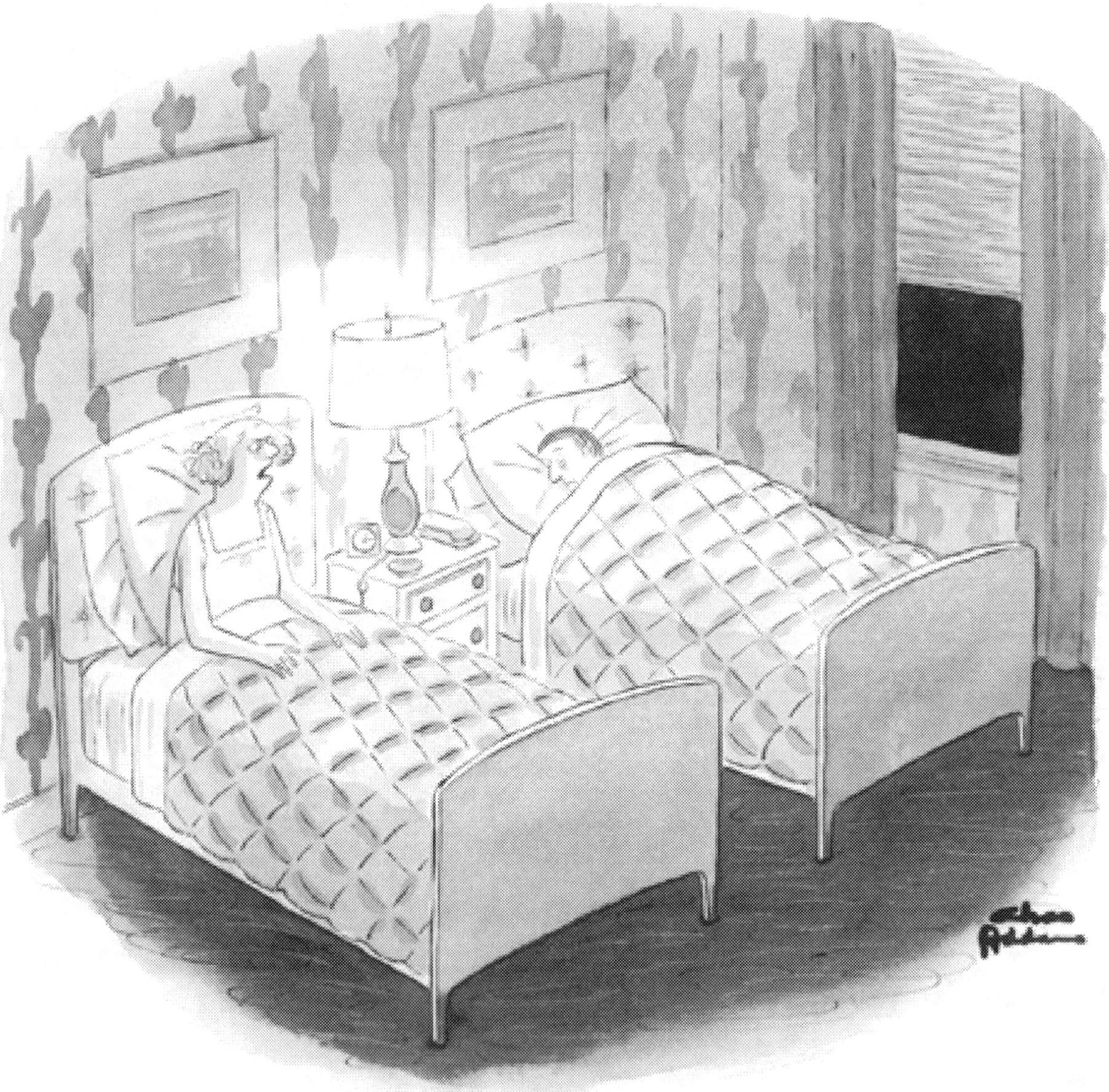

"How can you just lie there and *accept* continental drift?"

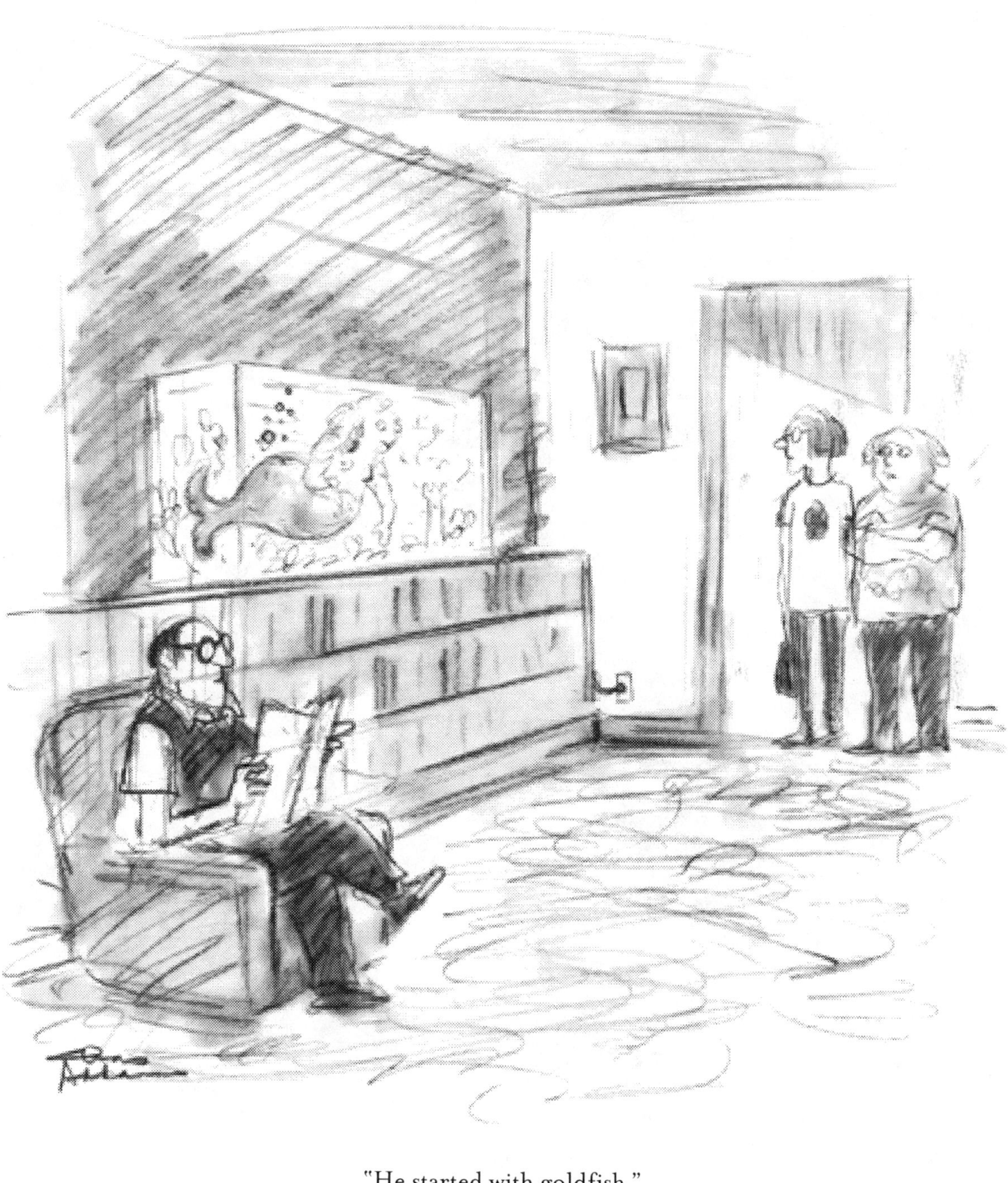

"He started with goldfish."

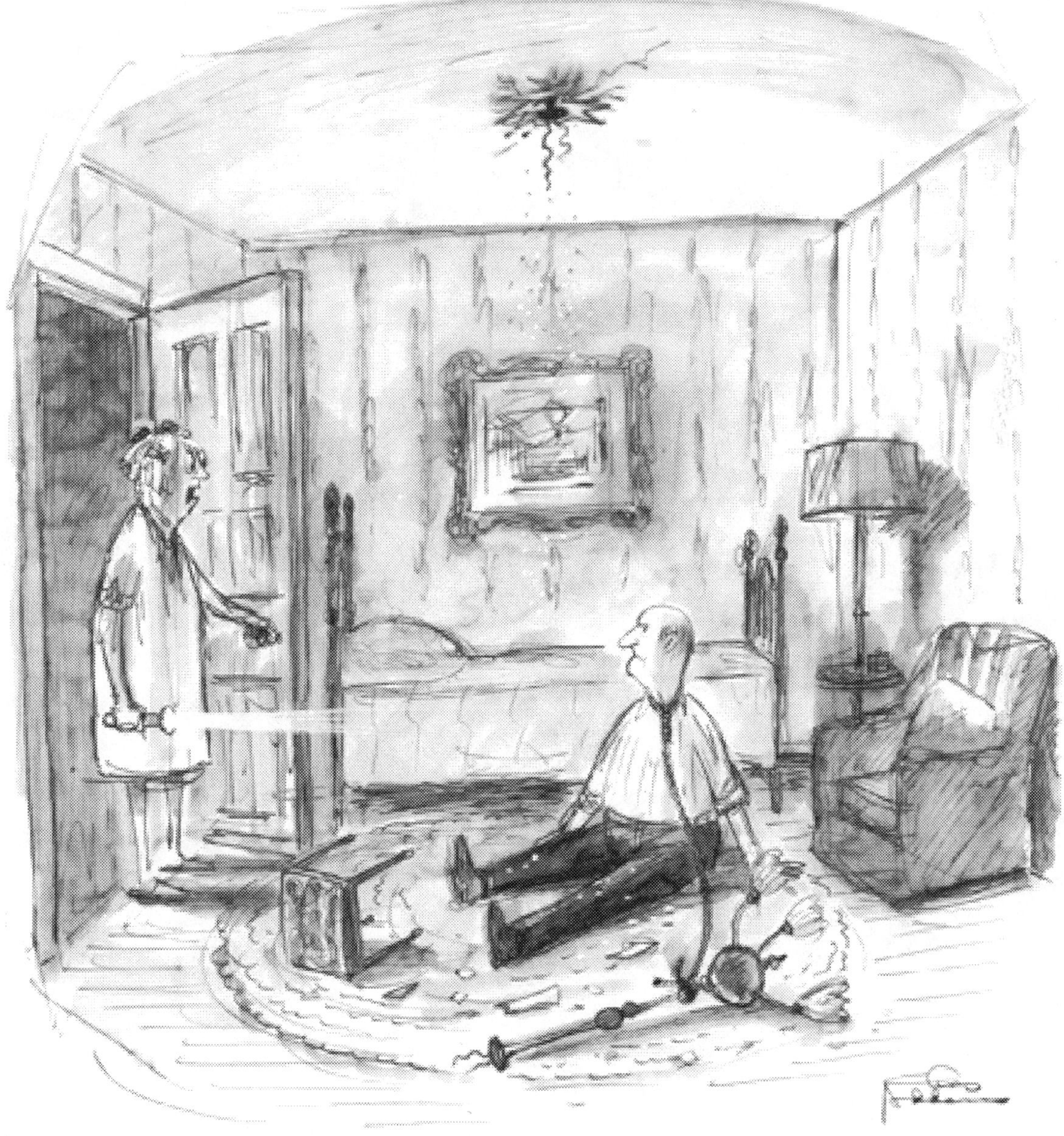

"Albert! You've gone and blown another fuse!"

"There, there, dear. It's only a commercial."

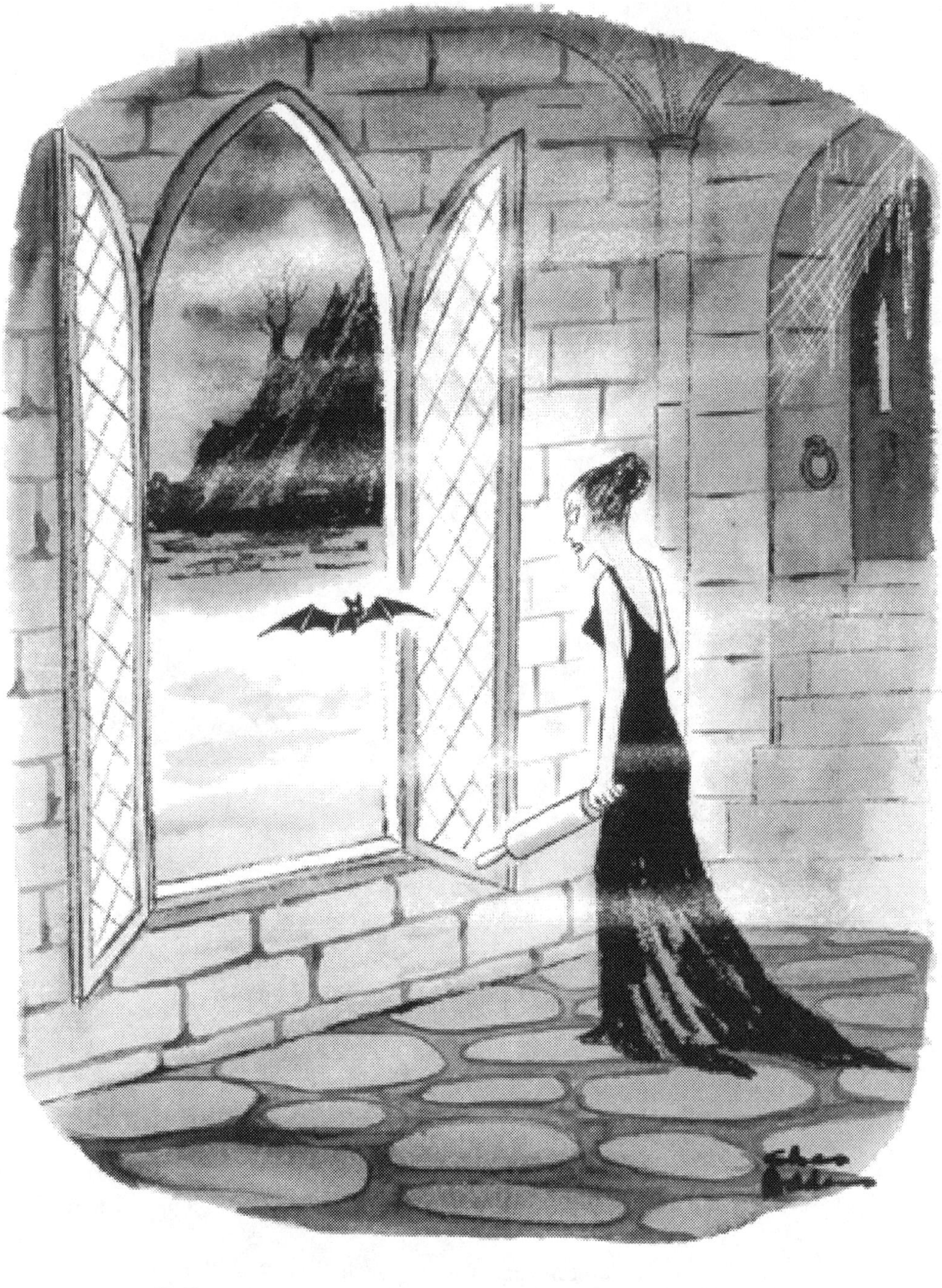

"Where have *you* been until this hour of the morning?"

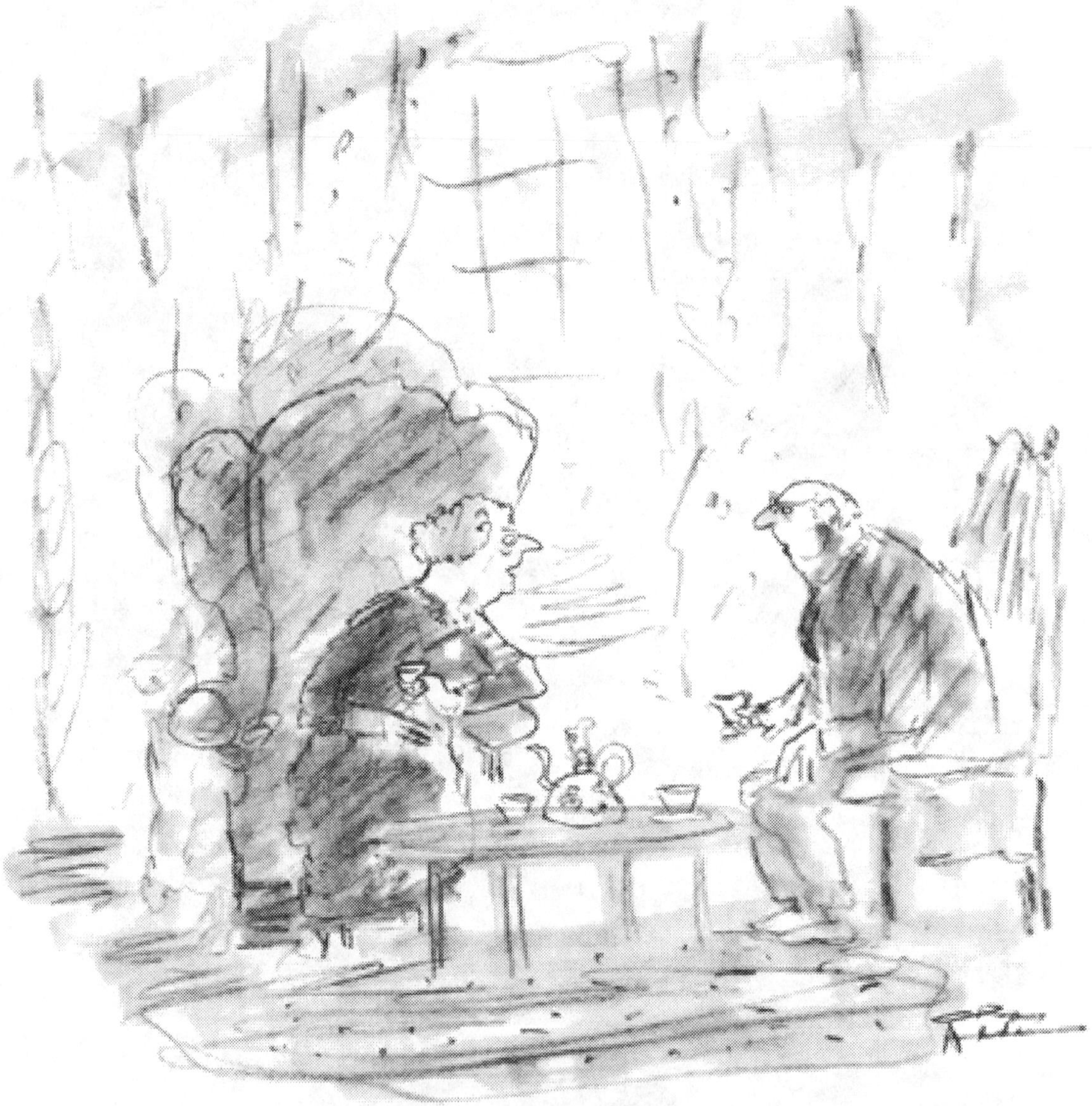

"Now, if my husband comes home, you hide in the closet."

"Please, let's not talk about your day."

"To think I could have married a CRO-MAGNON!"

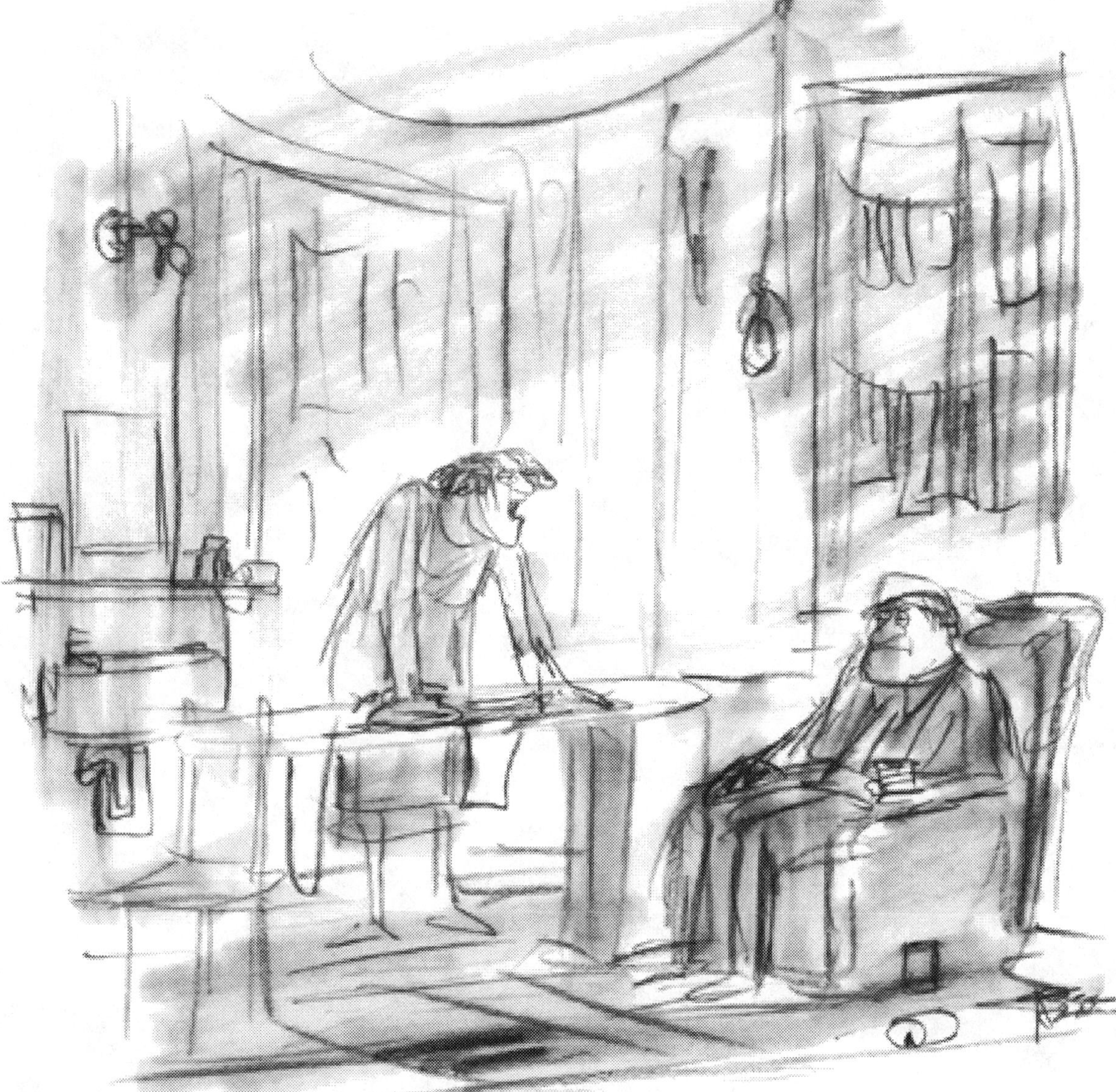

"So when are we supposed to look back and laugh at this already?"

His Resolve

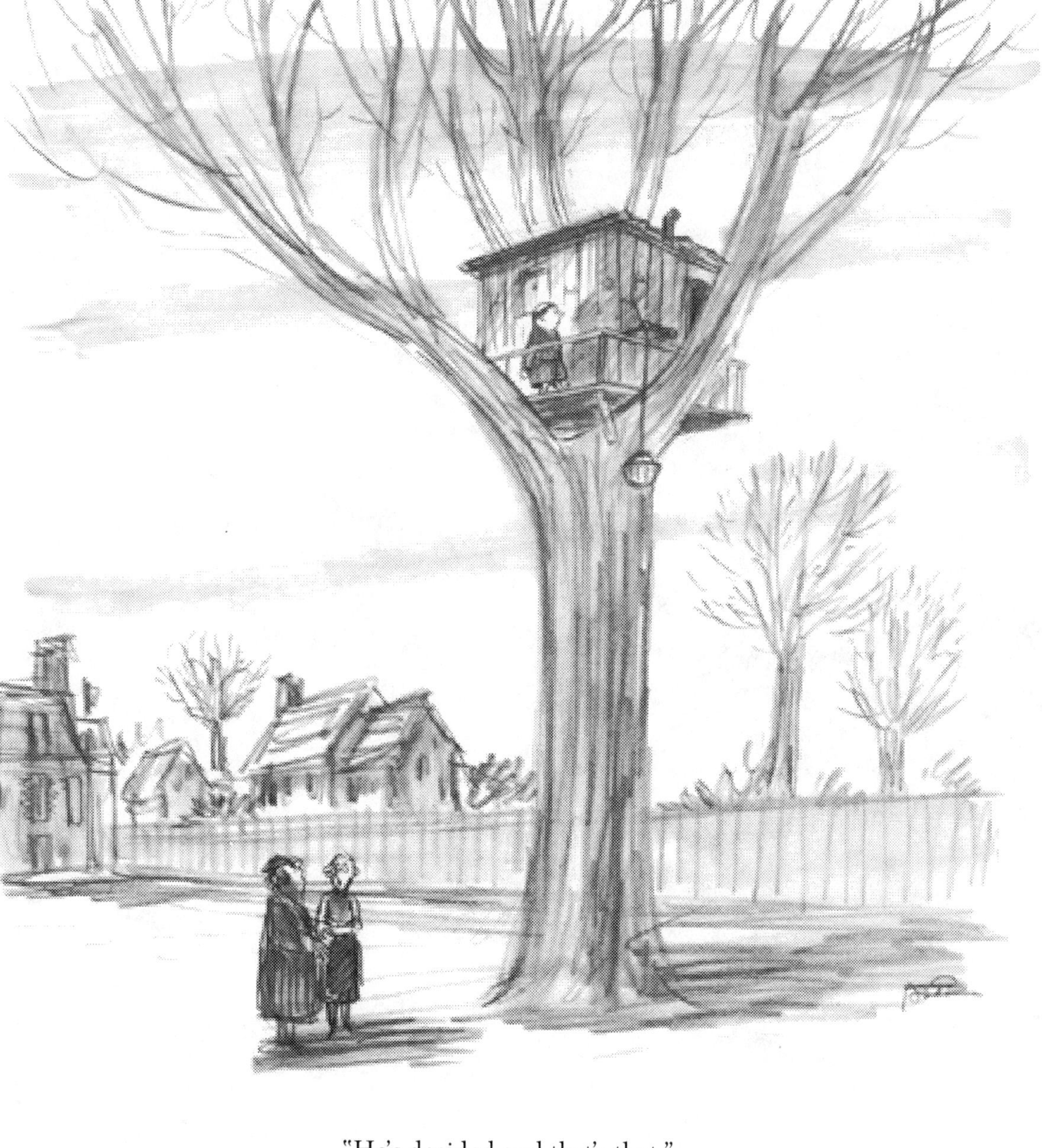

"He's decided and that's that."

"Just back up a little, dear, so you won't cut my head off."

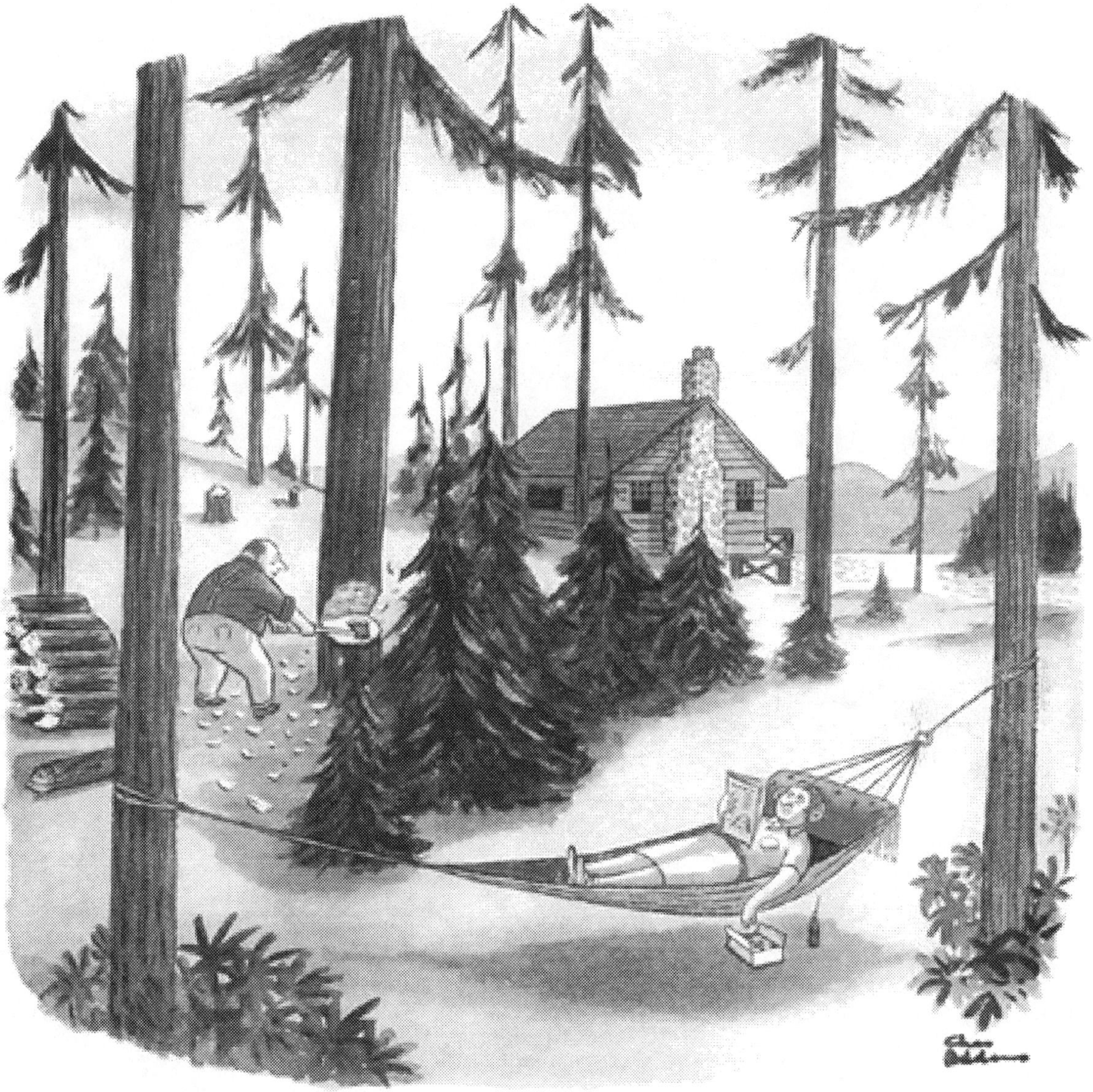

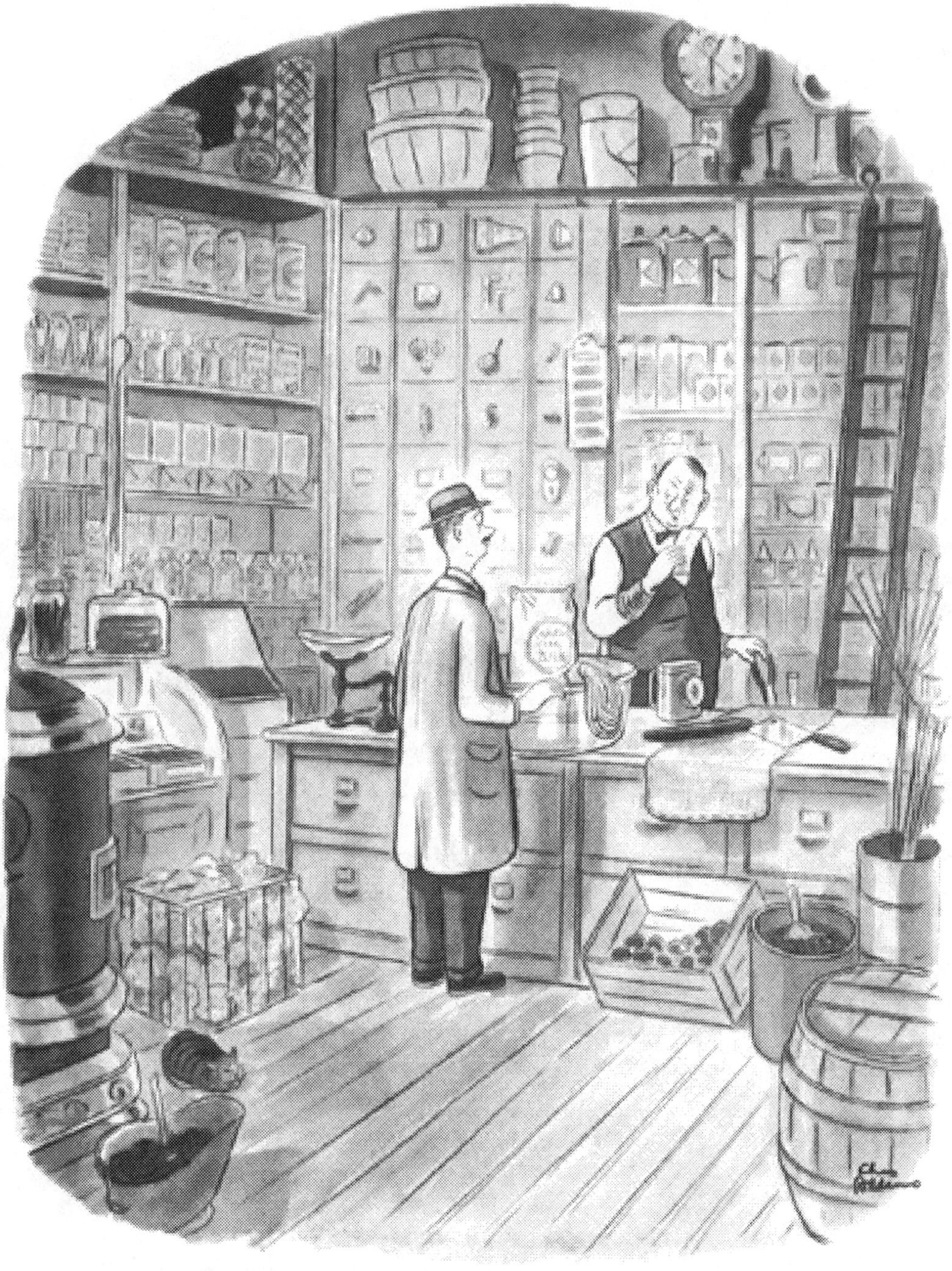

"Now, let's see—one sash weight, one butcher's cleaver, one galvanized-iron tub, fifty feet of half-inch rope, one gunnysack, one electric torch, one pickaxe, one shovel, twenty pounds of quicklime, a box of cigars, and a beach chair."

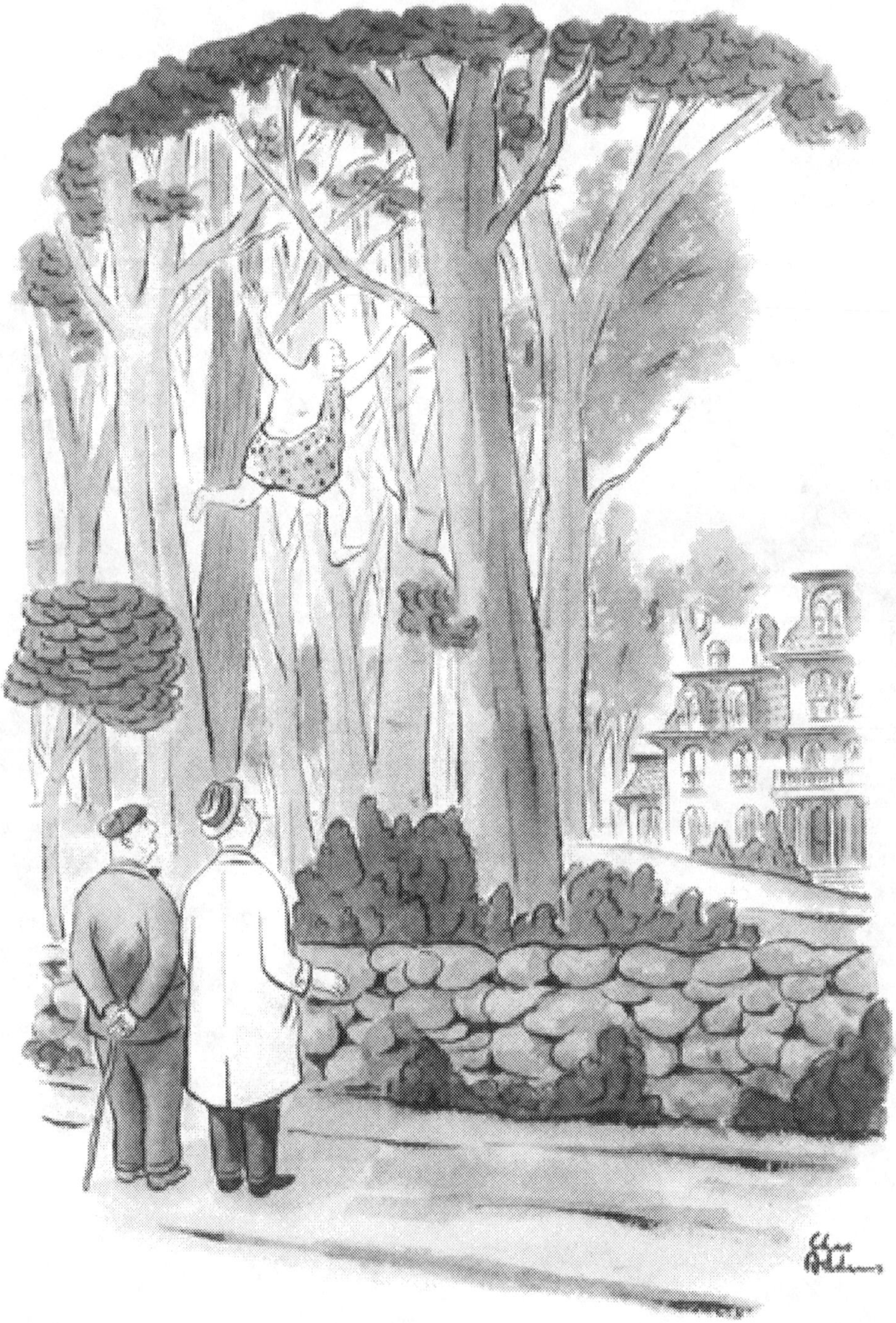

"Latham's been living that way ever since his wife gave him his freedom."

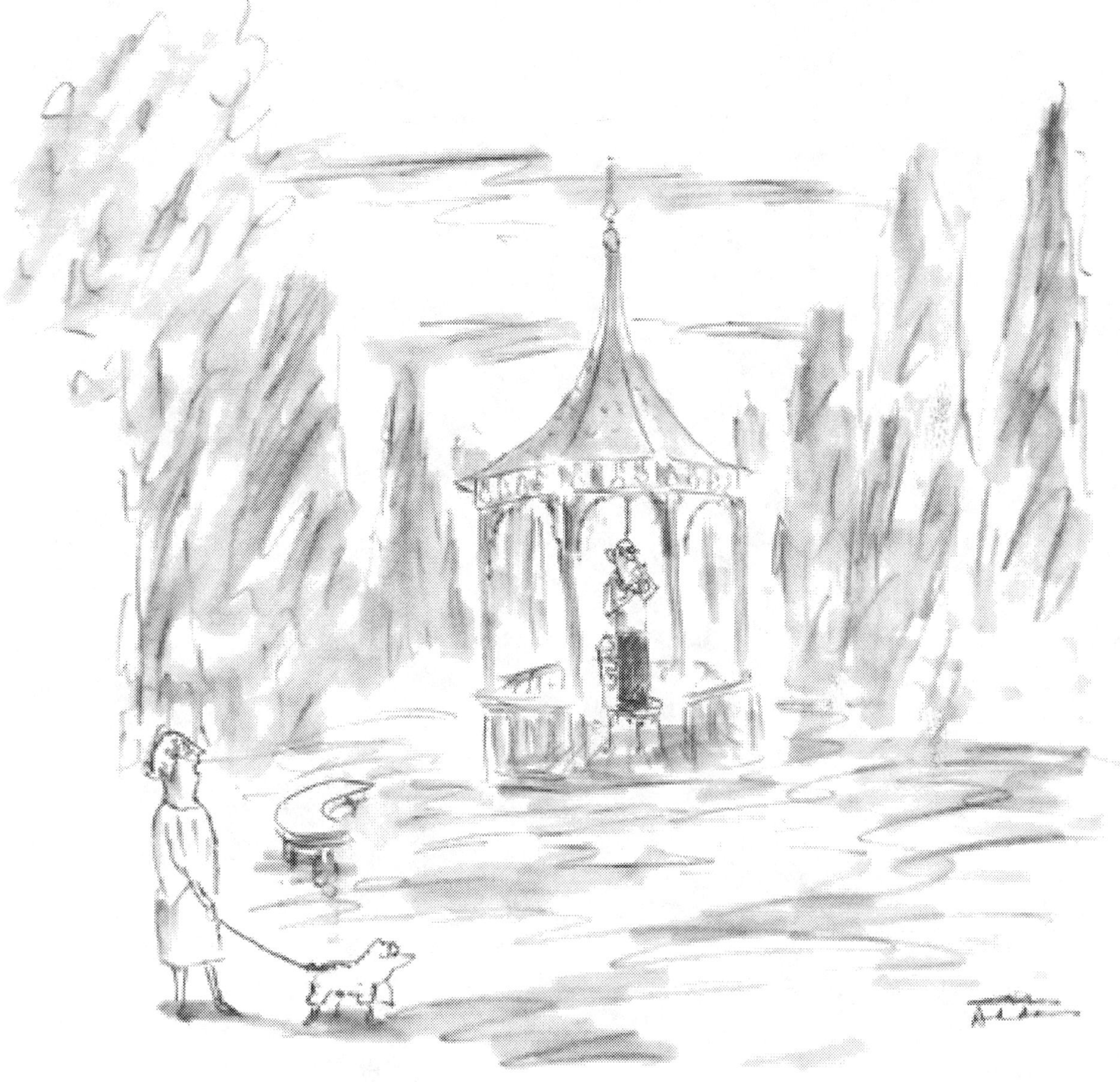

"Please, Elliot . . . not in the gazebo."

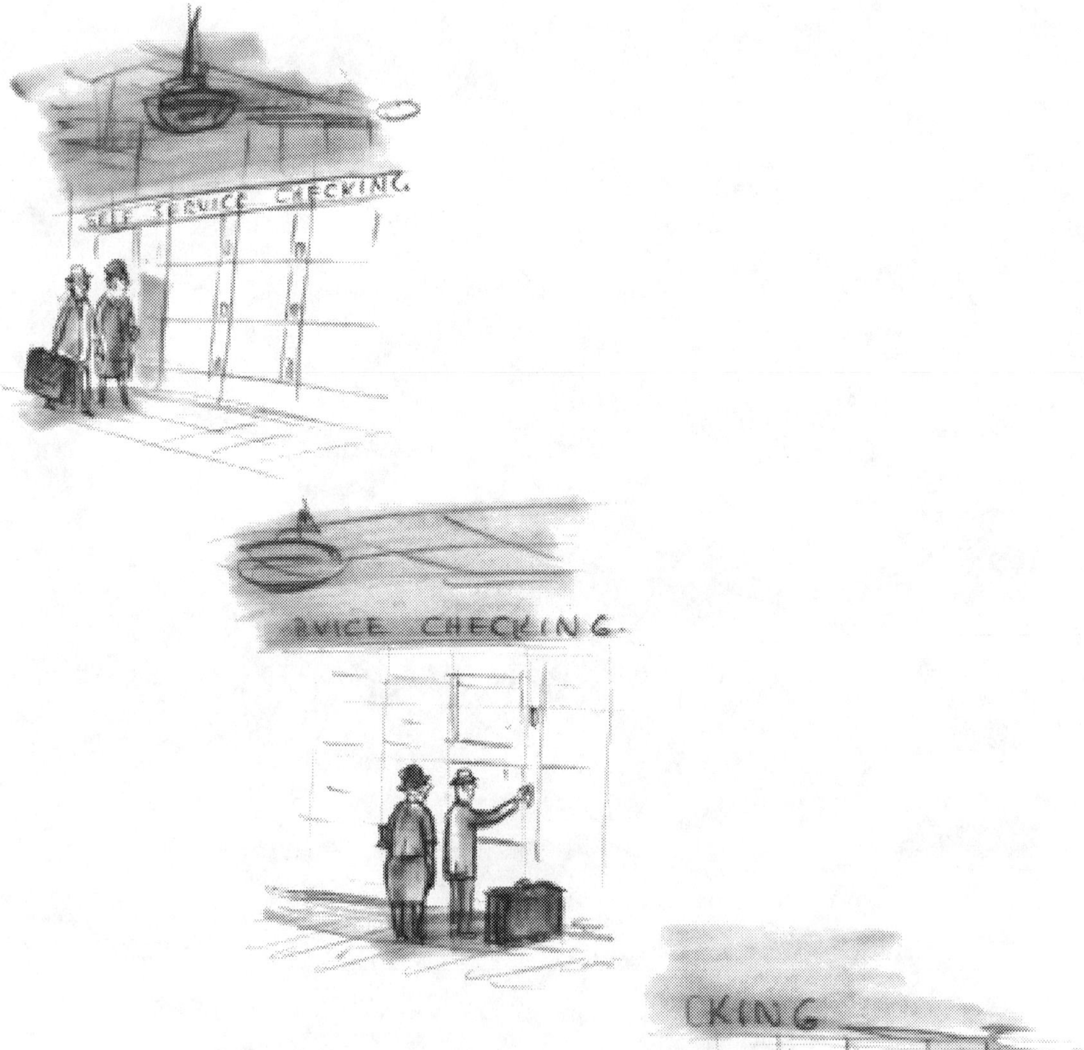

RVICE CHECKING
CKING

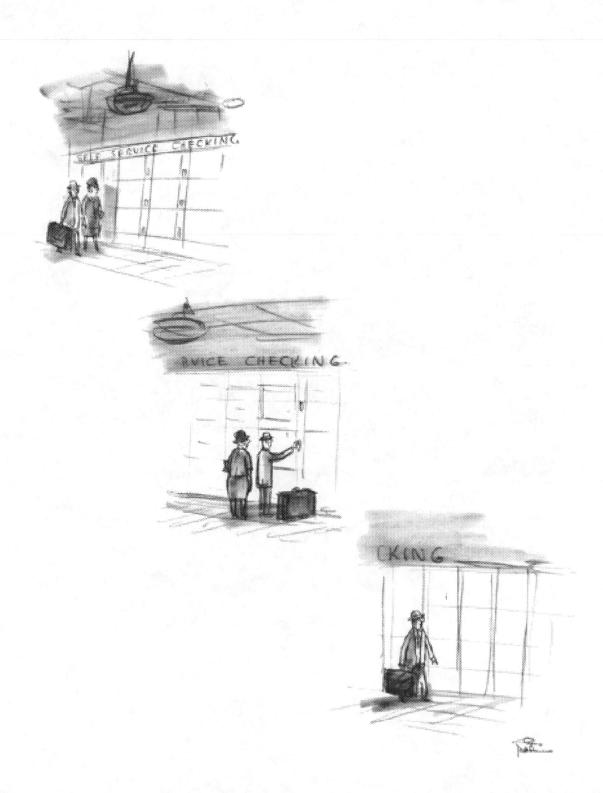

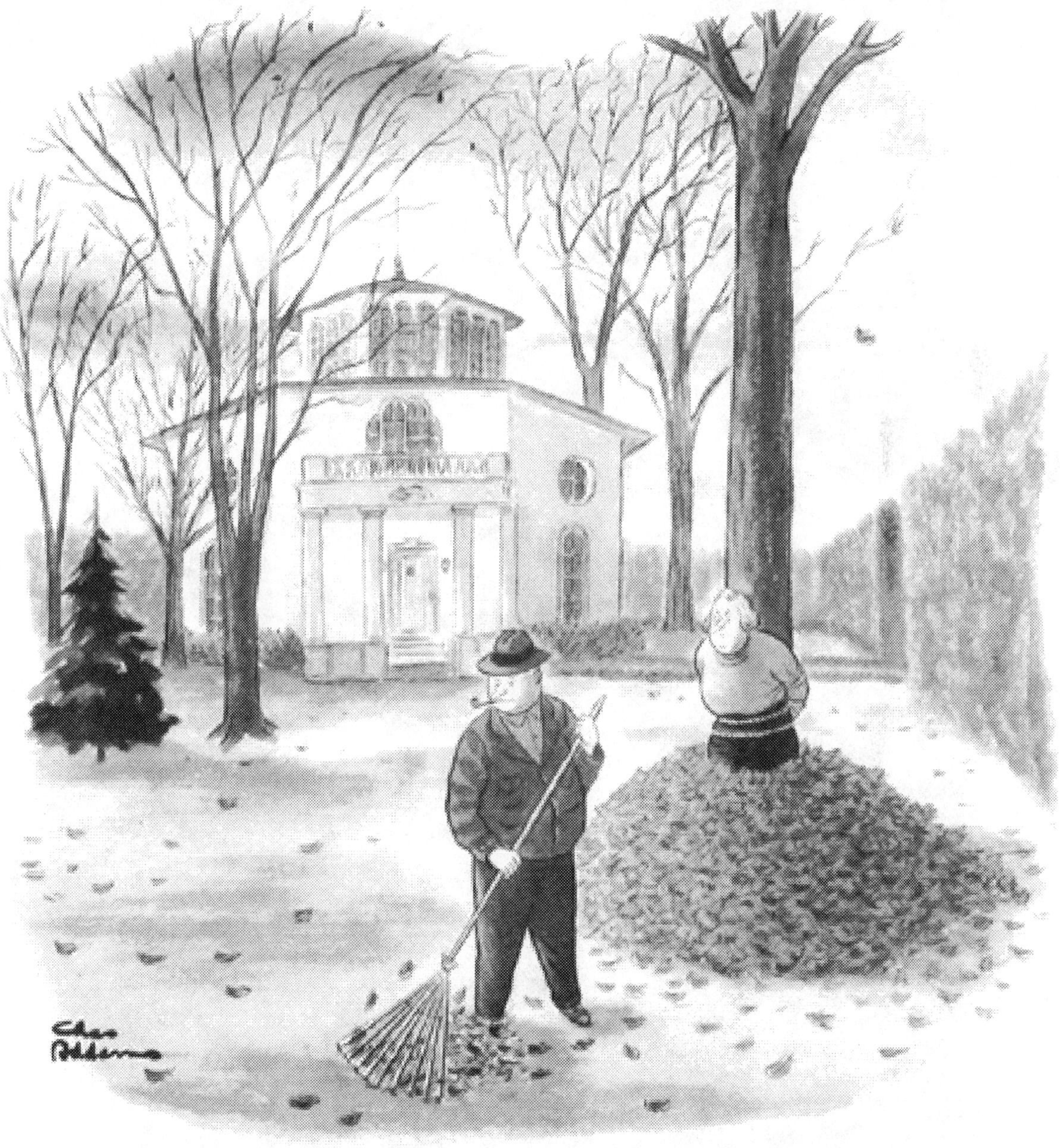
Chas Addams

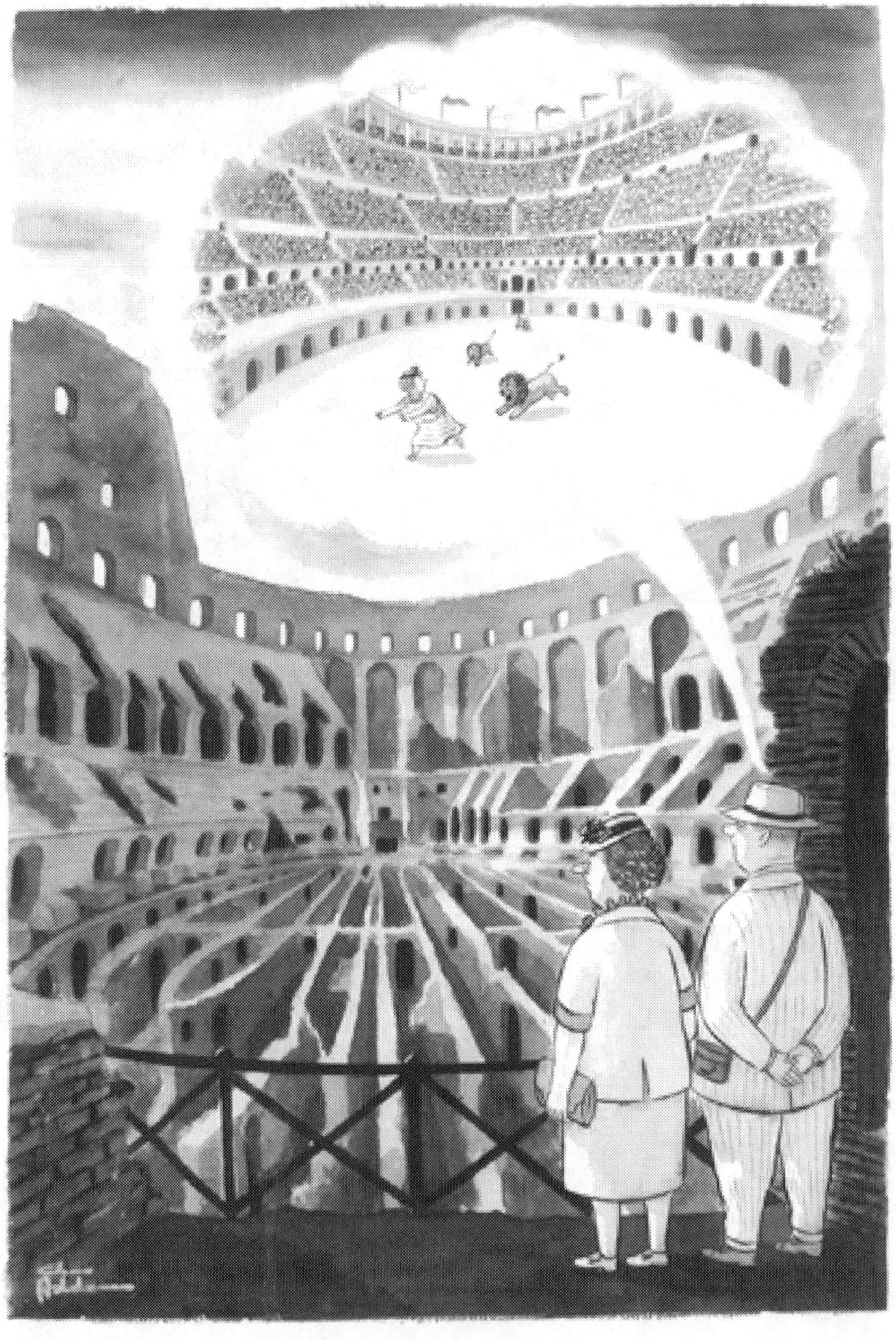

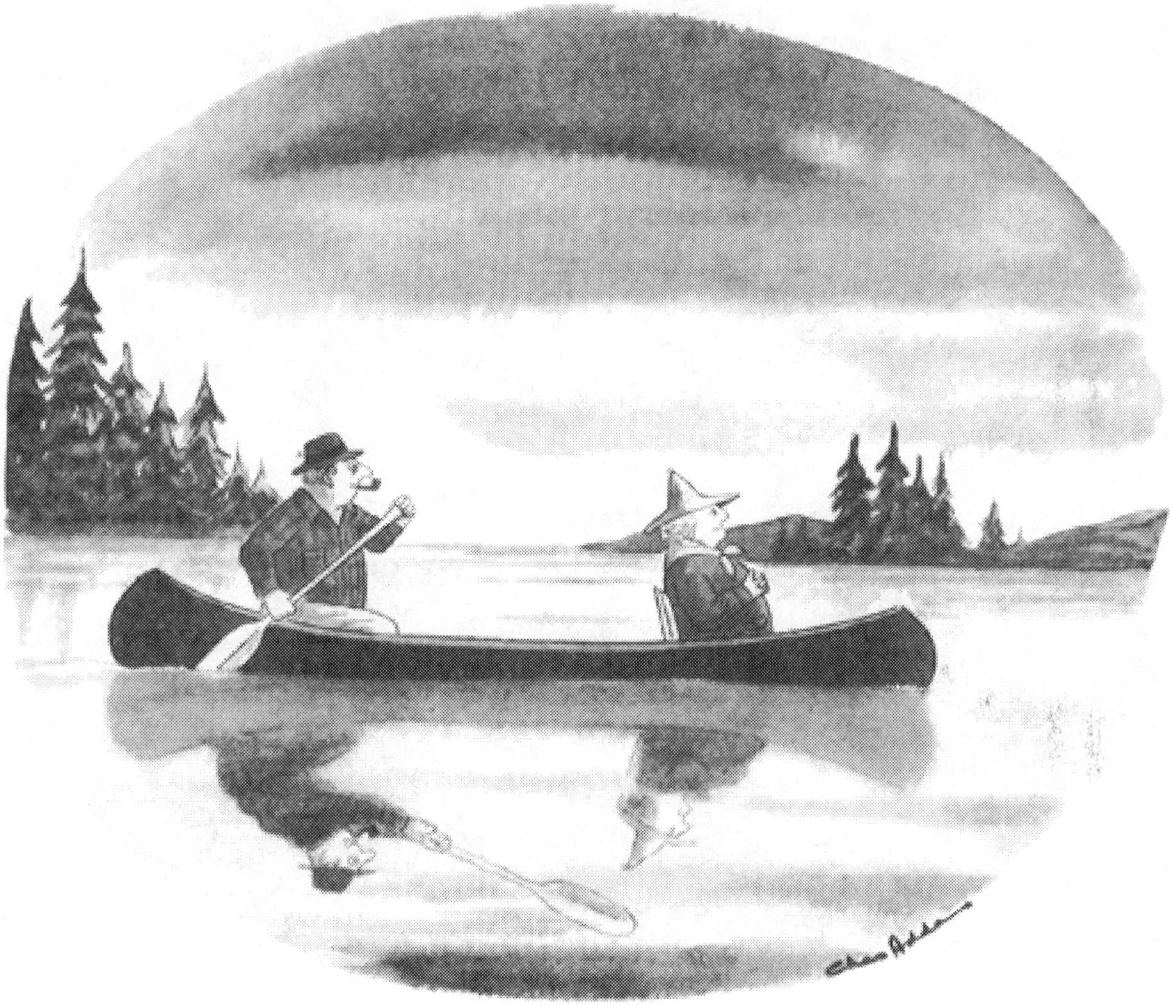

"Wallace, isn't that already too deep for glads?"

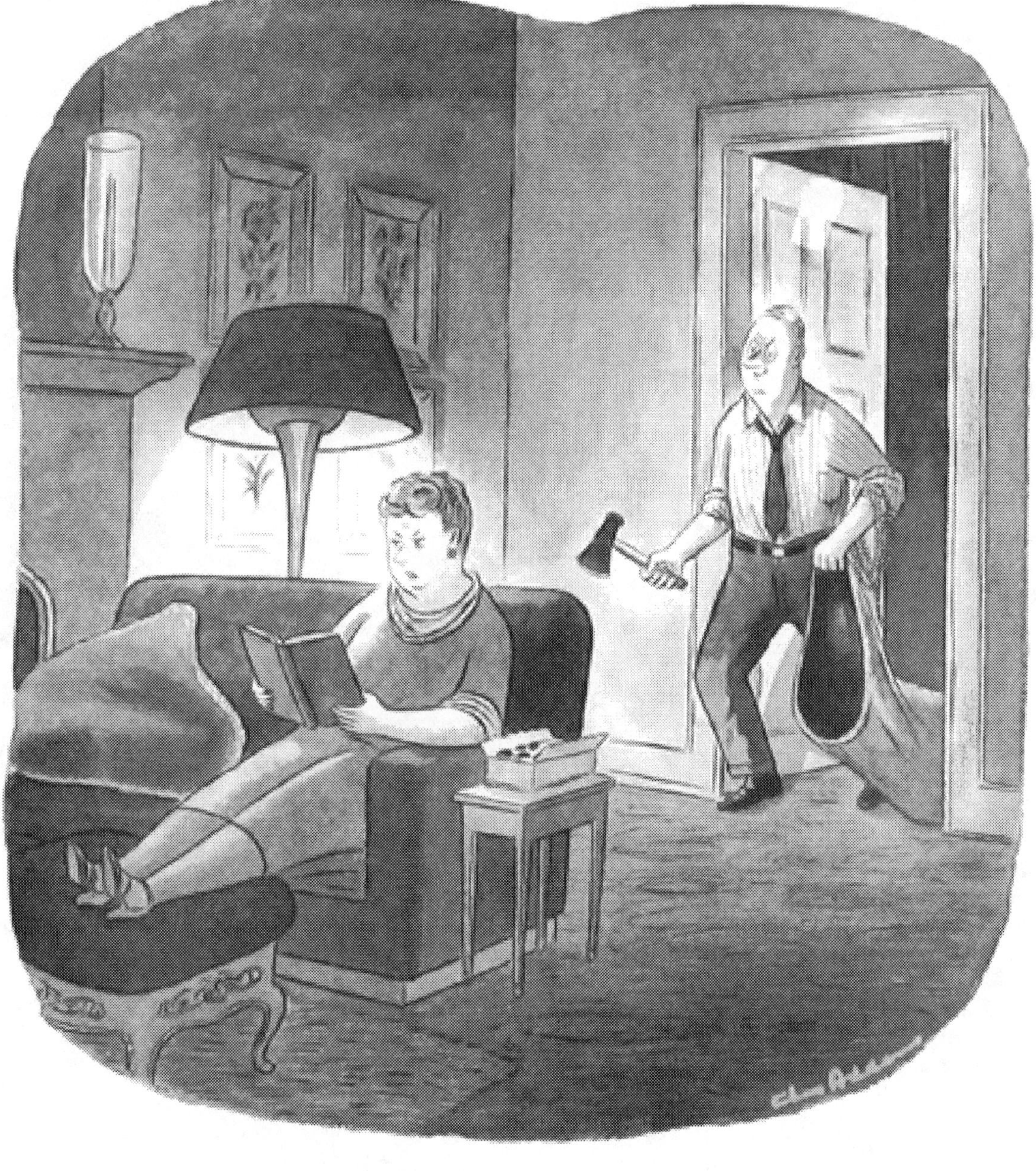

"Now, don't come crawling back asking me to forgive you."

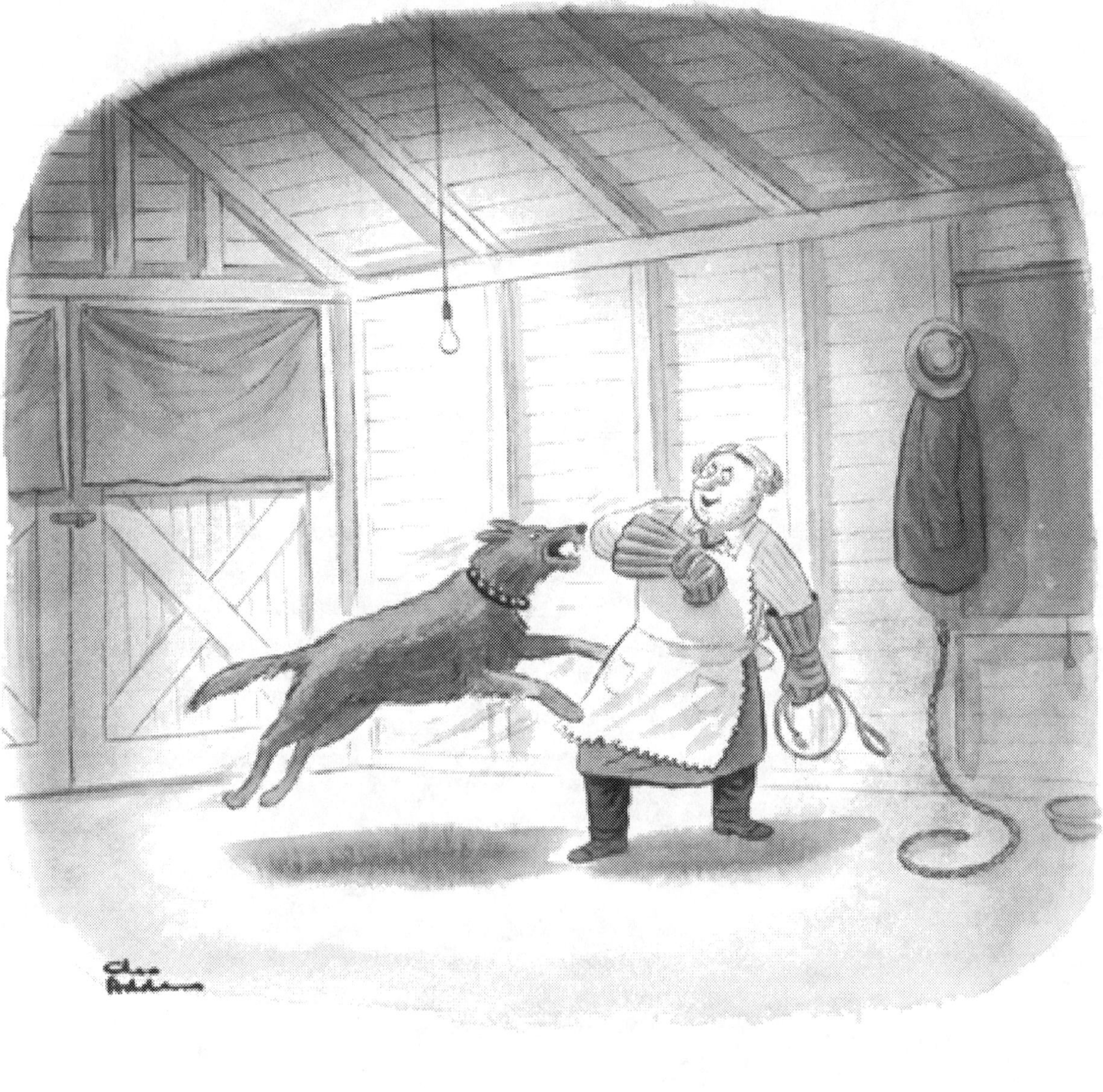

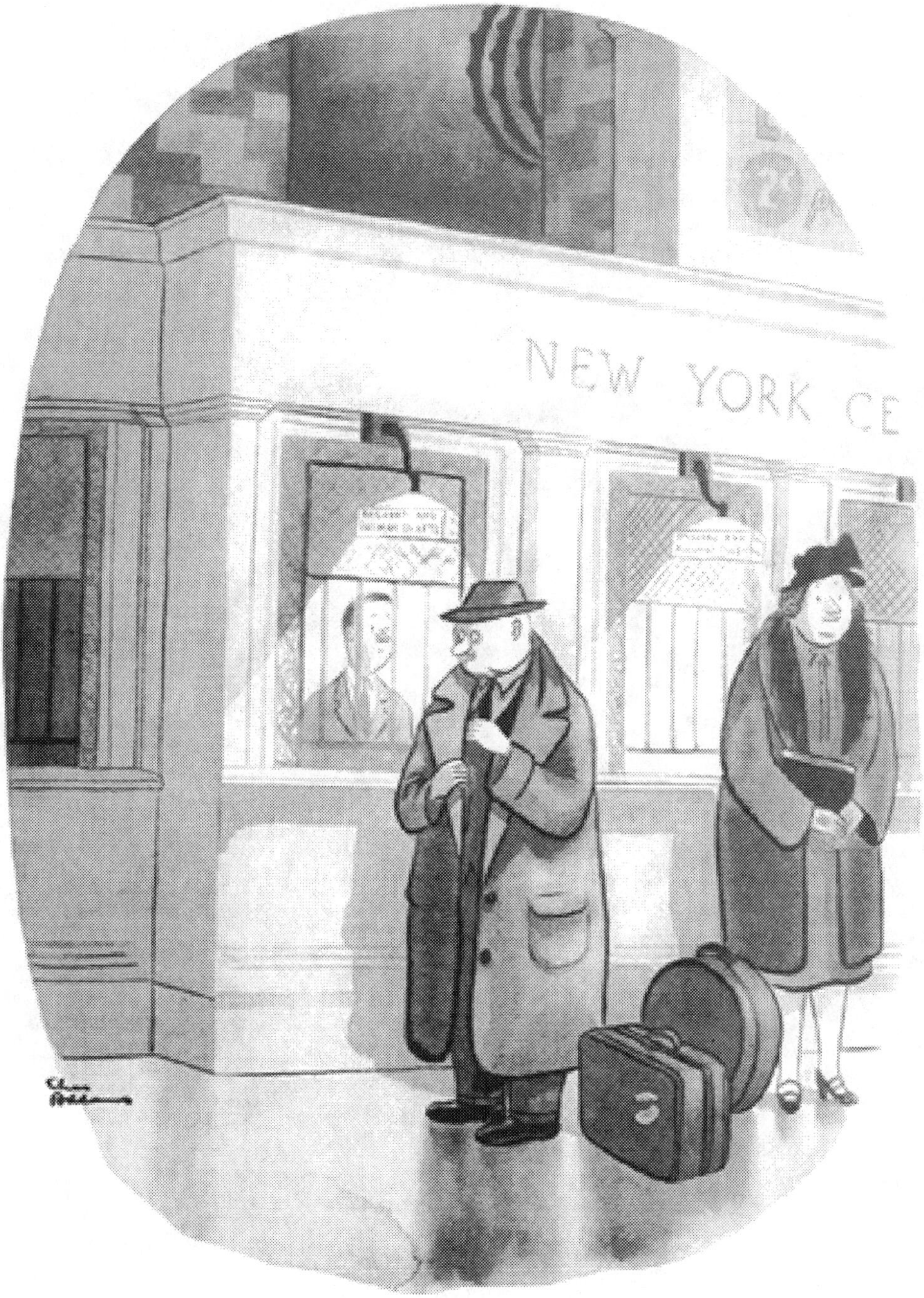
NEW YORK CE

"A round-trip and a one-way to Ausable Chasm."

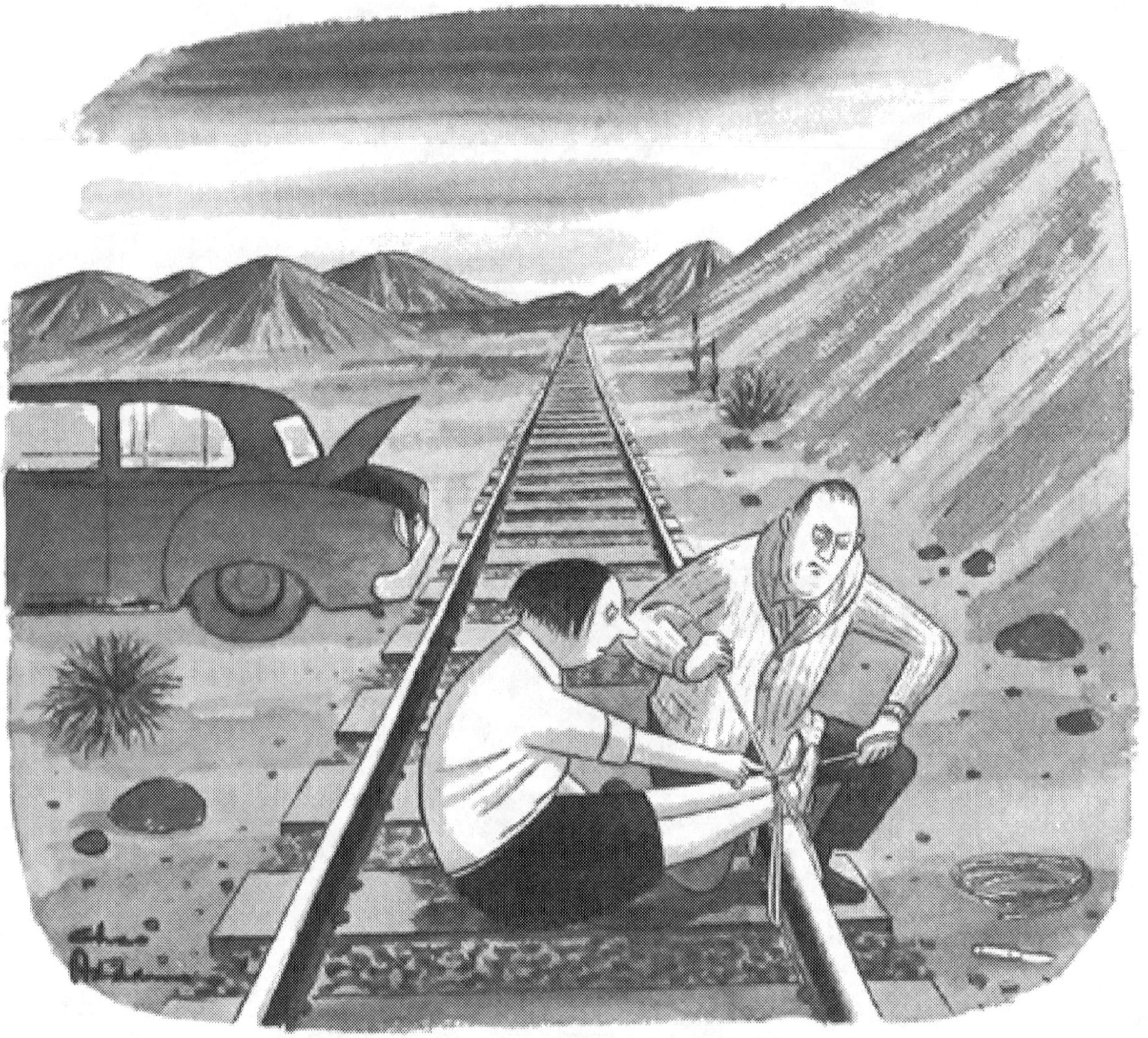

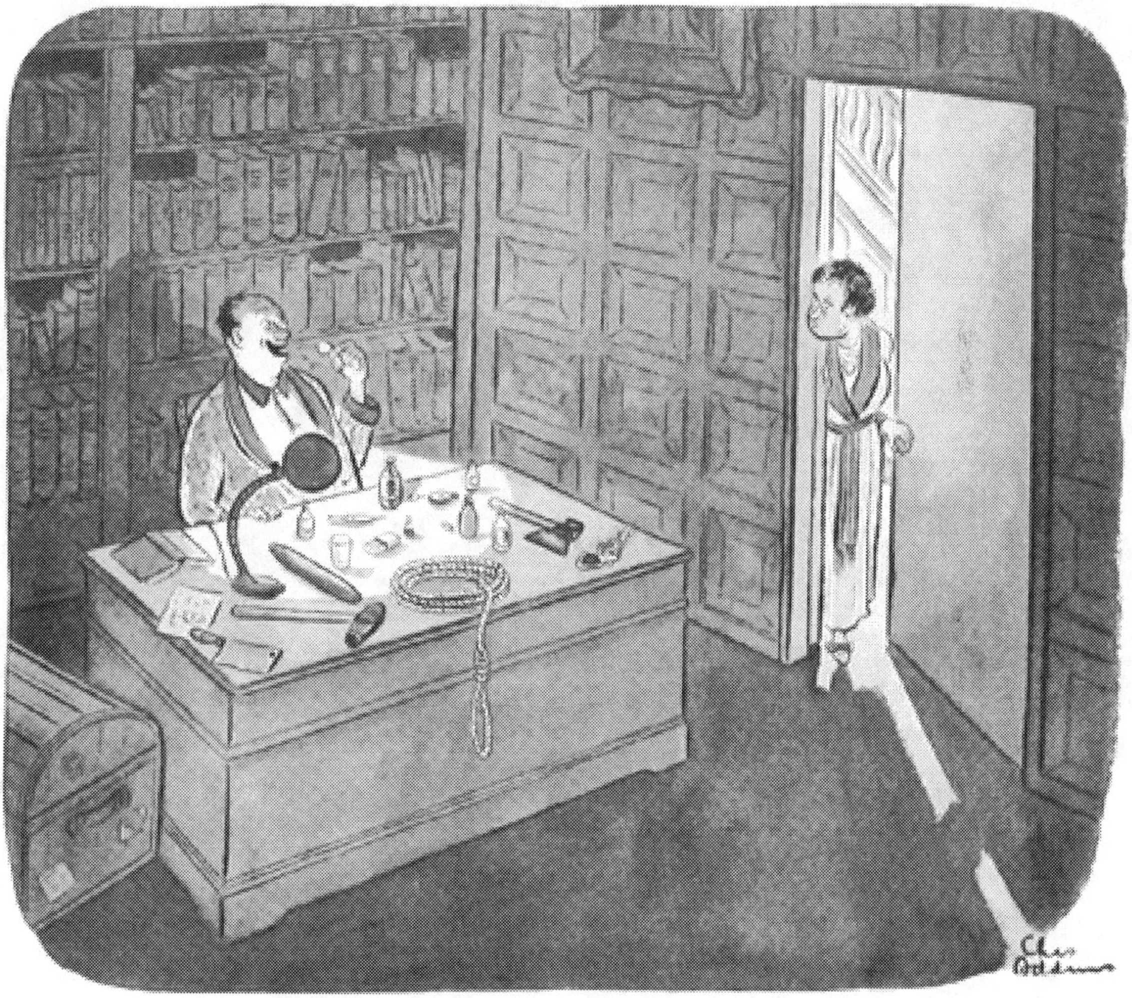
Chas Addams

"Why, *hello*, Sugar. I was just thinking about you."

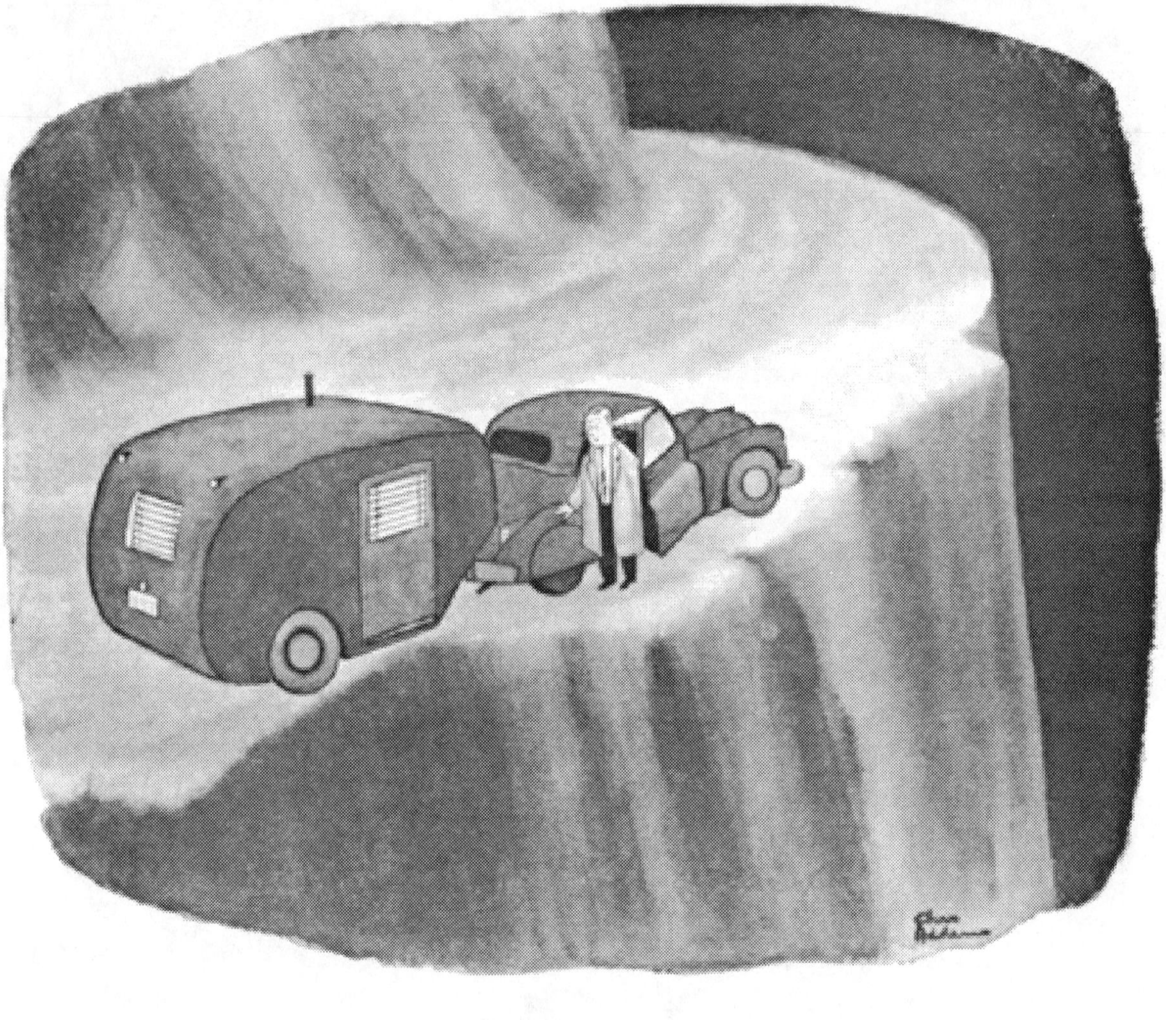

"Oh, darling, can you step out for a moment?"

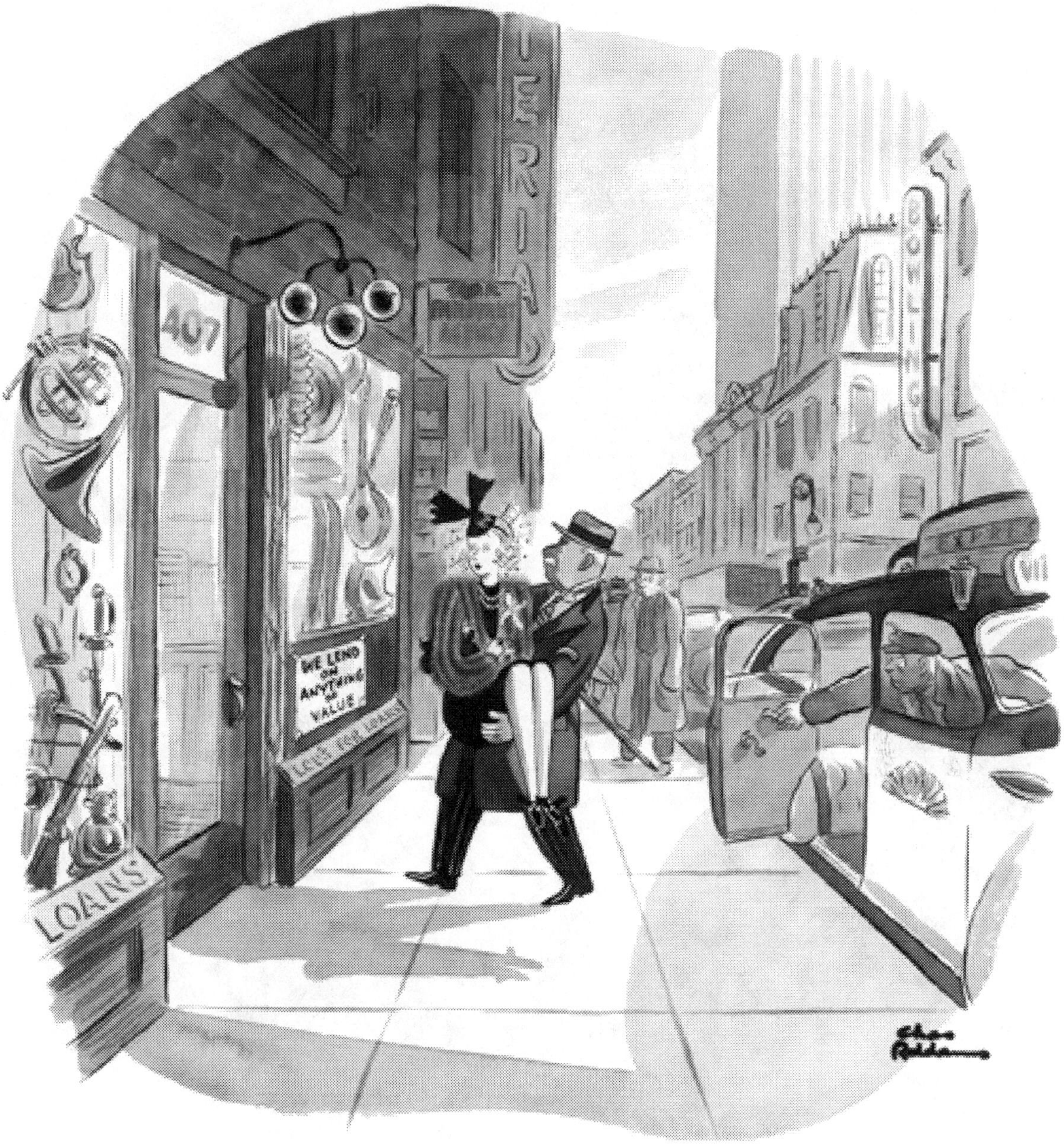
407
WE LEND ON ANYTHING OF VALUE
LOANS
BOWLING

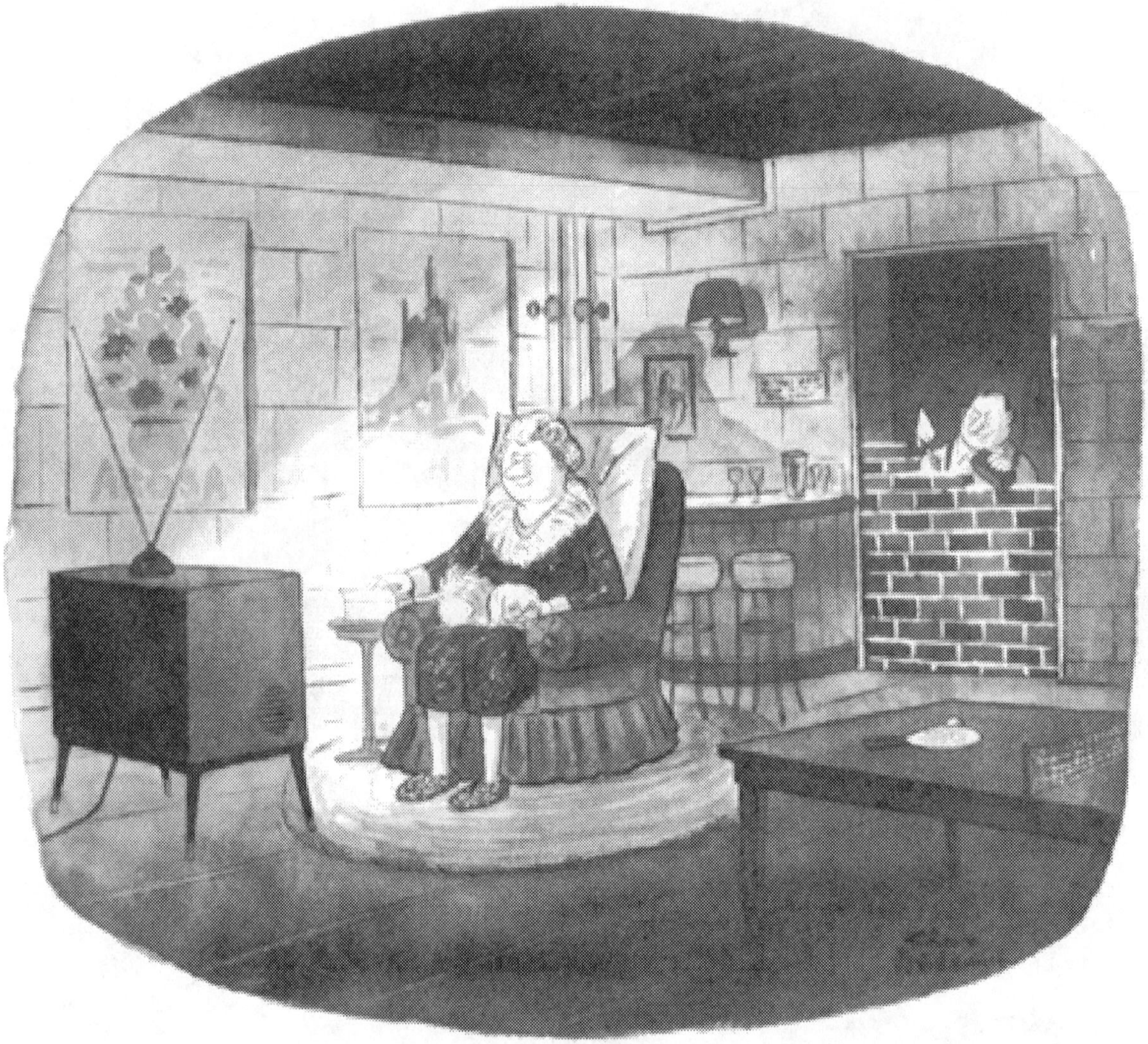

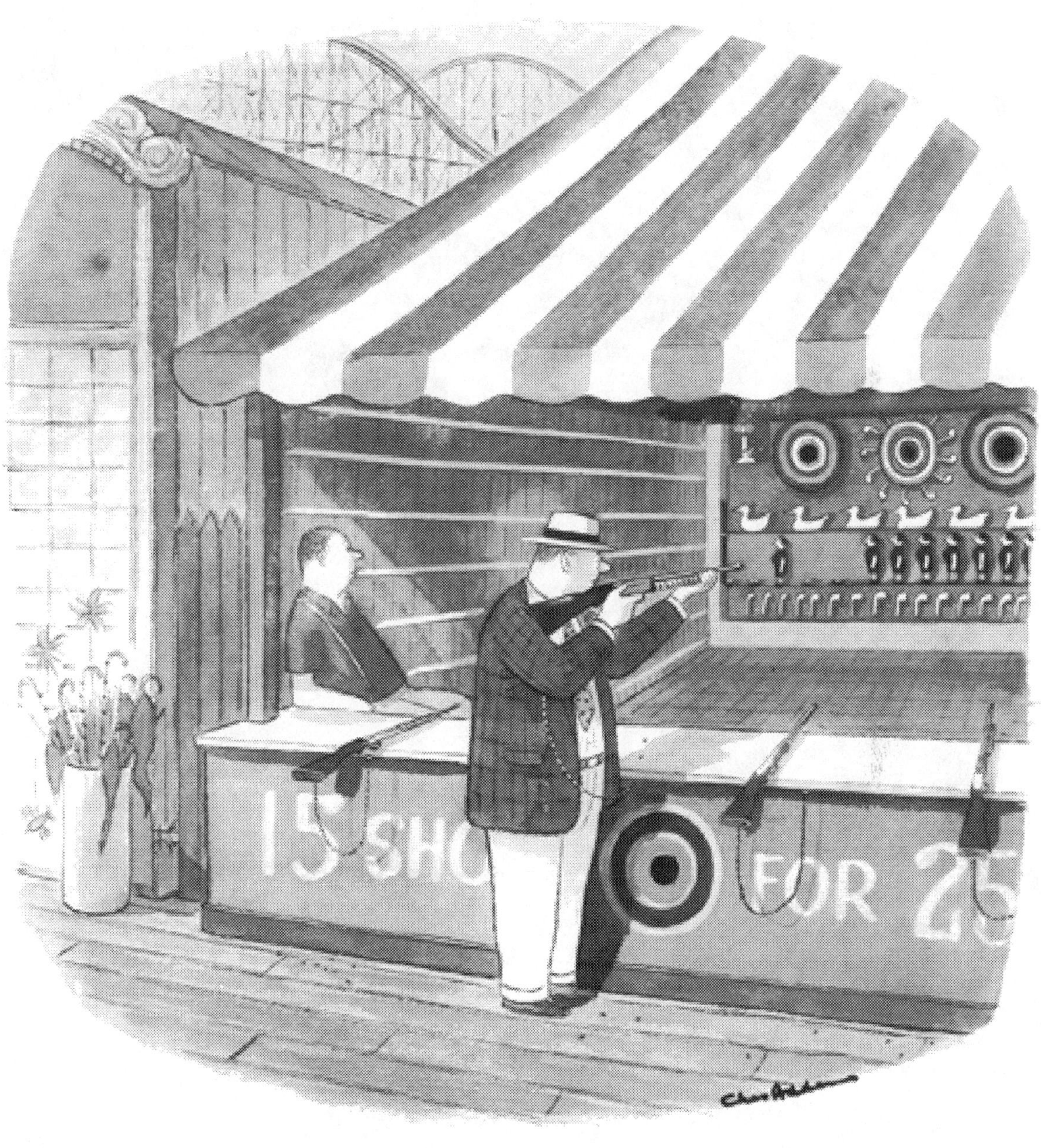
15 SHO
FOR 25

Her Resolve

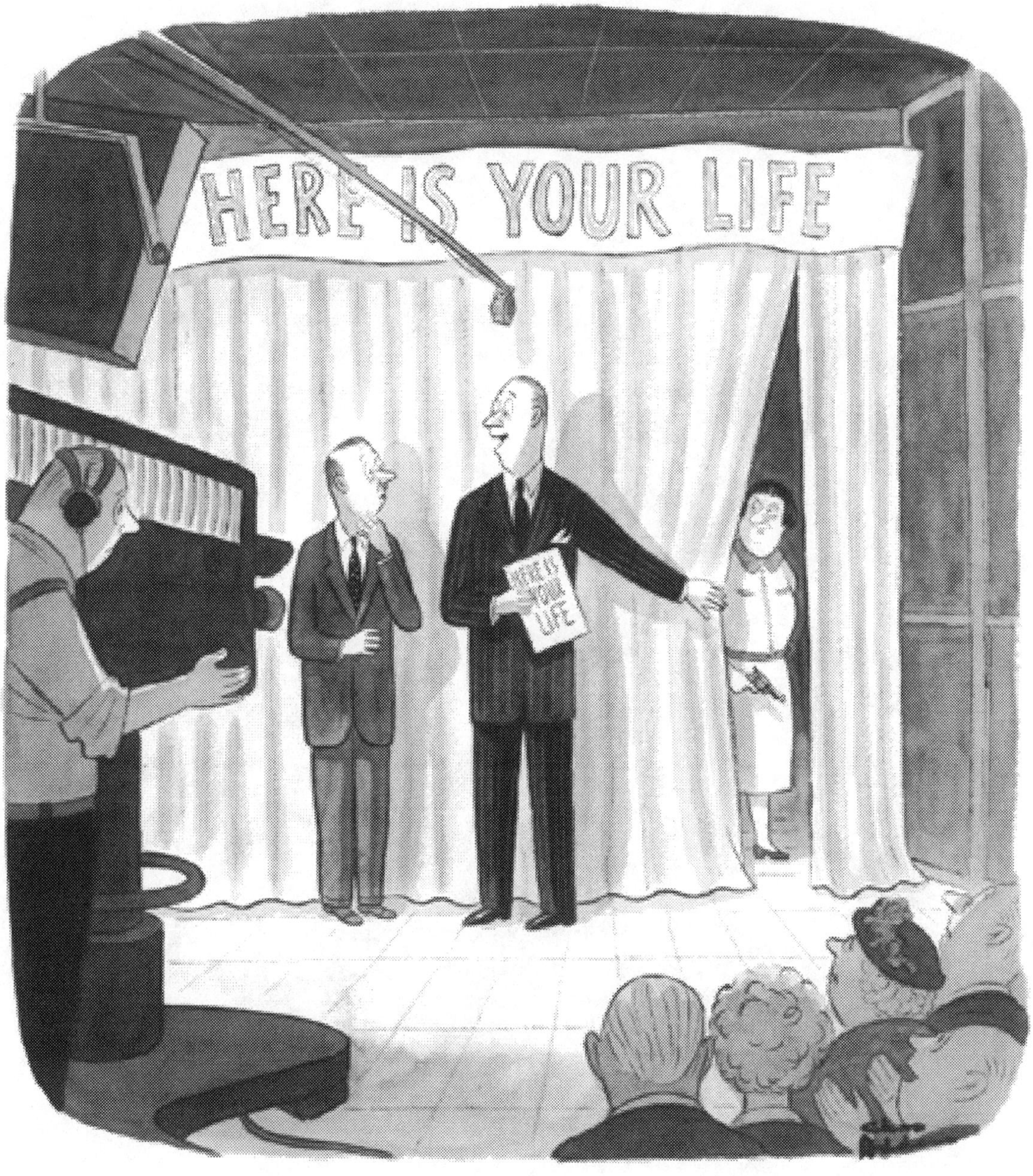
HERE IS YOUR LIFE
HERE IS YOUR LIFE

". . . and now, George Pembrook, here is the wife you haven't seen in eighteen years!"

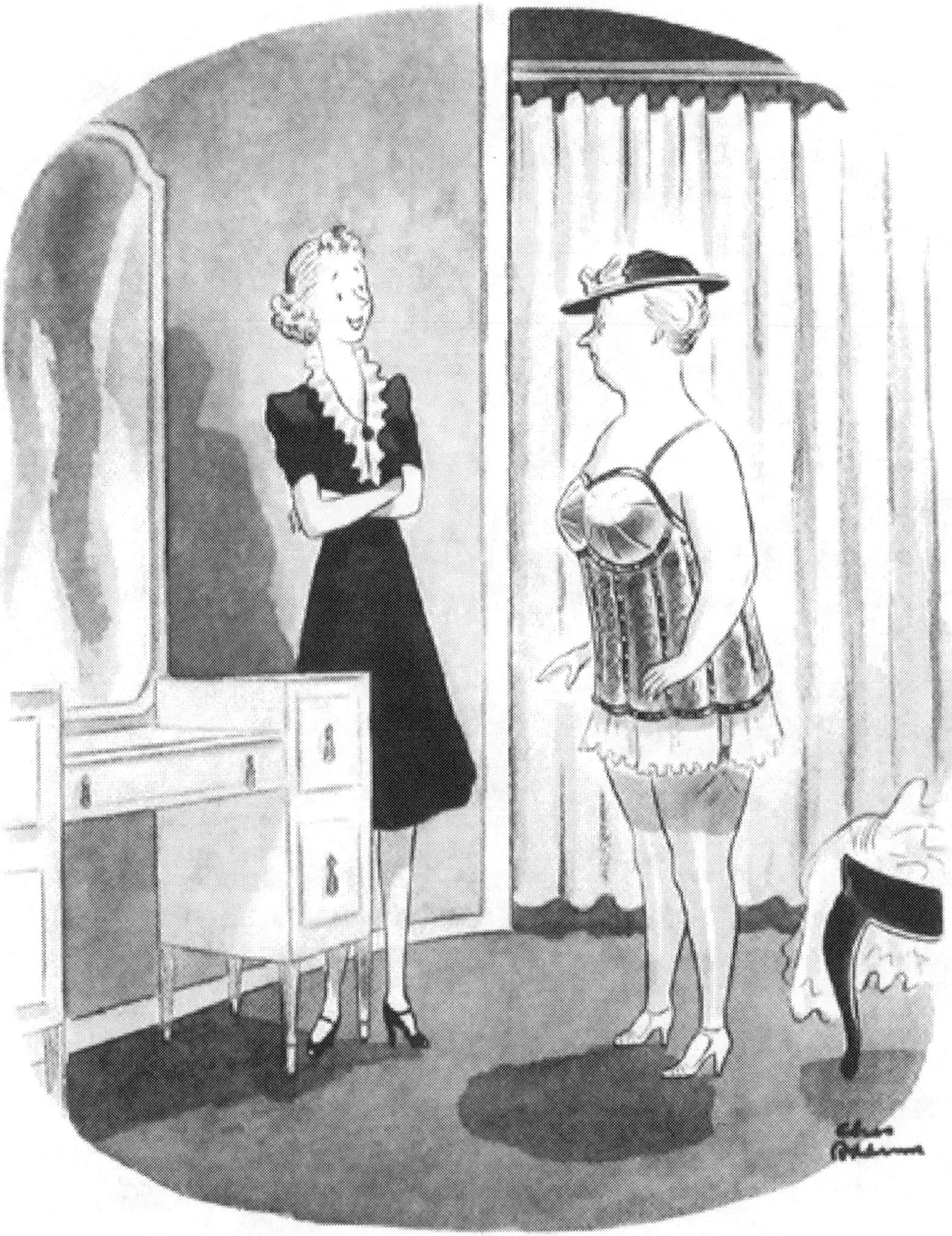

"Now, this one has the added advantage of being bulletproof."

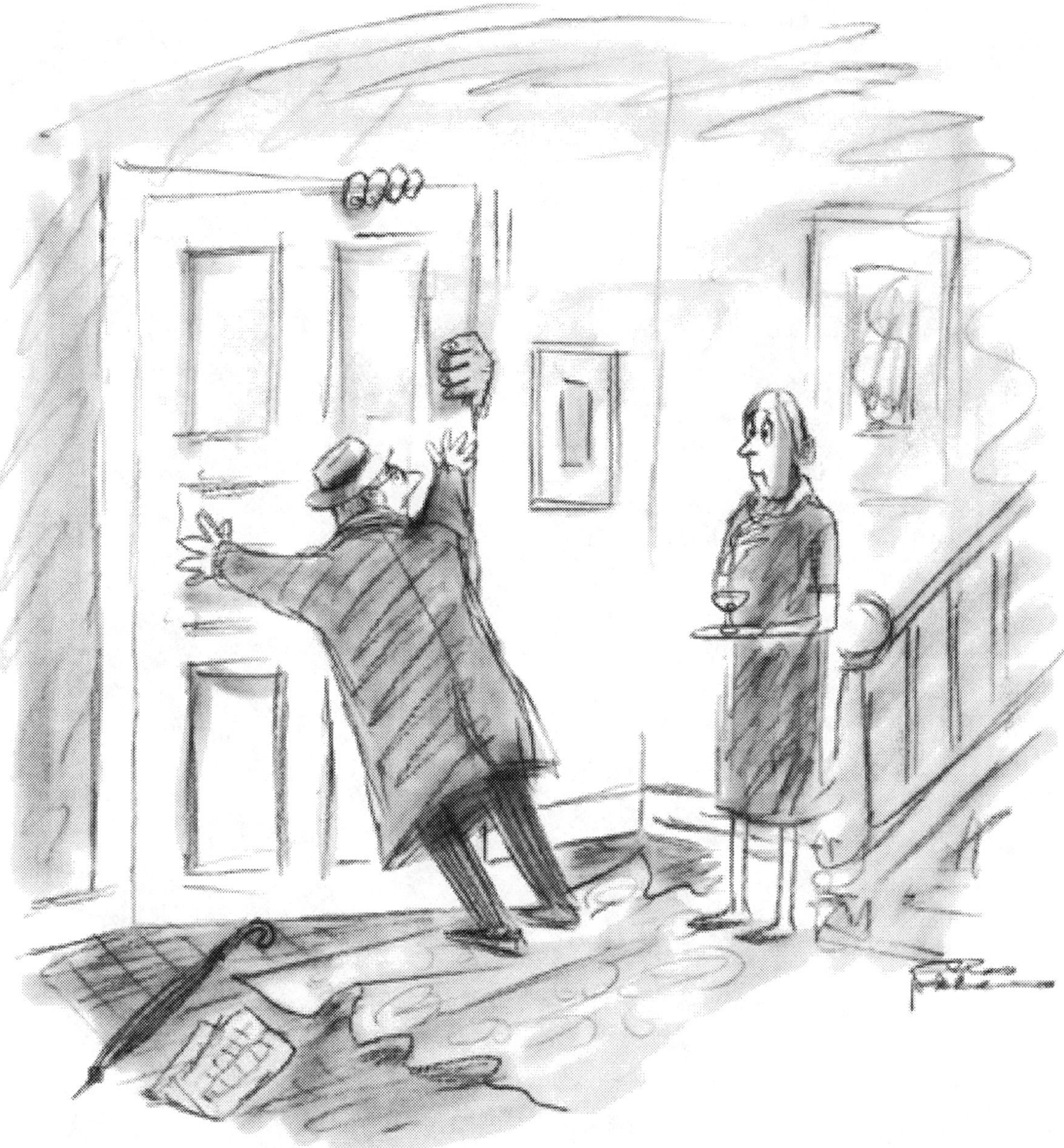

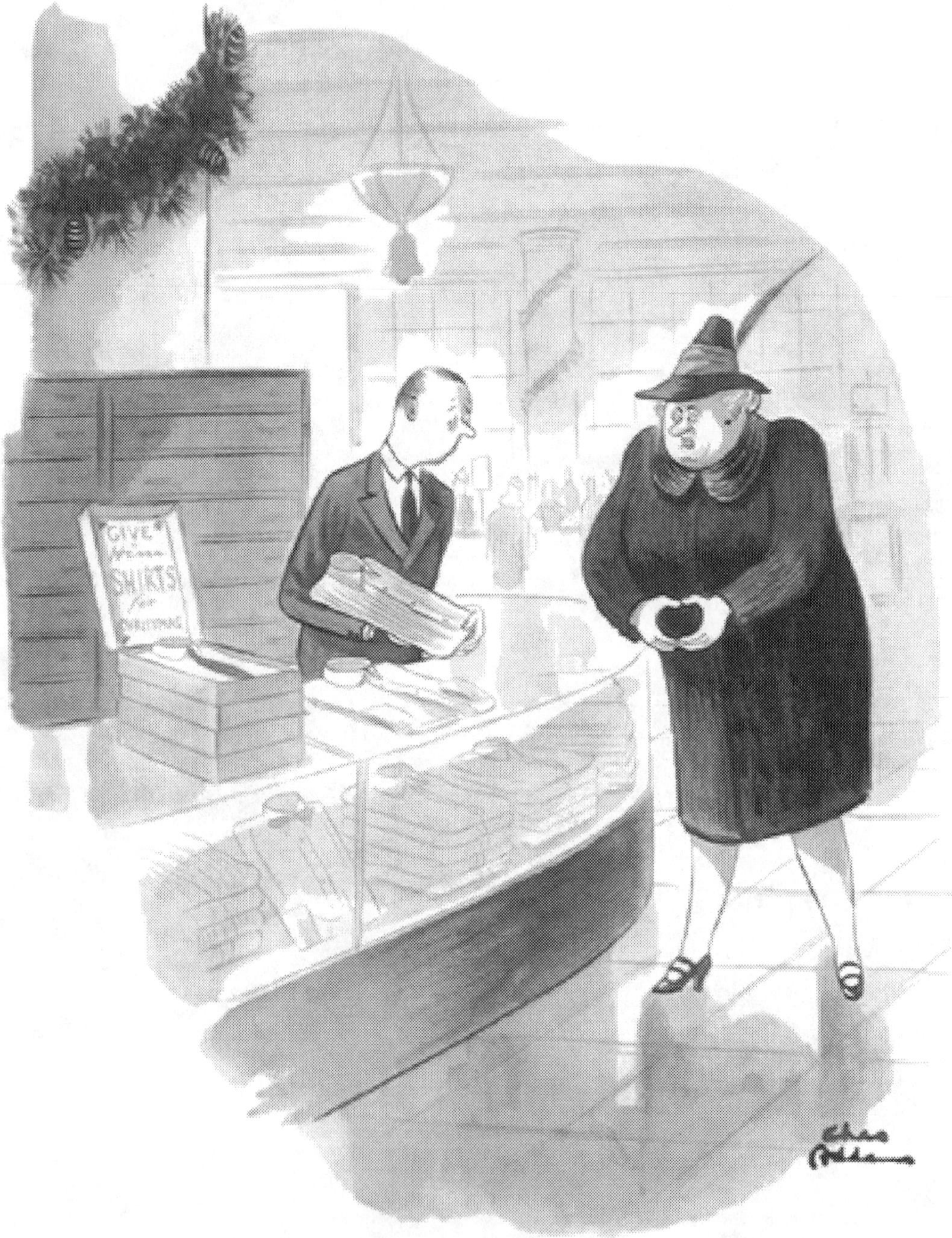
GIVE
SHIRTS

"I don't know his sleeve length, but his neck is about like *that*."

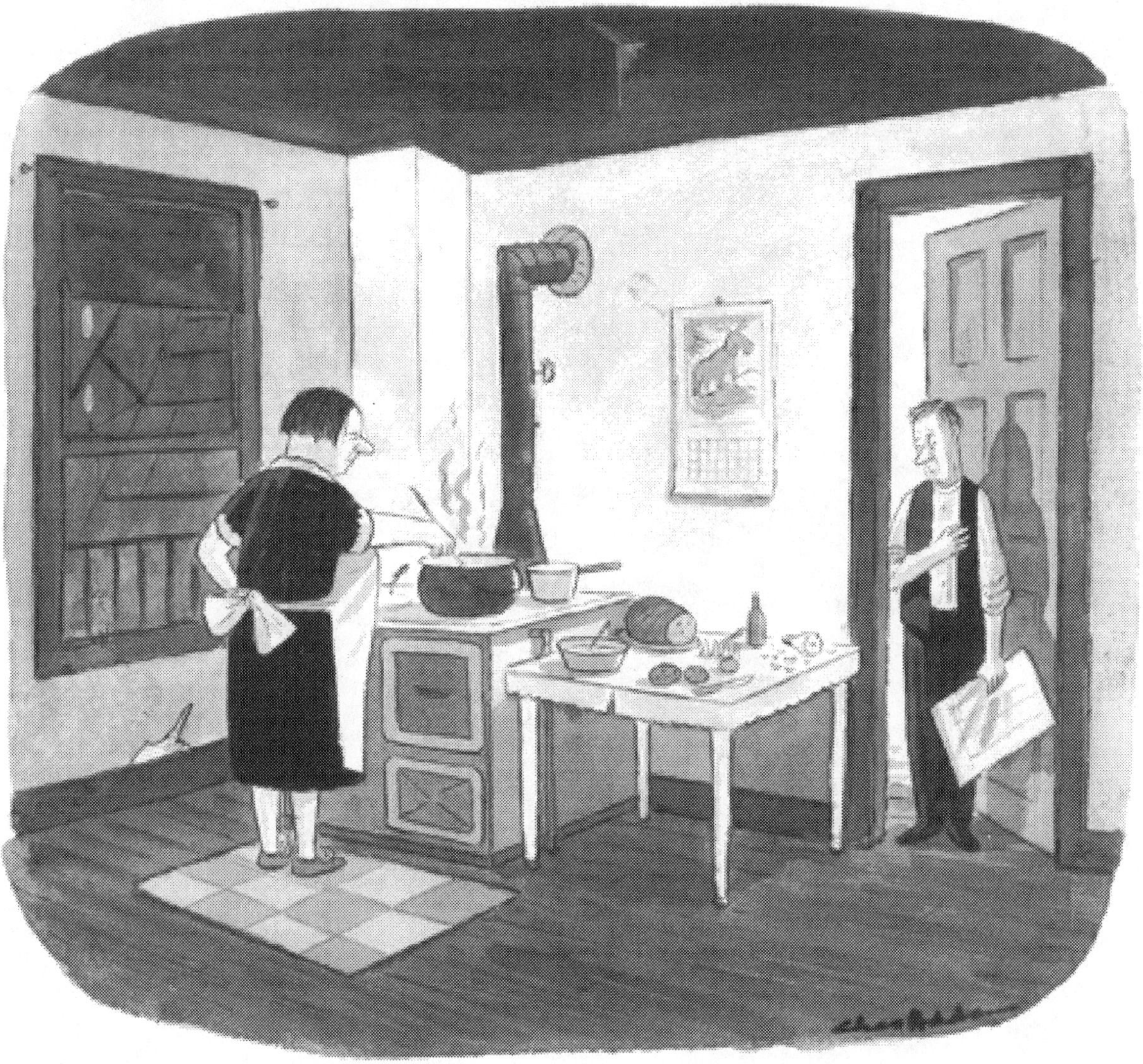

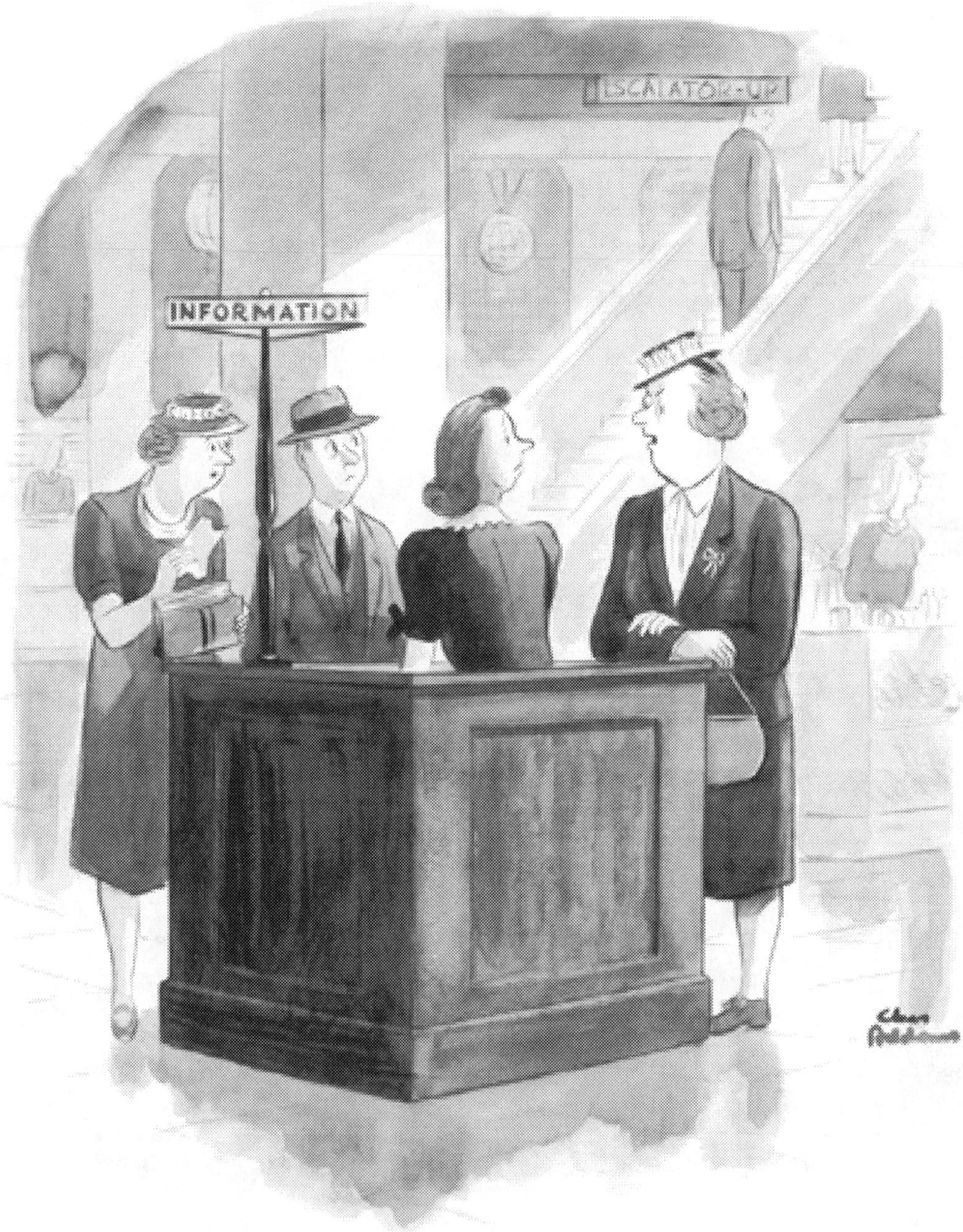
ESCALATOR-UP
INFORMATION
Chas Addams

"Blunt instruments?"

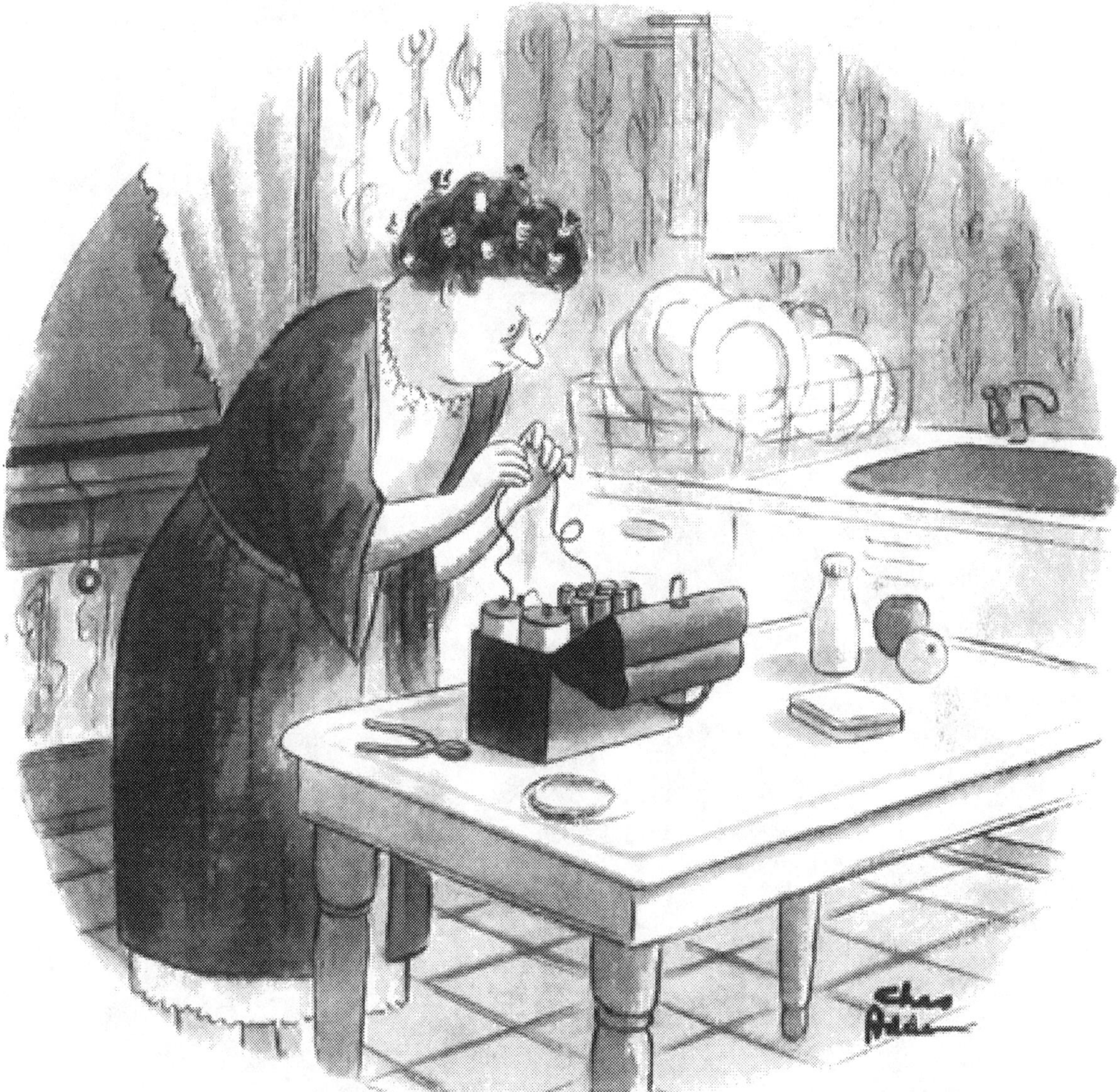

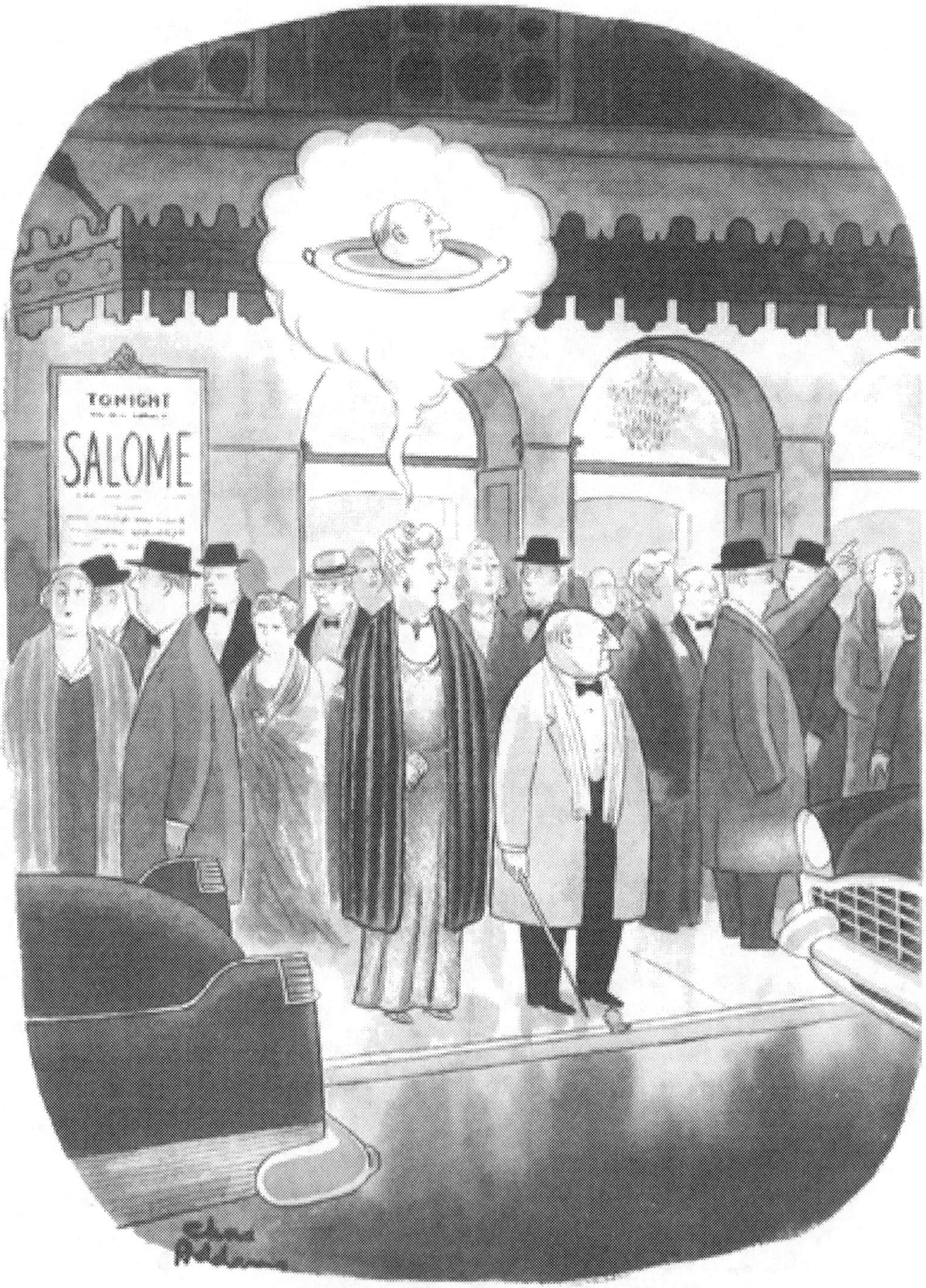
TONIGHT
SALOME

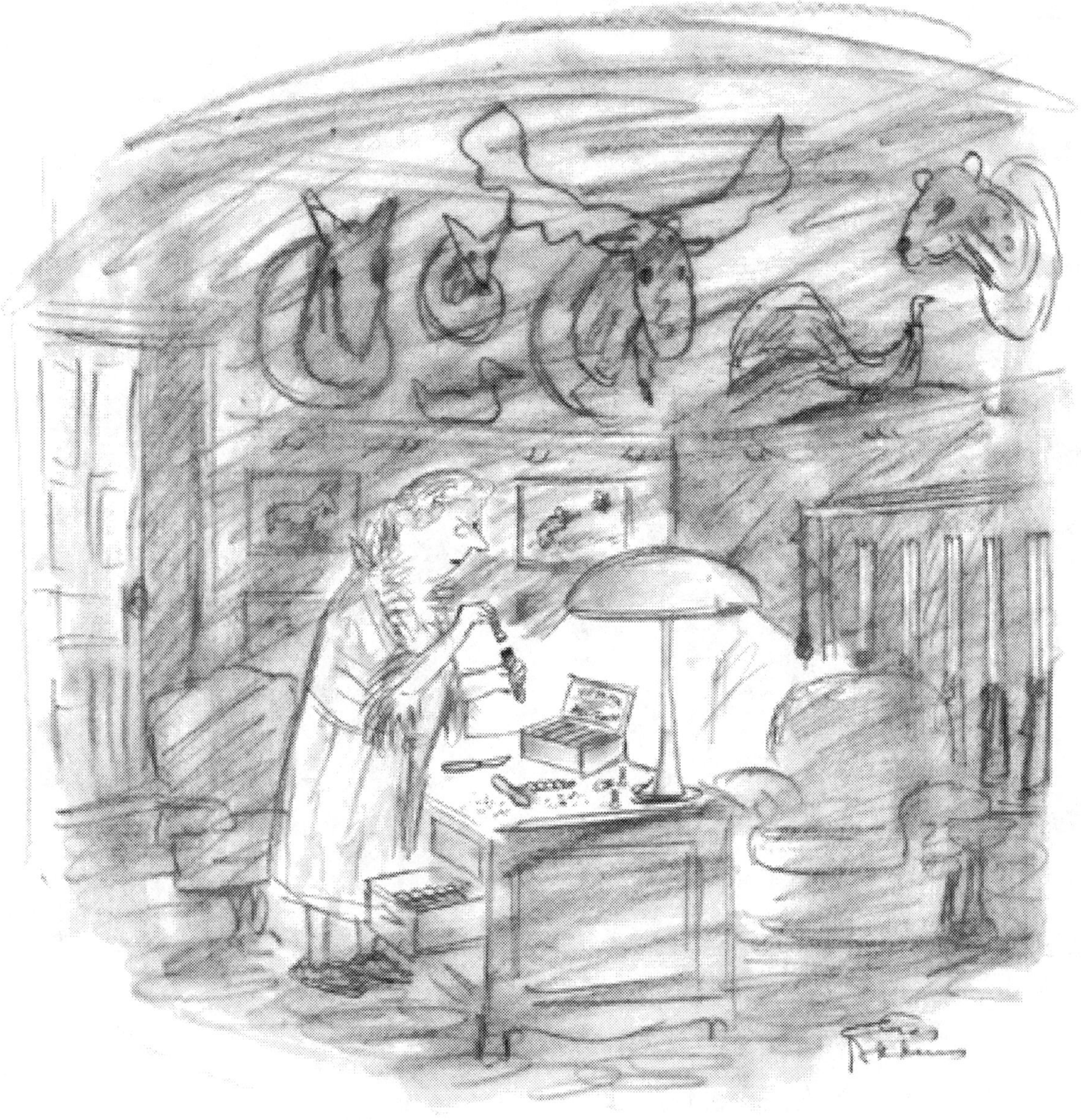

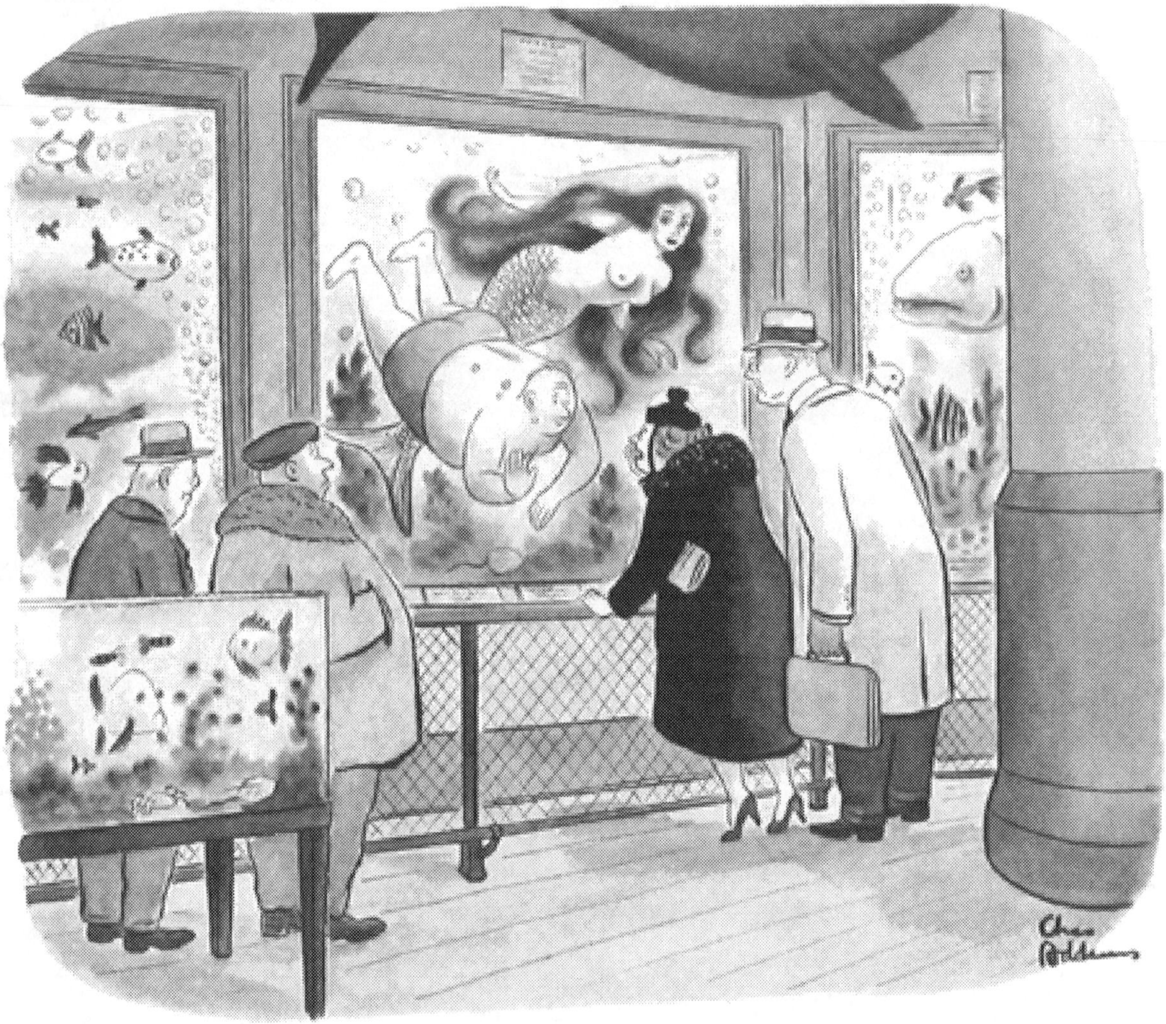

"Richard! I said I want you to meet my lawyer."

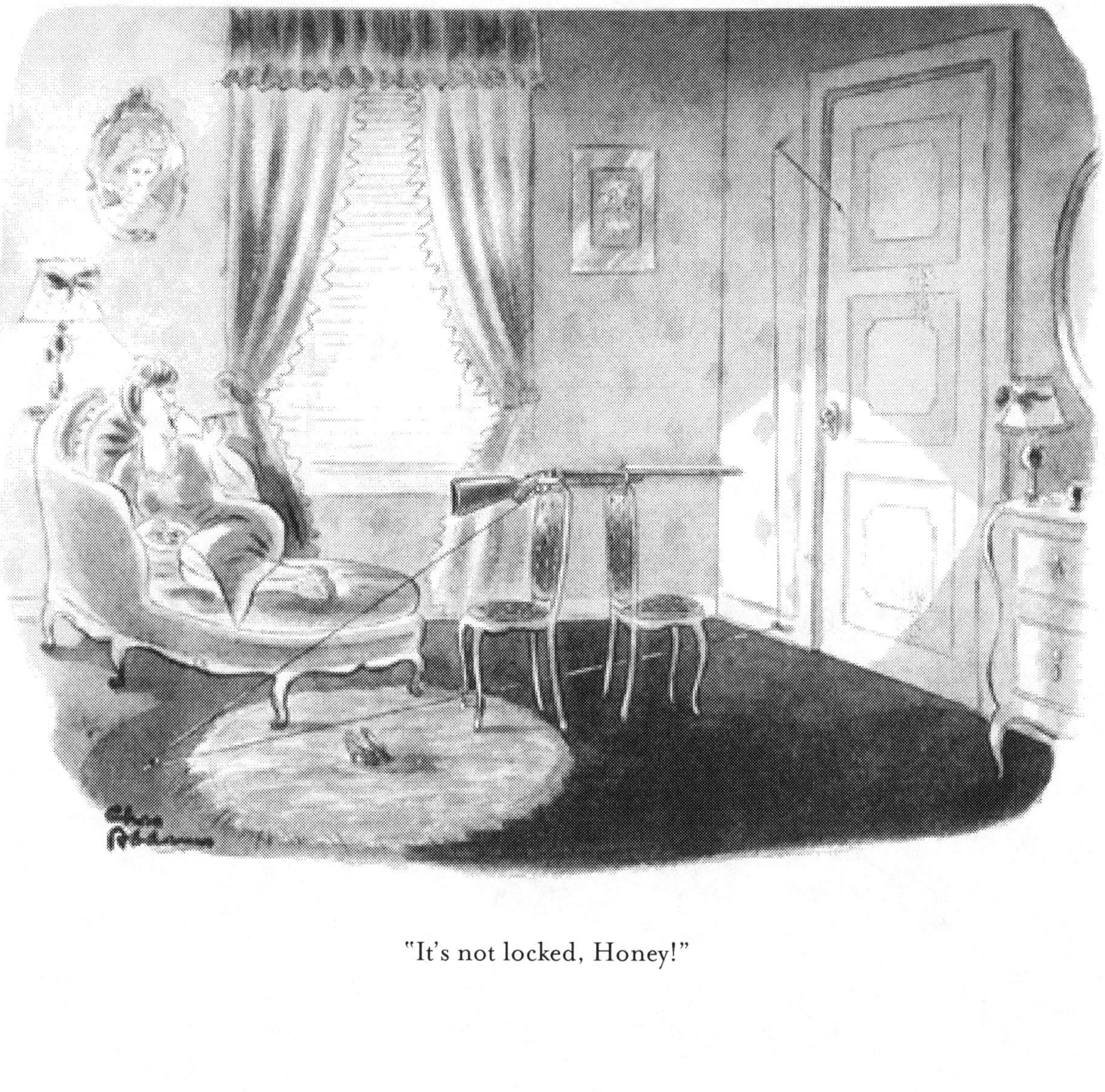

"It's not locked, Honey!"

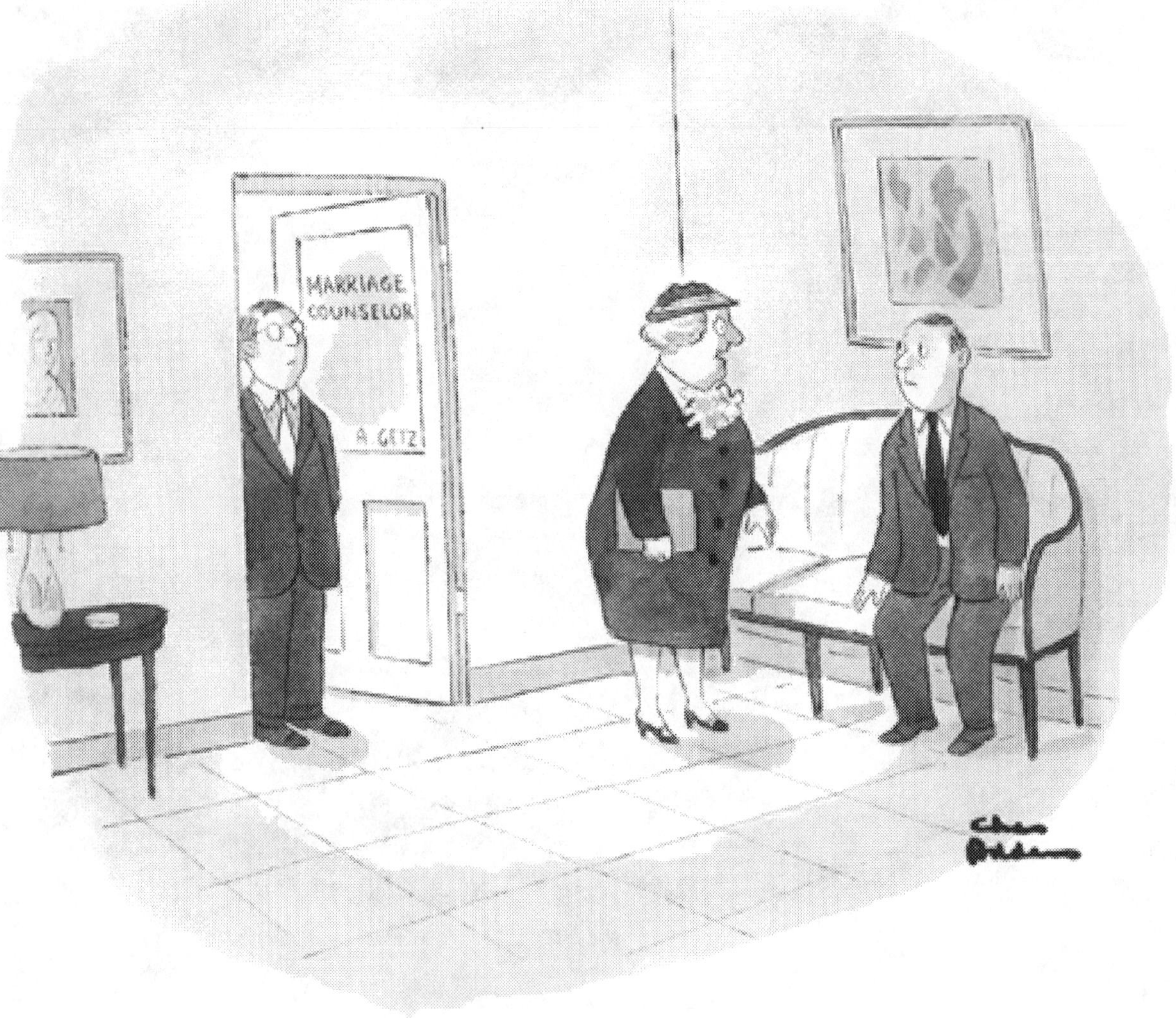
MARRIAGE
COUNSELOR
A. GETZ

"You wait here. I'll talk to him."

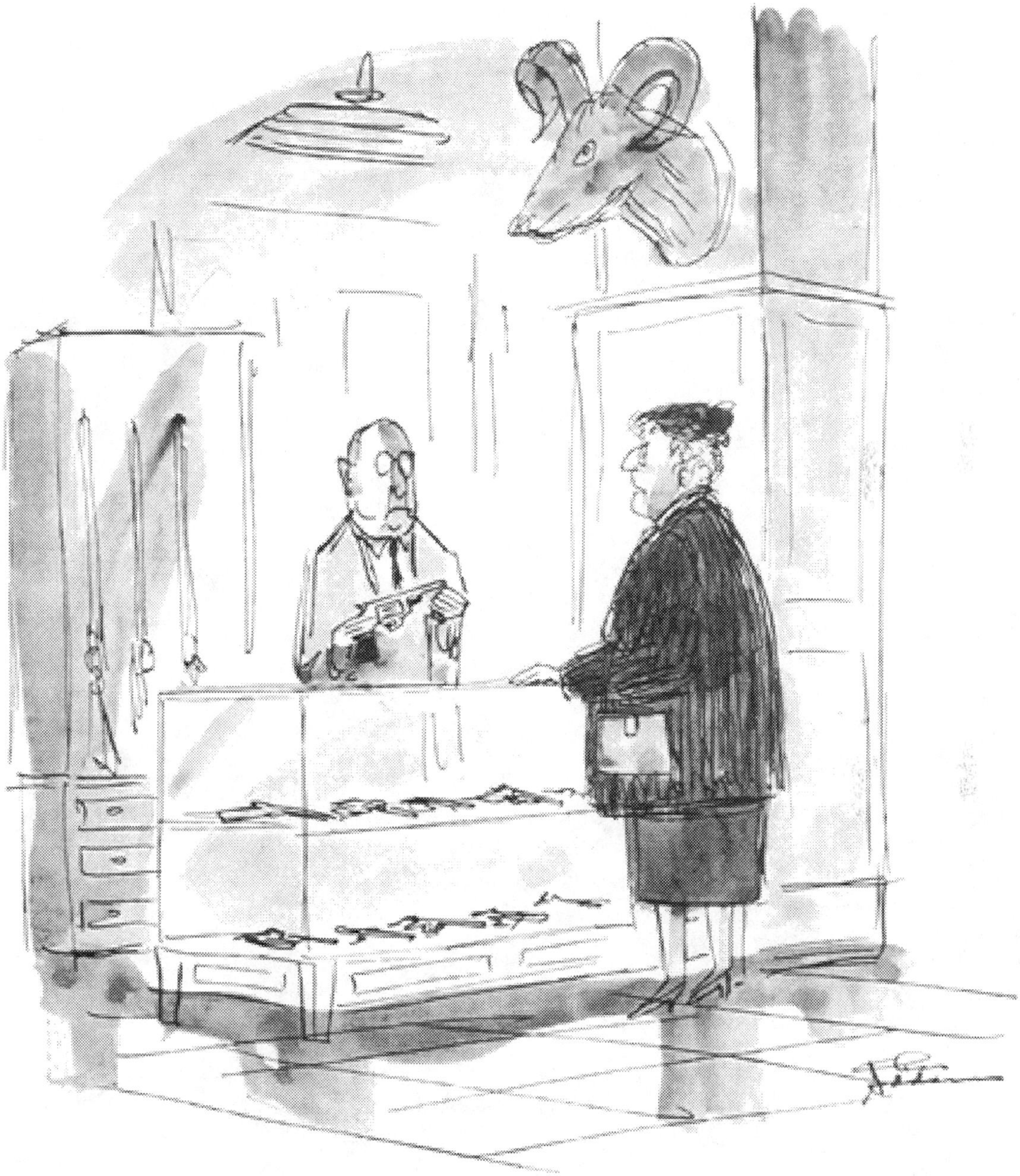

"But why do I need a license? It's only for use around the house."

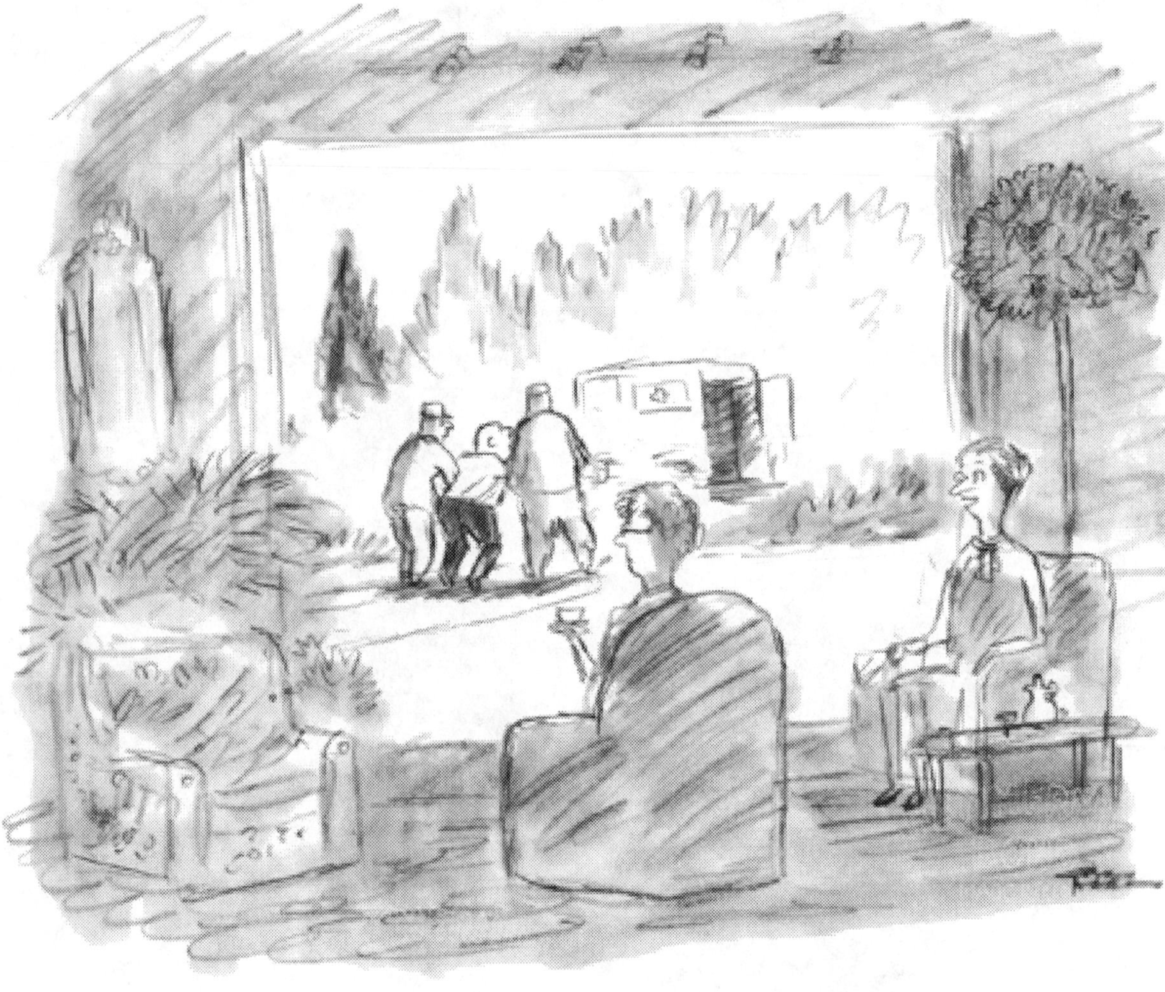

"I can't take full credit. Having Foster committed was another one of the decorator's ideas."

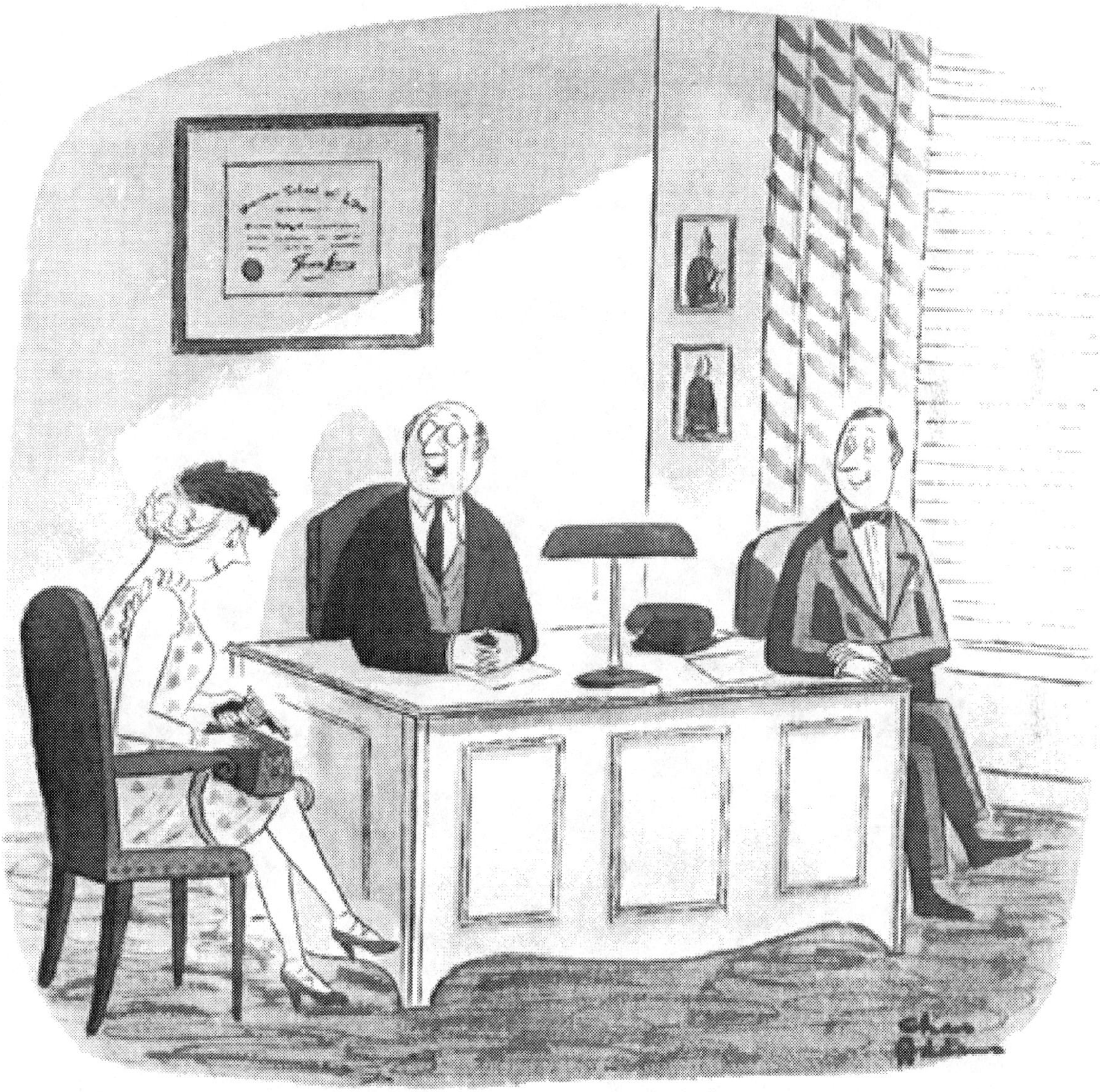

"We're delighted to hear, Mrs. Sinclair, that you've finally decided to settle out of court."

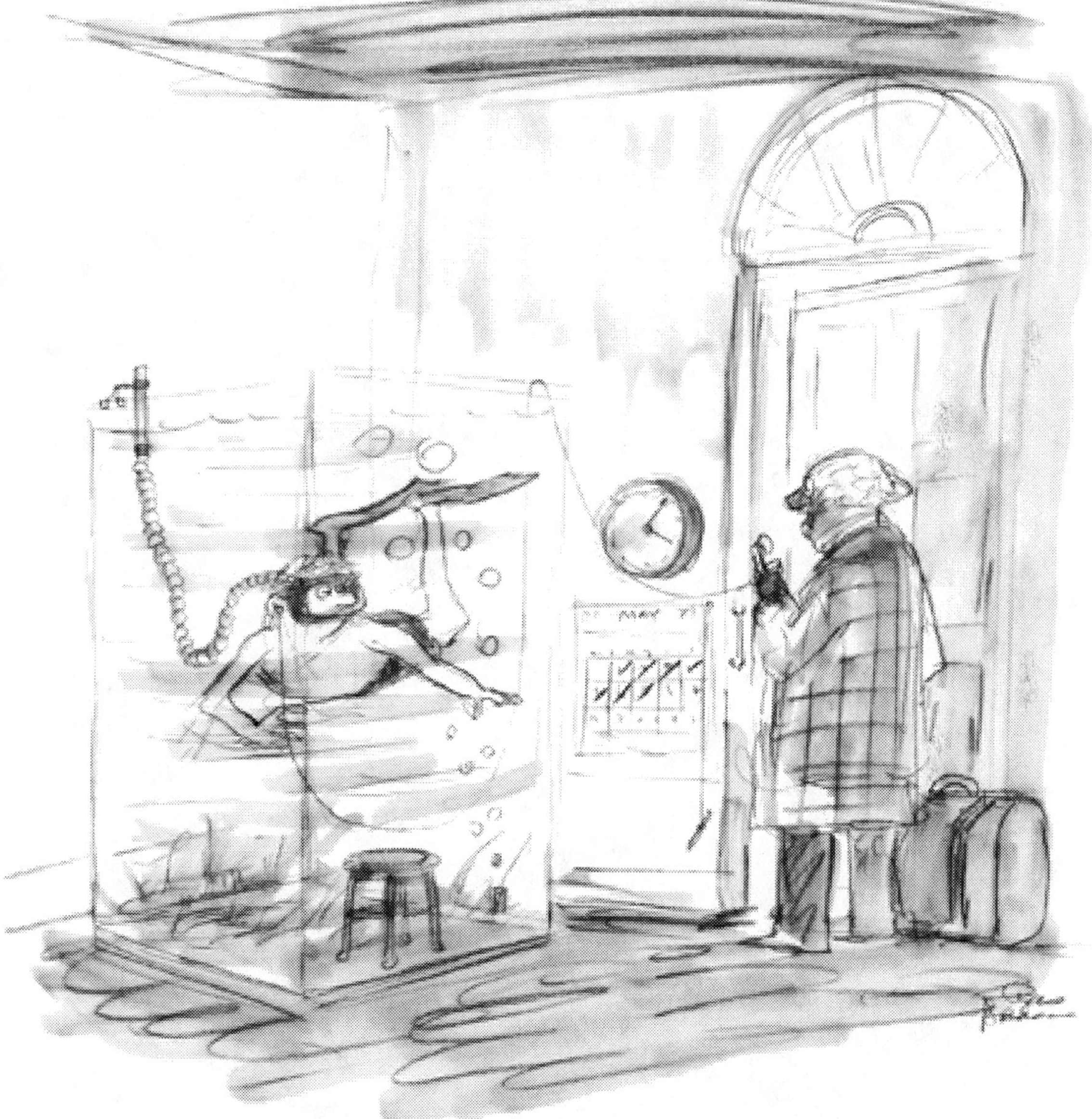

"Now hear this. I'm walking out on you and *The Guinness Book of World Records.*"

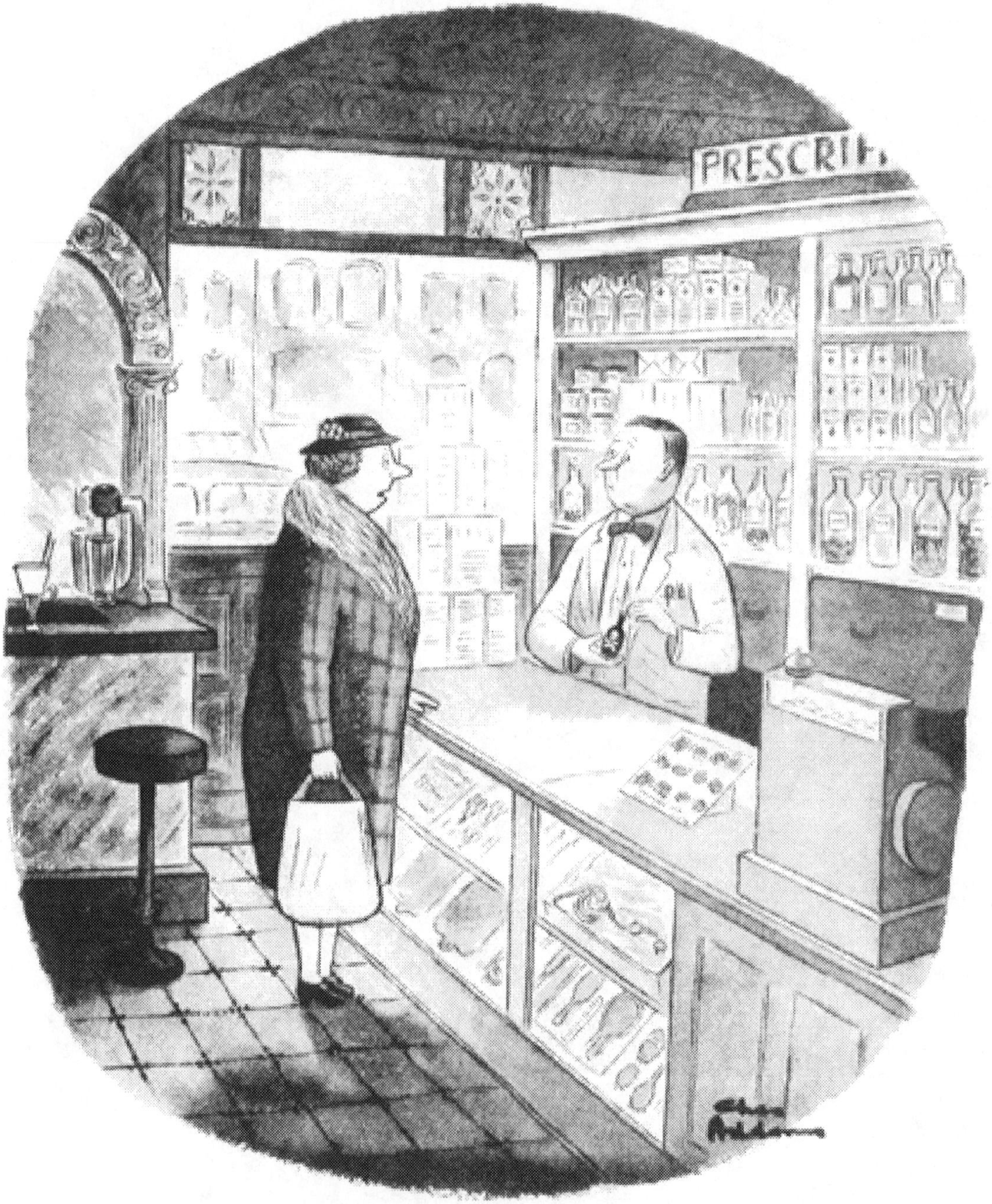

"Don't you carry the large economy size?"

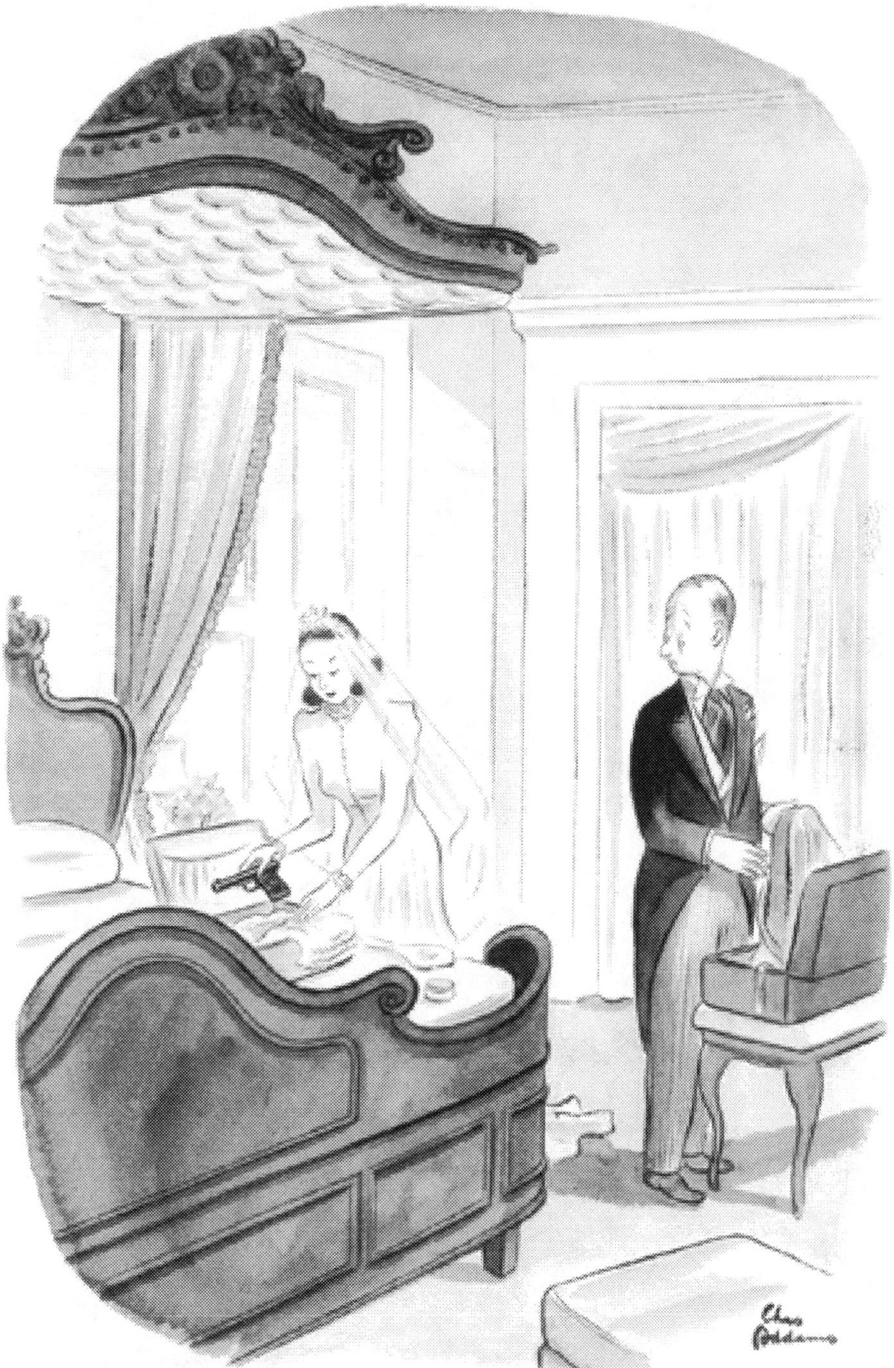
Chas Addams

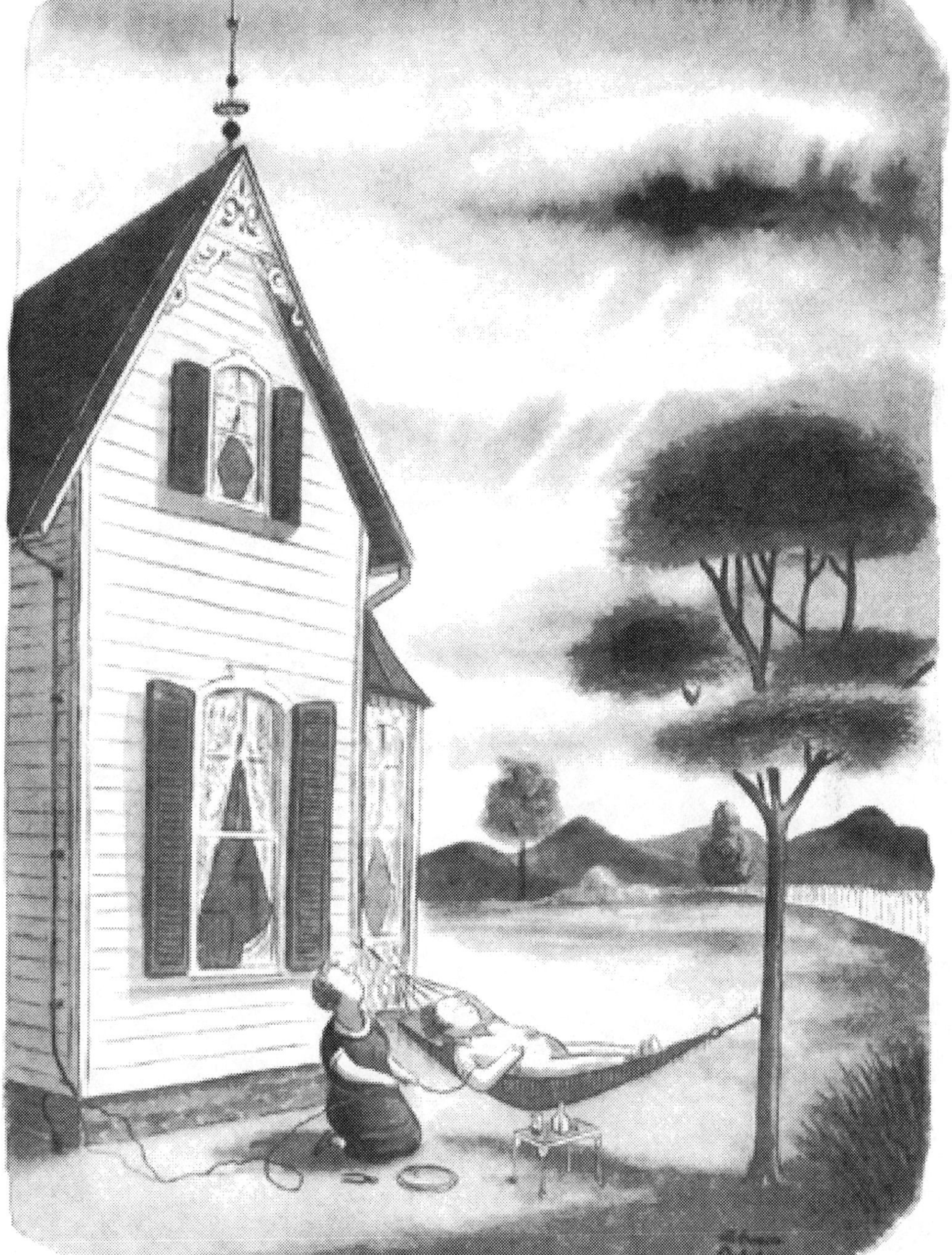

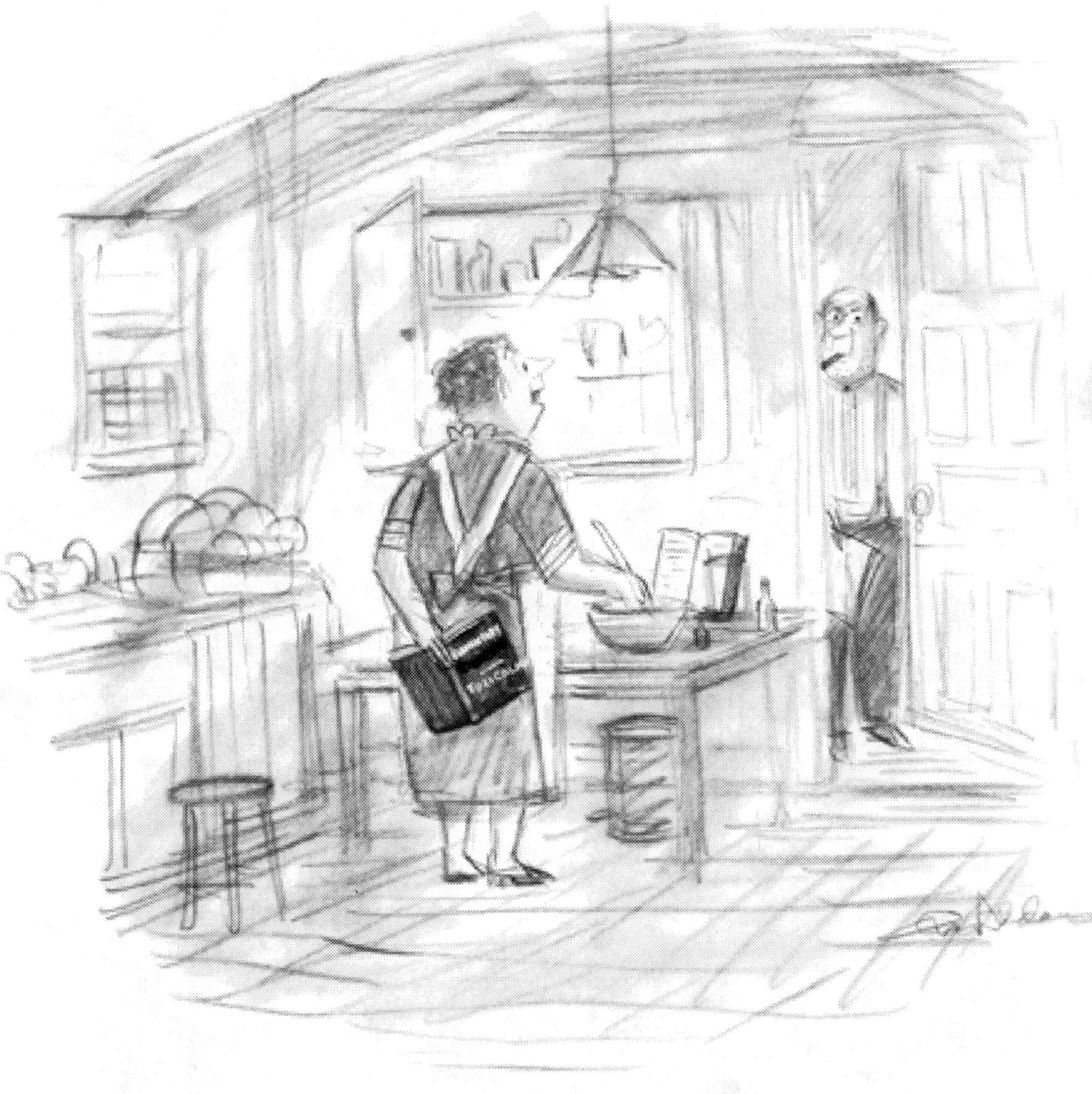

"Now, don't come prowling around–I'm preparing a little surprise for you."

135

The Final Score

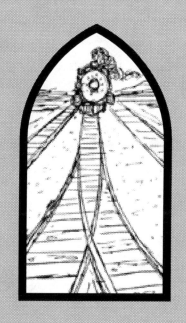

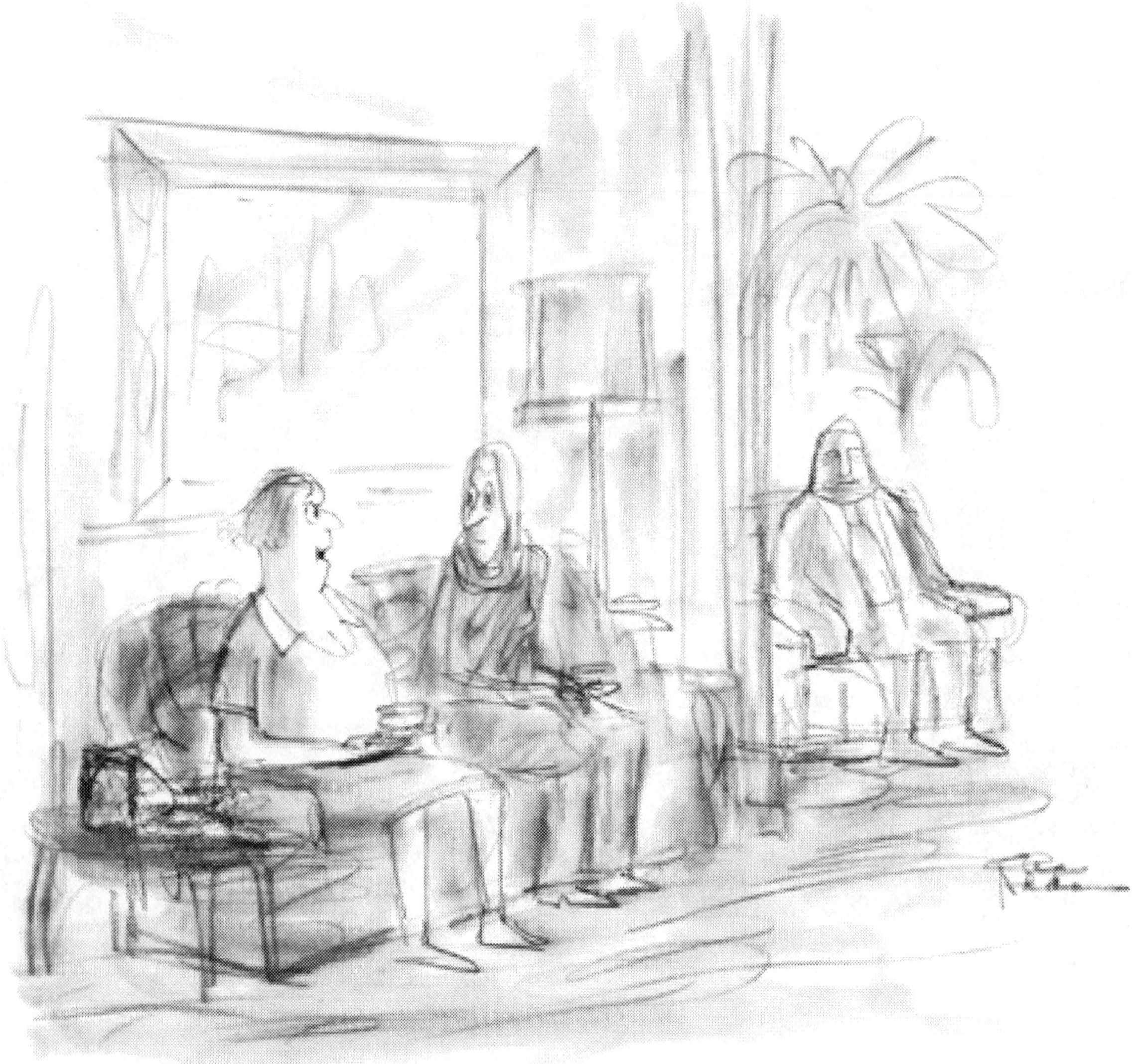

"Dan? Oh, I had him bronzed last fall."

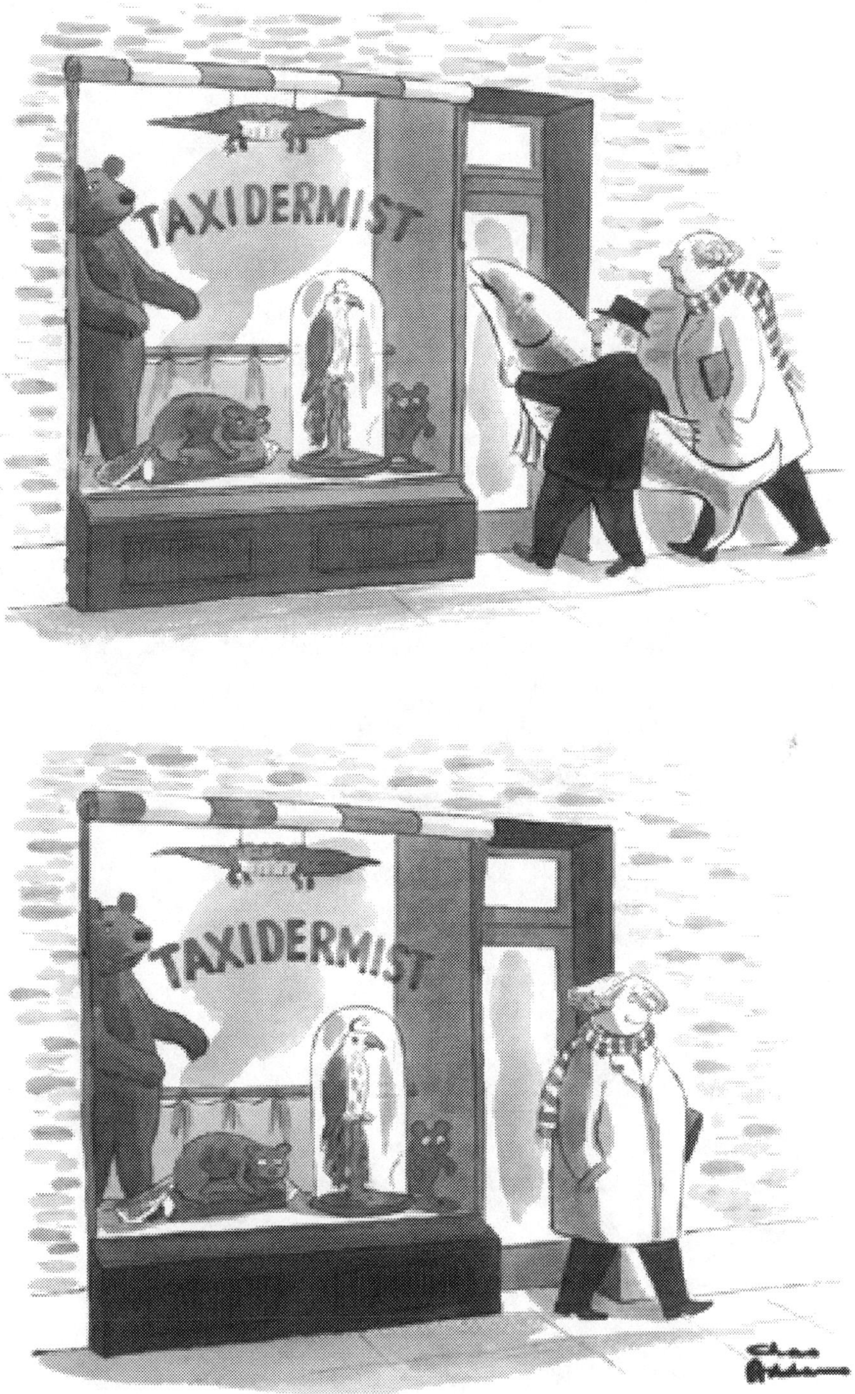
TAXIDERMIST
TAXIDERMIST
Chas Addams

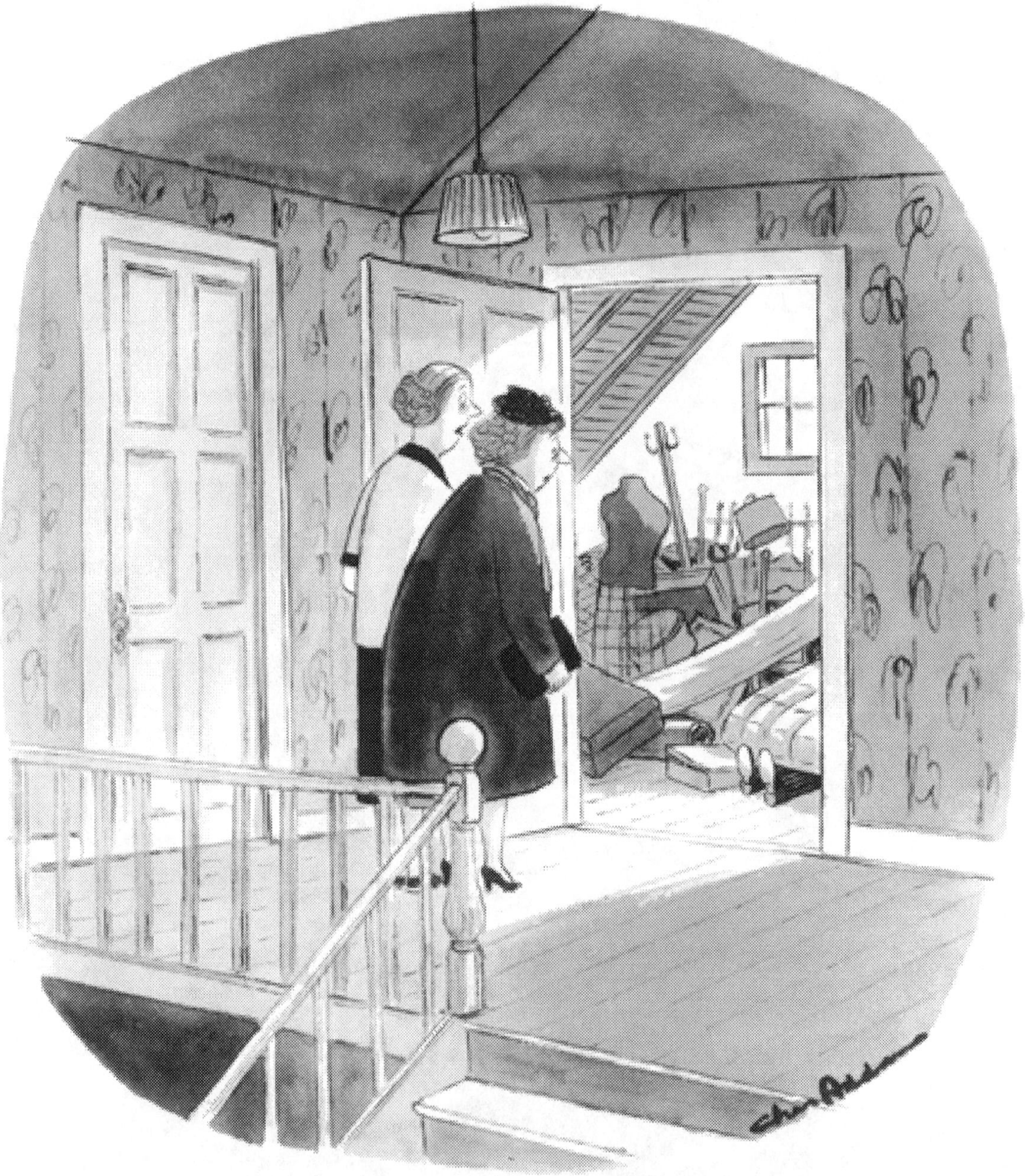

"This room's a sort of catch-all."

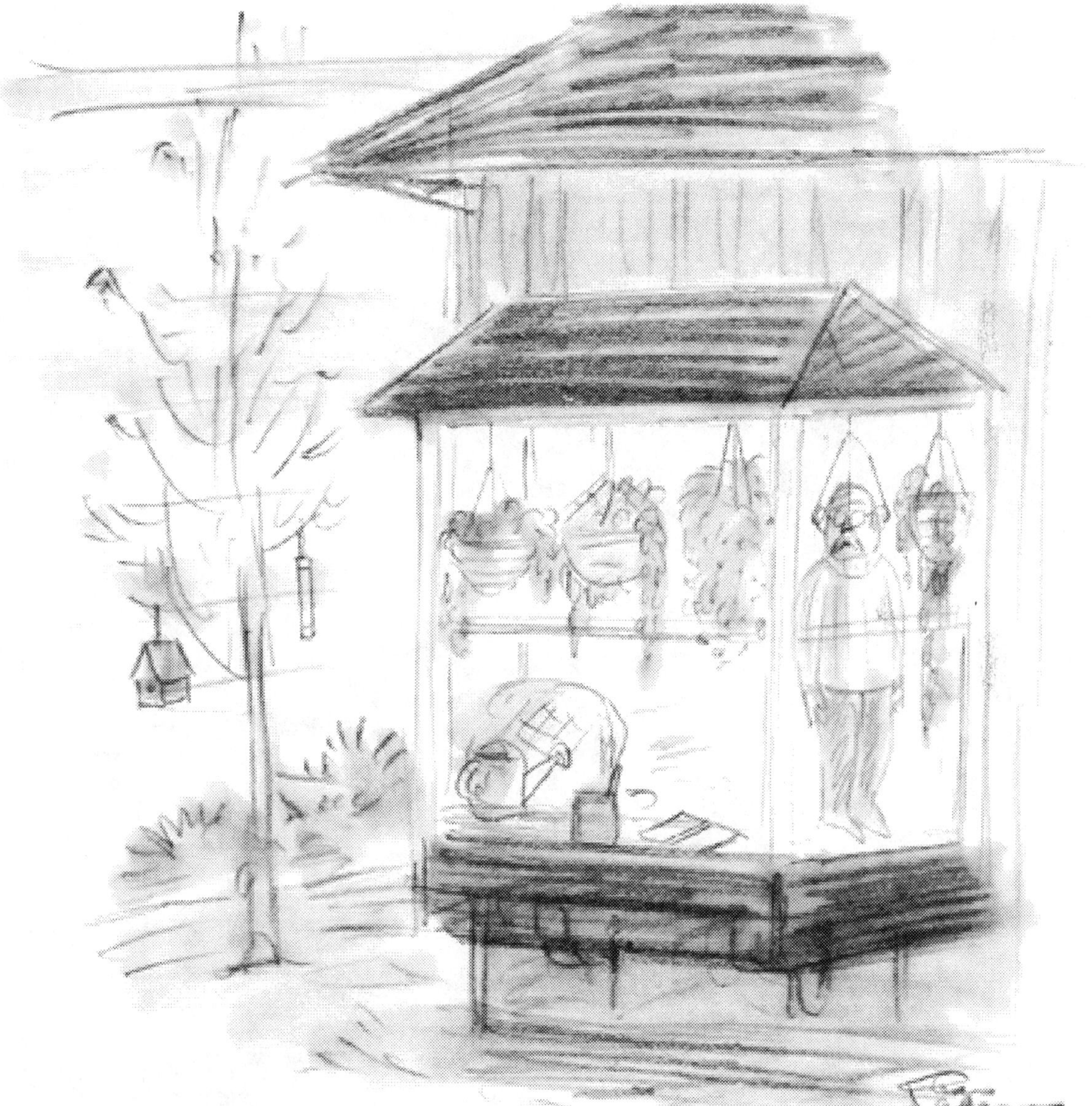

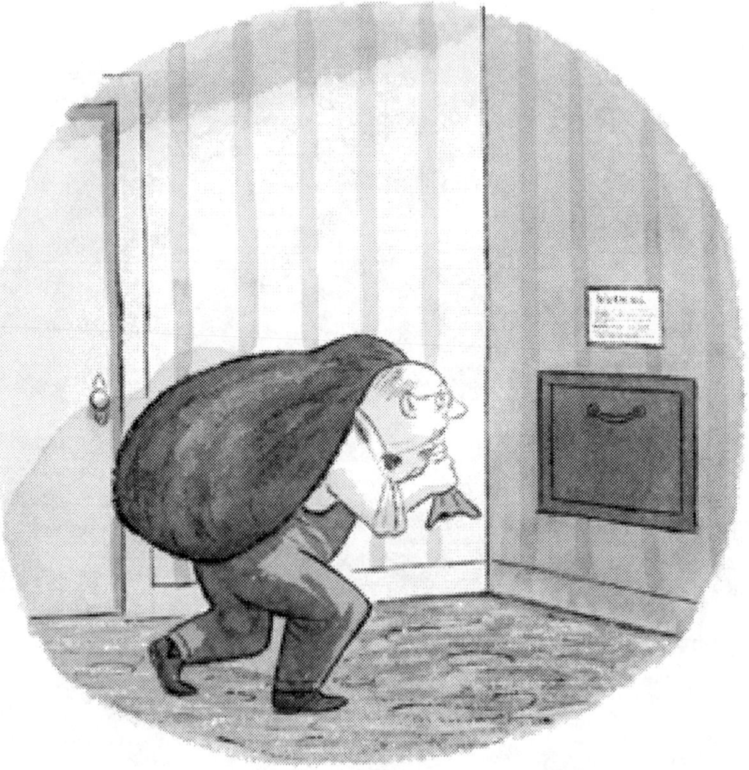

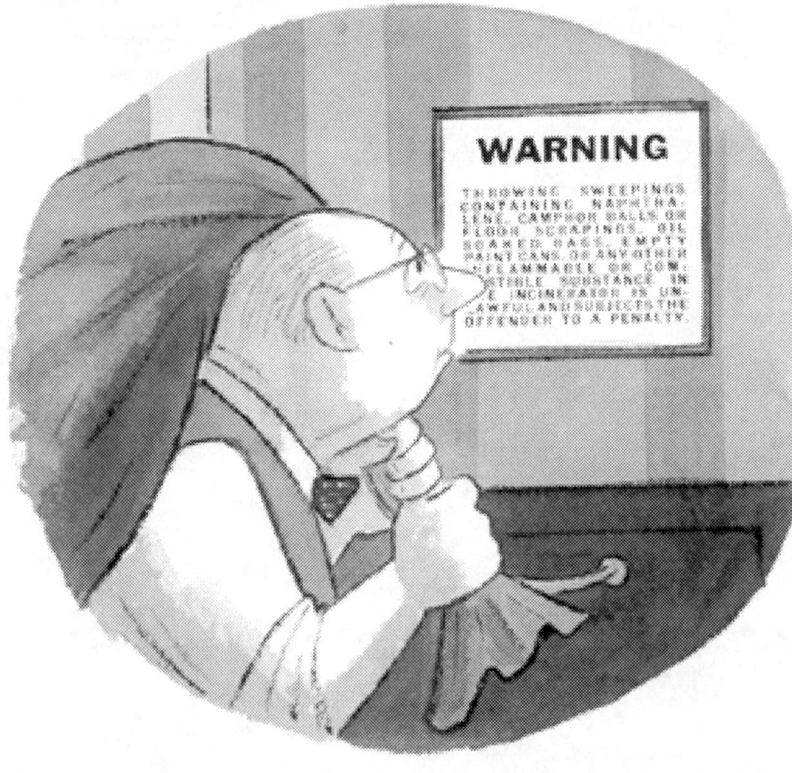
WARNING
THROWING SWEEPINGS
CONTAINING NAPHTHA-
LENE, CAMPHOR BALLS OR
FLOOR SCRAPINGS, OIL
SOAKED RAGS, EMPTY
PAINT CANS, OR ANY OTHER
FLAMMABLE OR COM-
TIBLE SUBSTANCE IN
E INCINERATOR IS UN-
AWFUL AND SUBJECTS THE
OFFENDER TO A PENALTY.

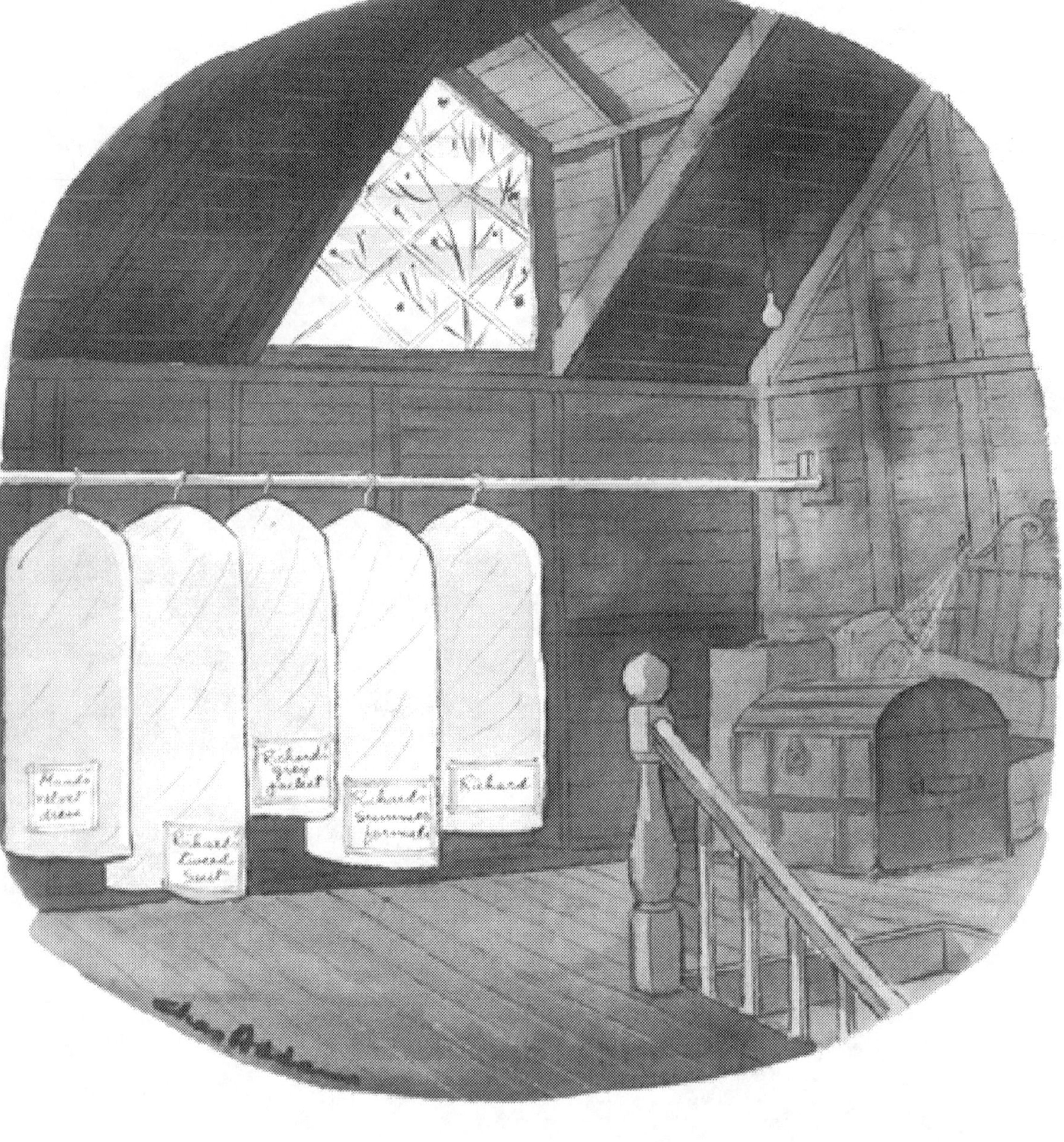
Richard's grey jacket
Richard

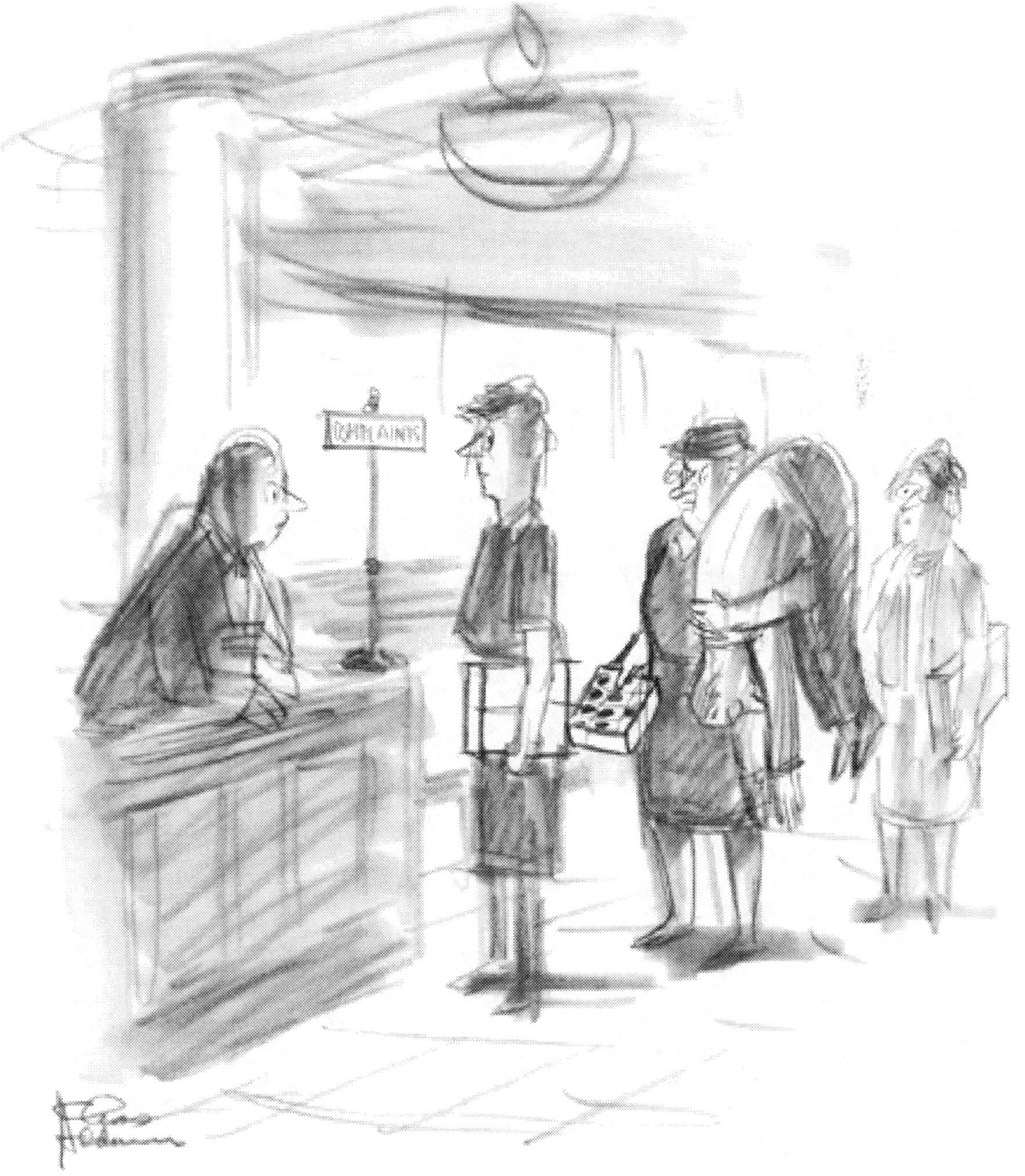

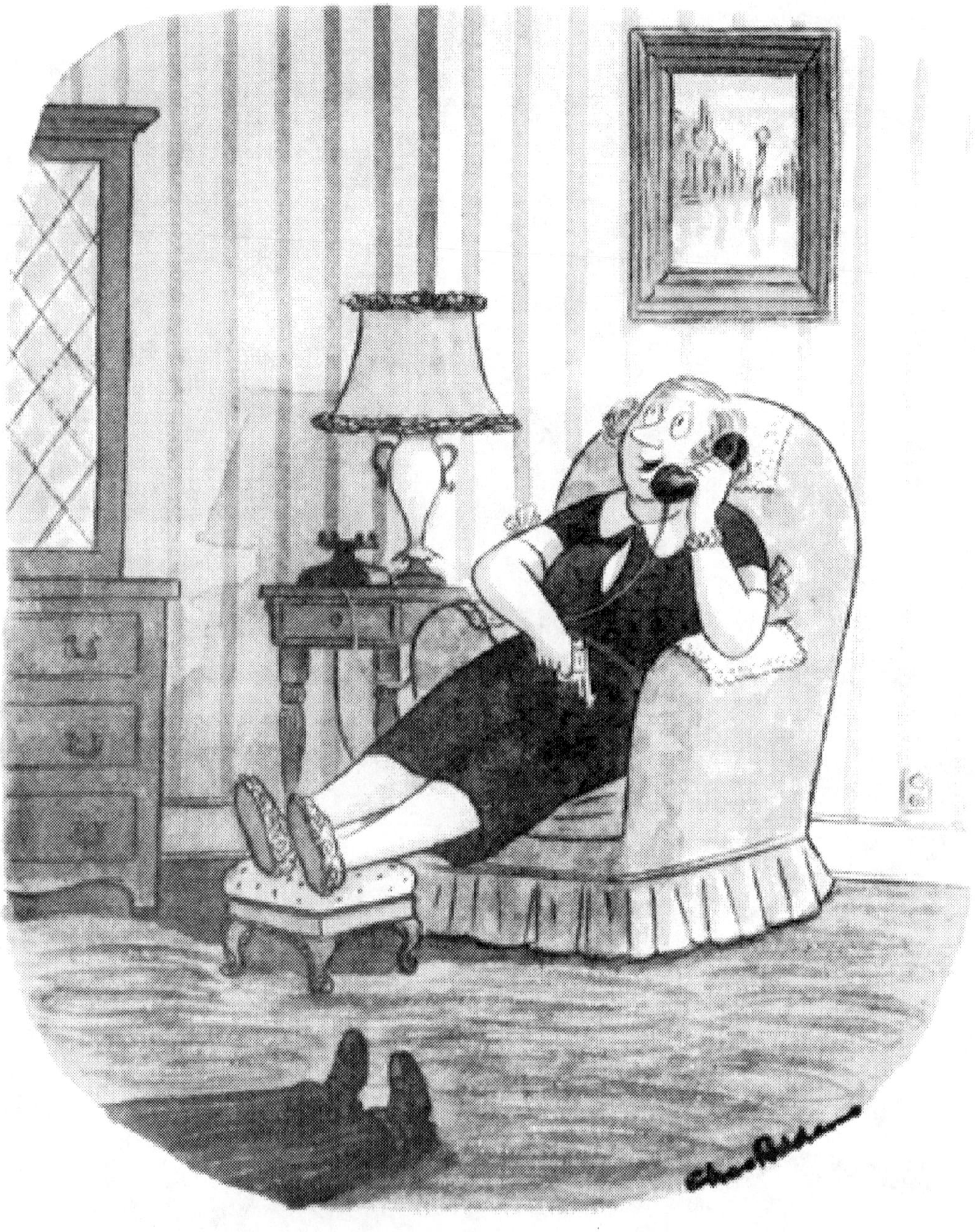

"Nothing much, Agnes. What's new with you?"

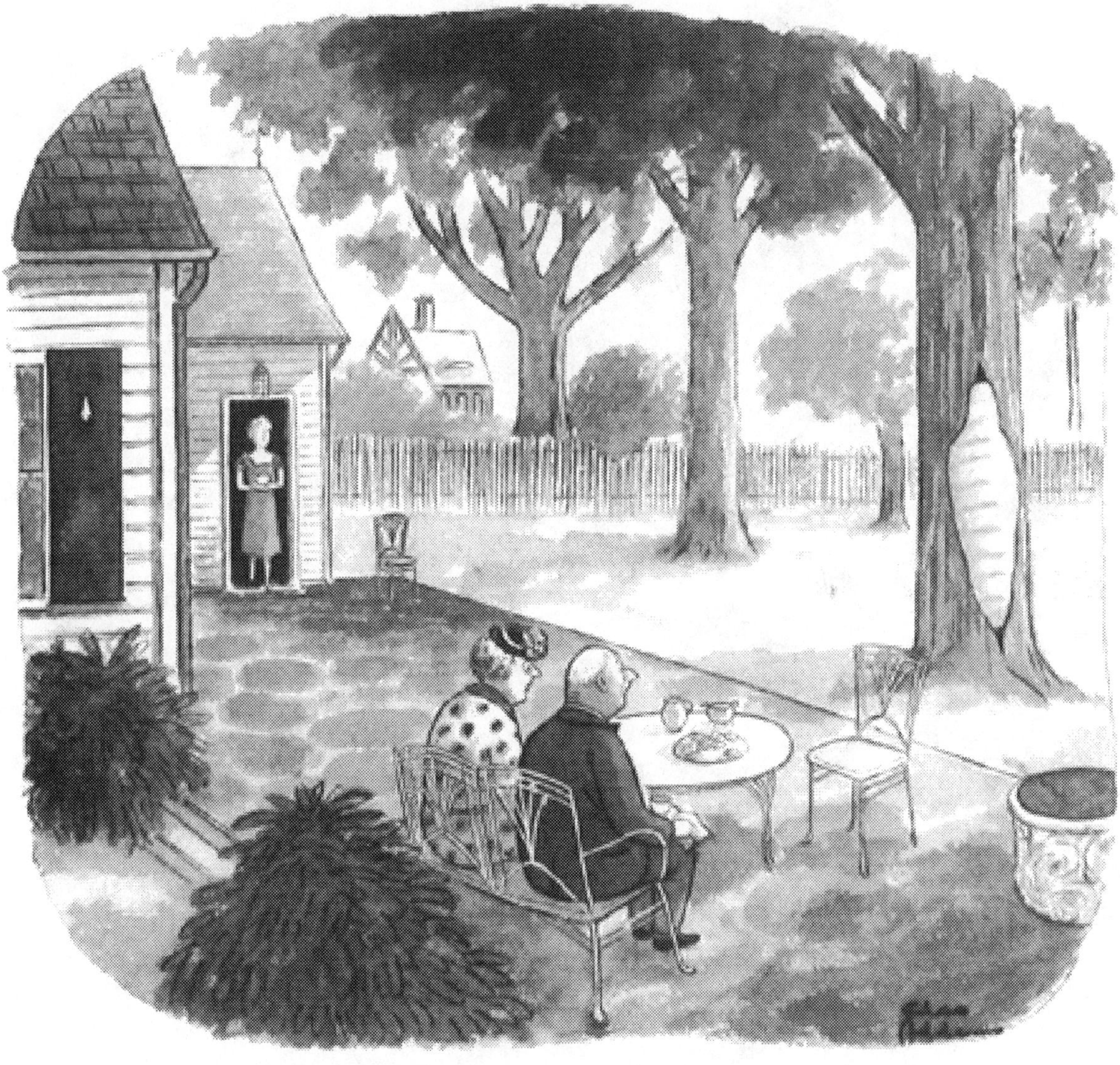

"You know, sometimes I can't help wondering if Mr. Lawrence really *did* go to Chicago."

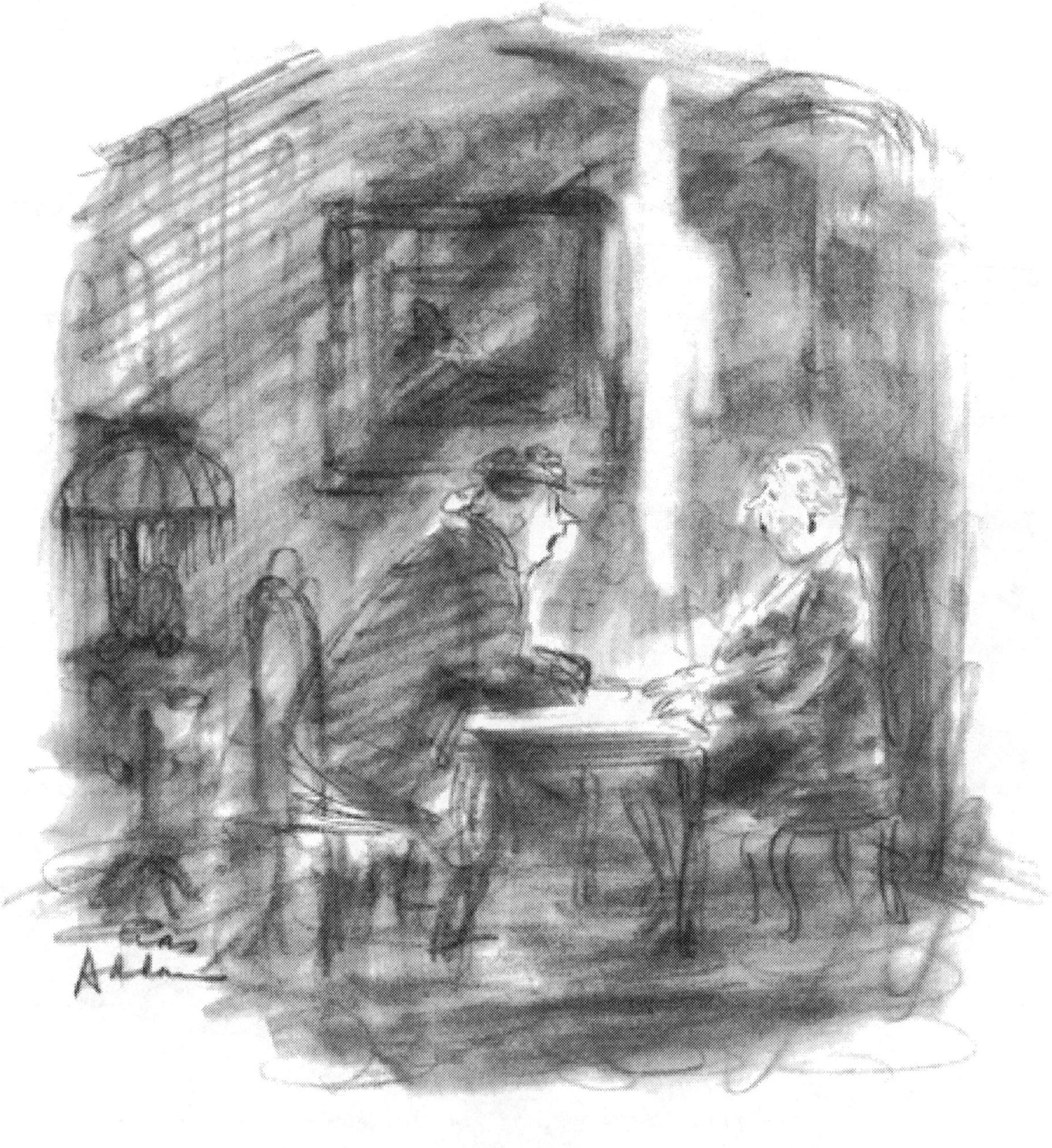

"If that's Harry, ask him where he hid the insurance policy."

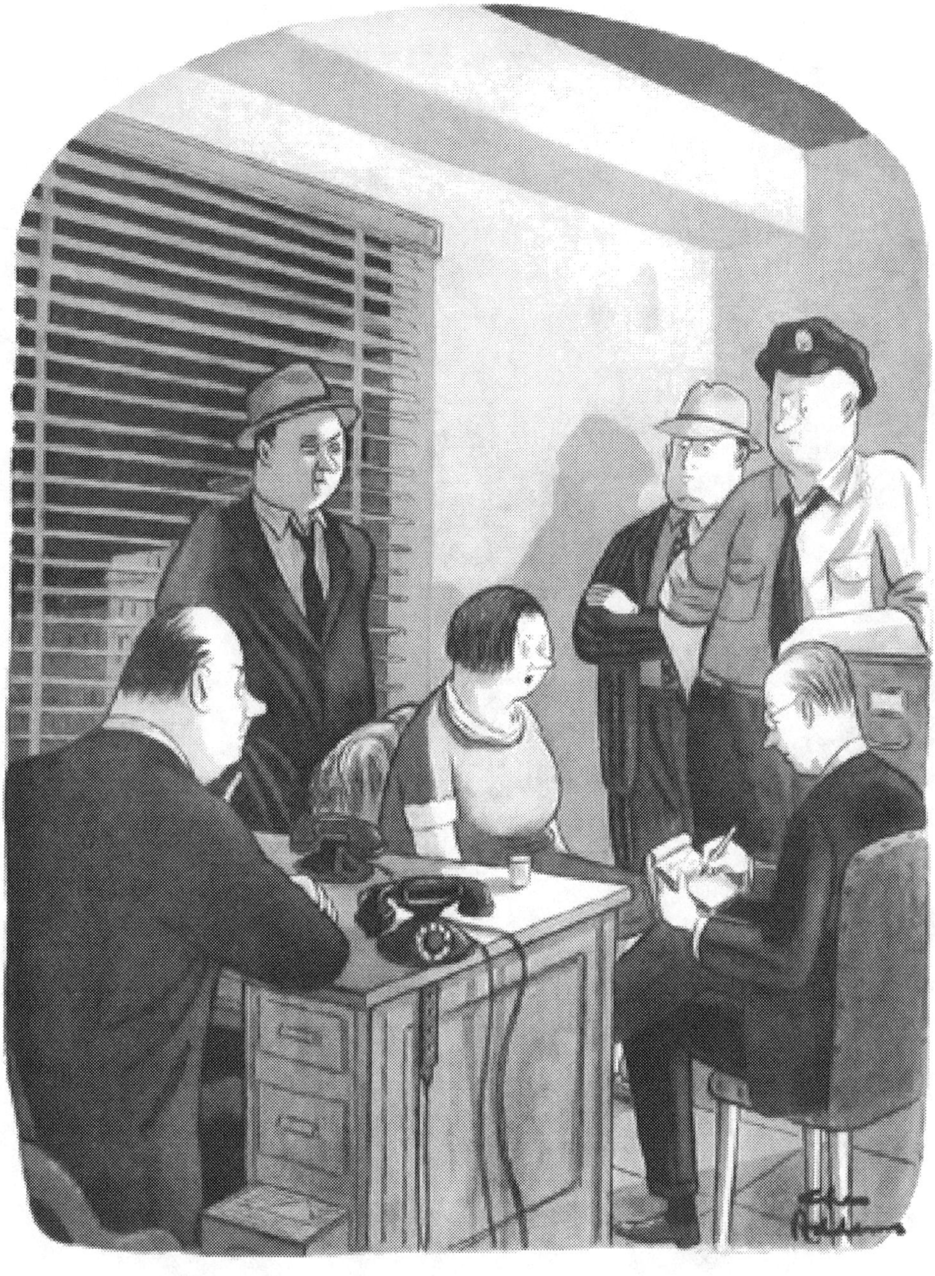

". . . and then I disconnected the booster from the Electro-Snuggie Blanket and put him in the deep-freeze. In the morning, I defrosted him and ran him through the Handi Home Slicer and then the Jiffy Burger Grind, and after that I fed him down the Dispose-All. Then I washed my clothes in the Bendix, tidied up the kitchen, and went to a movie."

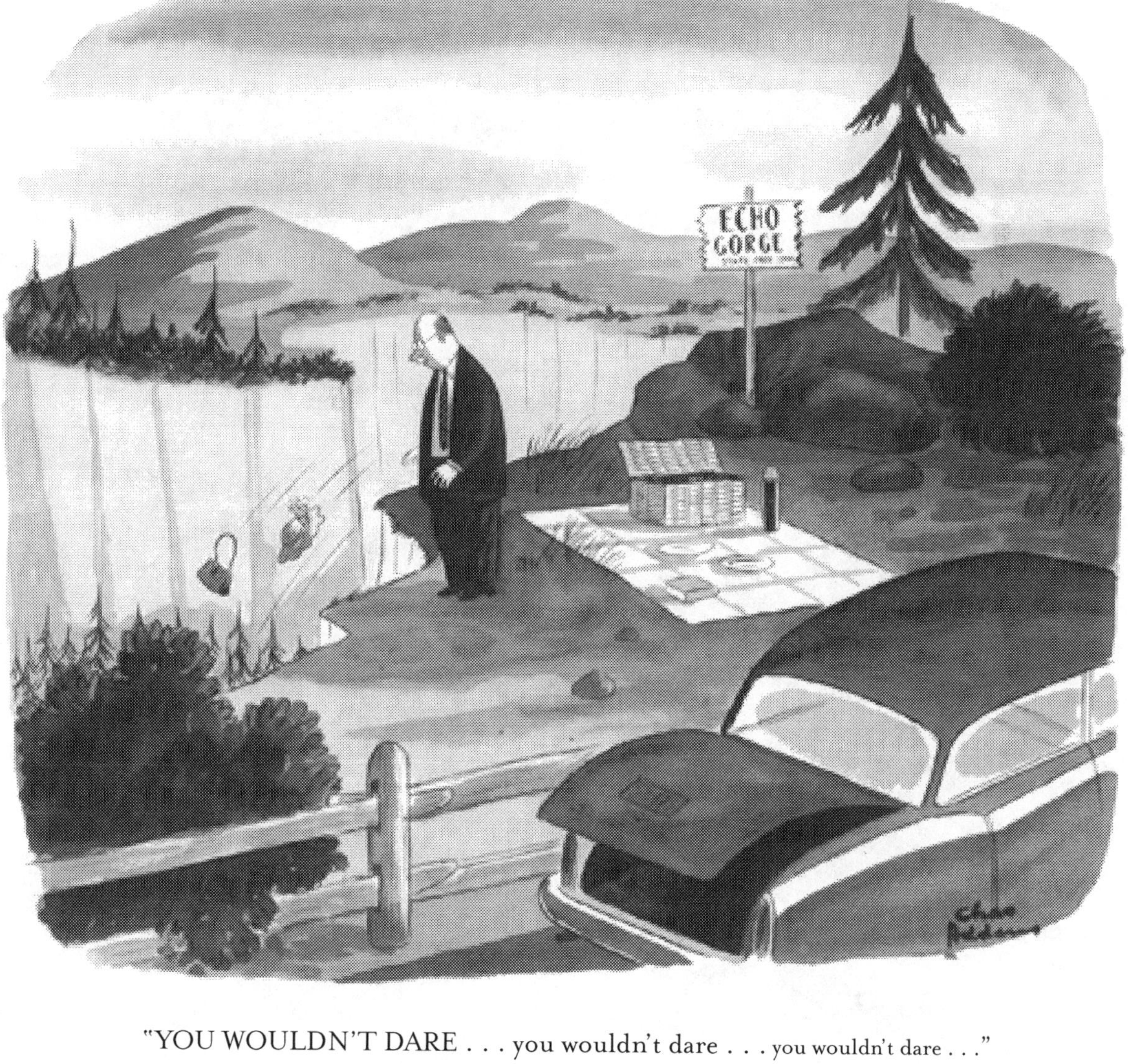
ECHO
GORGE

"YOU WOULDN'T DARE . . . you wouldn't dare . . . you wouldn't dare . . ."

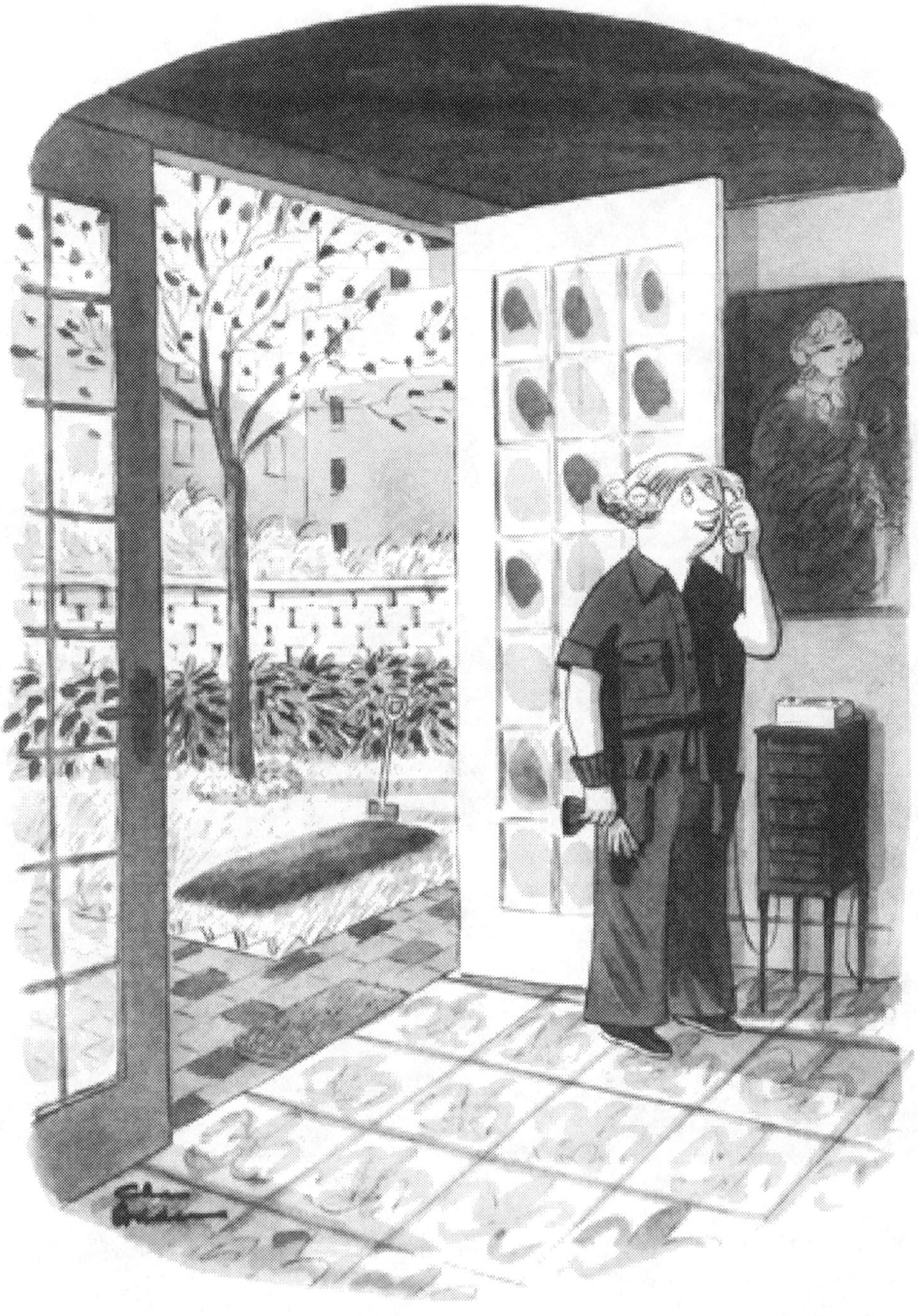

"He's in the garden."

"Chester gave me a rough time during the divorce,
but my lawyer finally got me what I wanted."

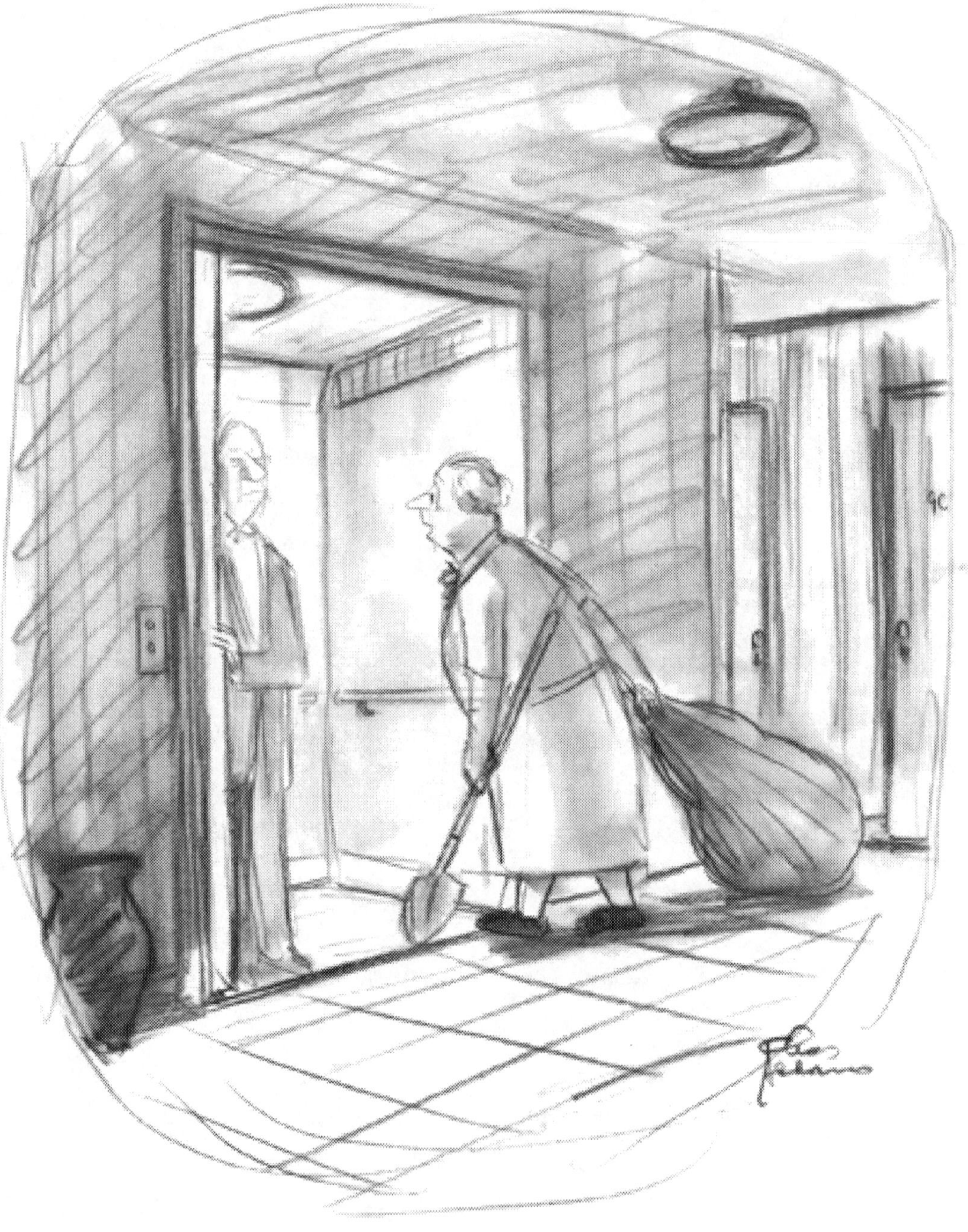

"Basement, Lou."

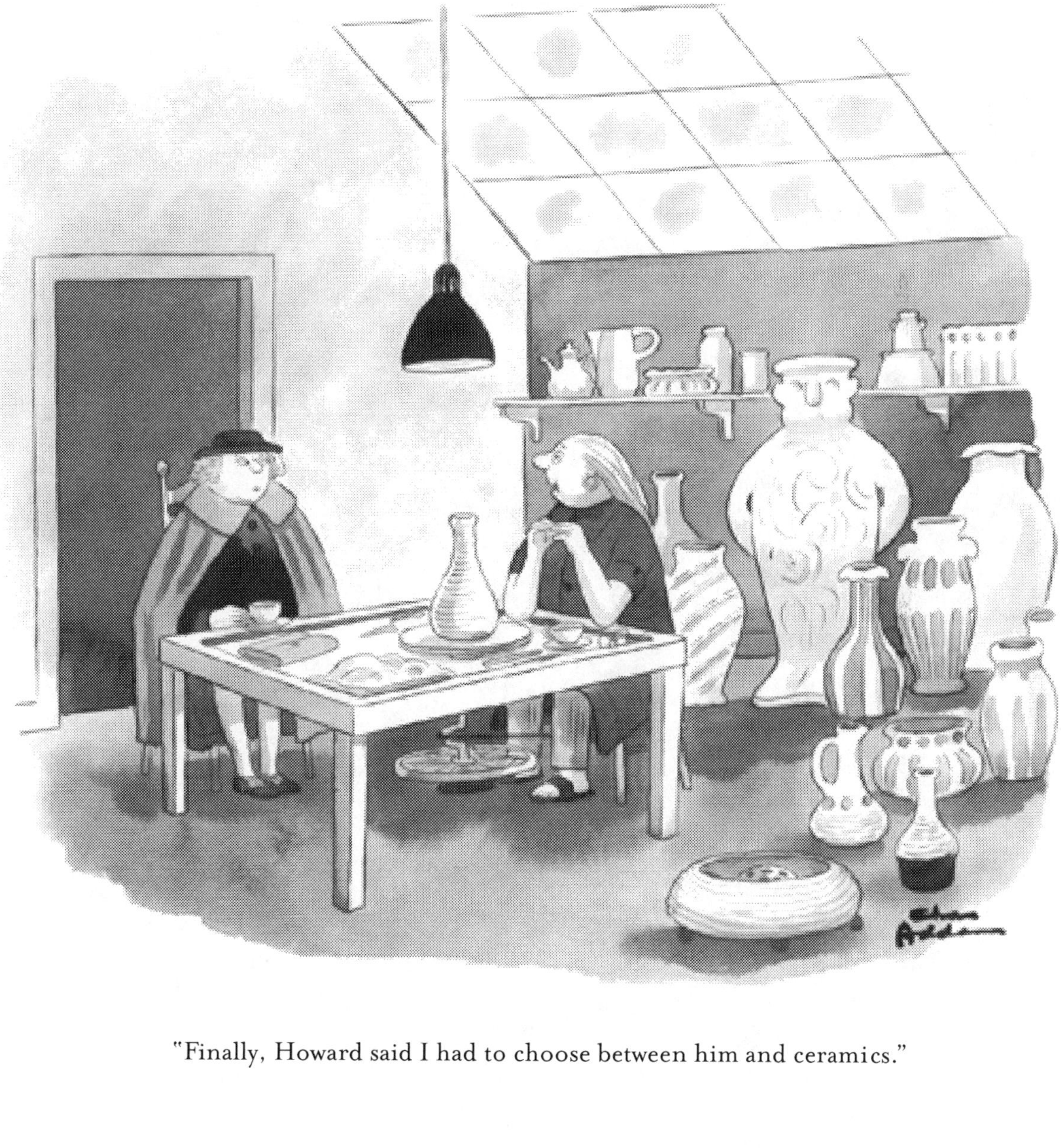

"Finally, Howard said I had to choose between him and ceramics."

"There simply is no place for a woman on safari."

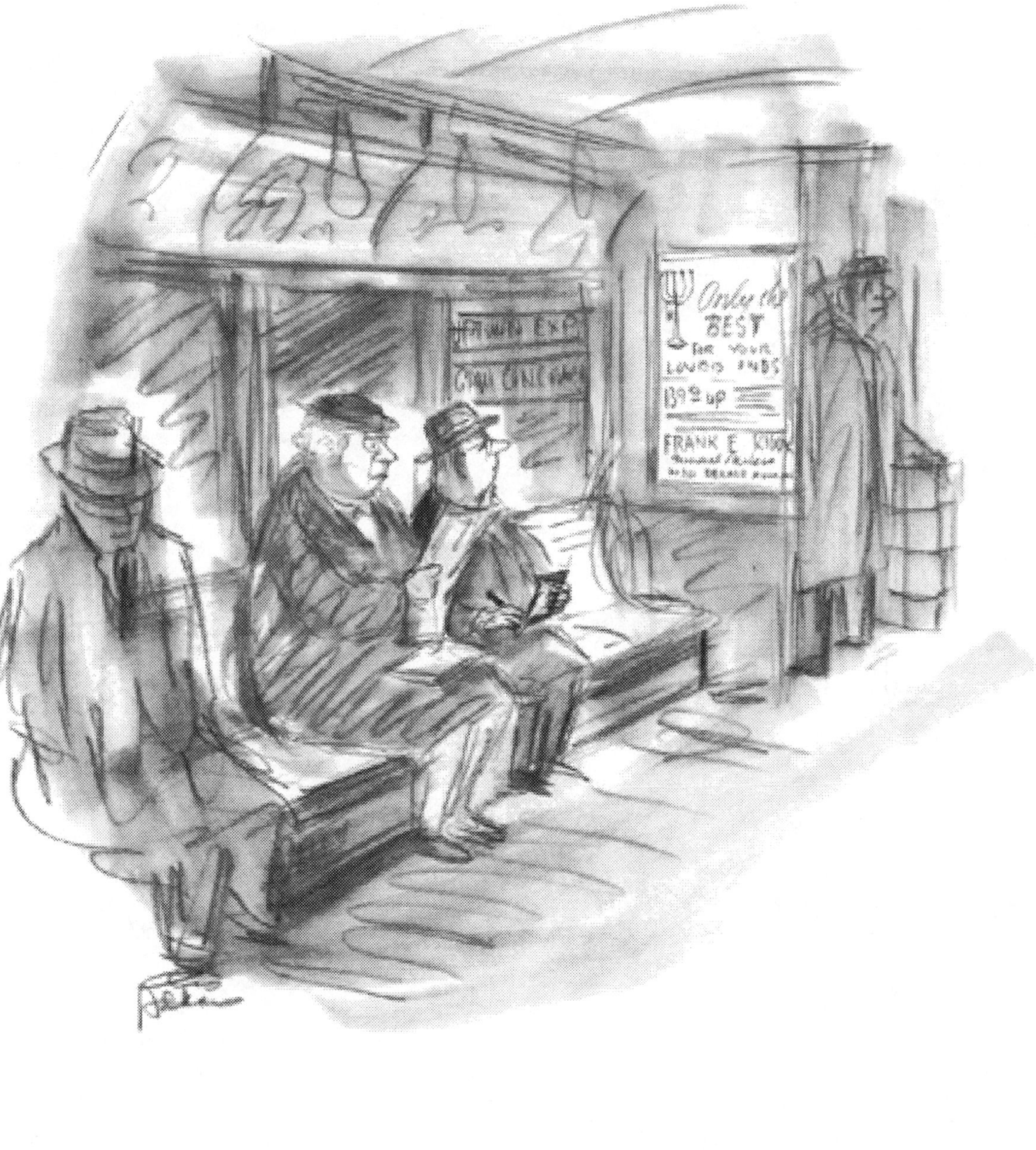
BEST
FOR YOUR
LOVED ONES
FRANK E.

Suicide Pact

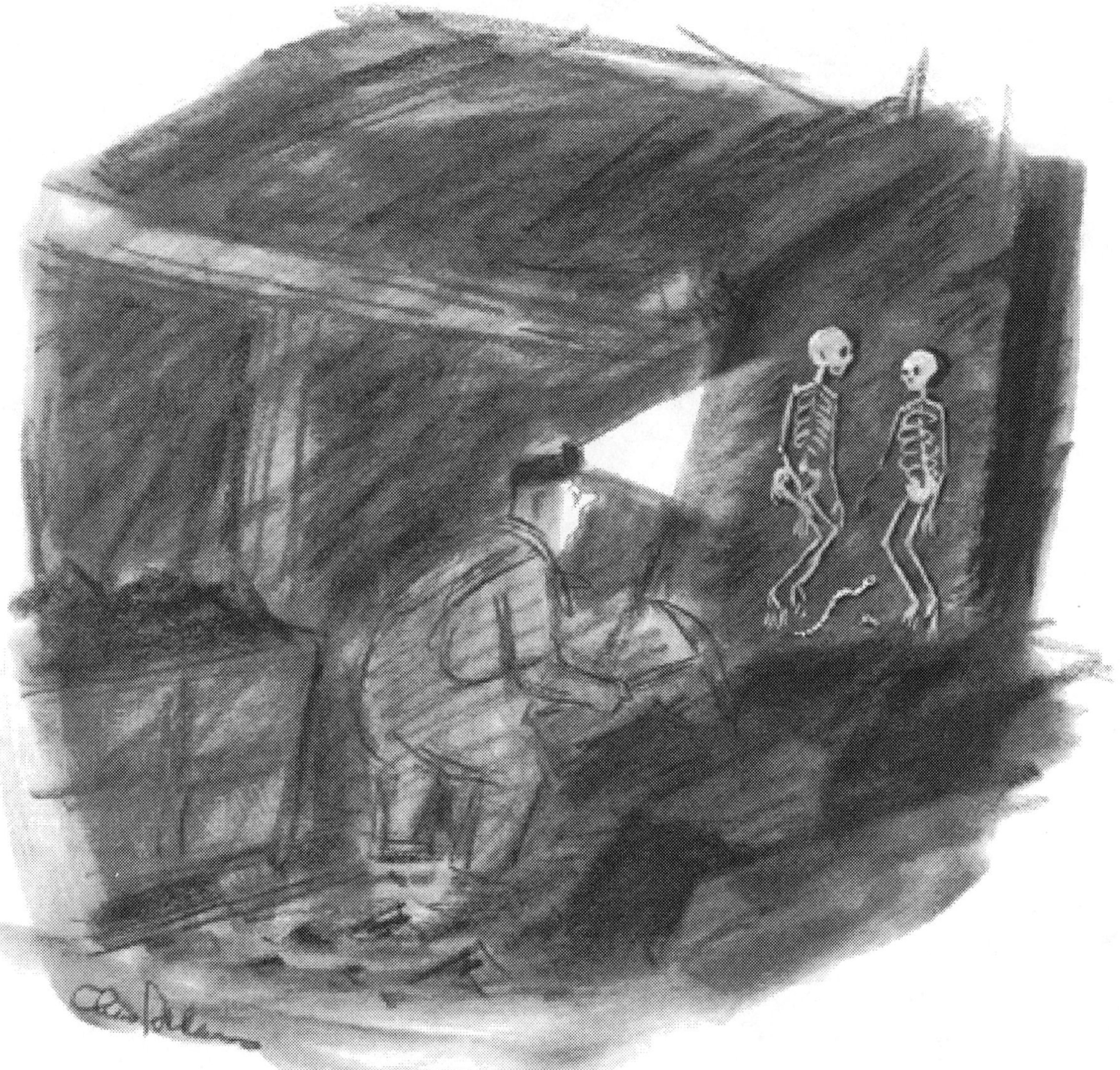

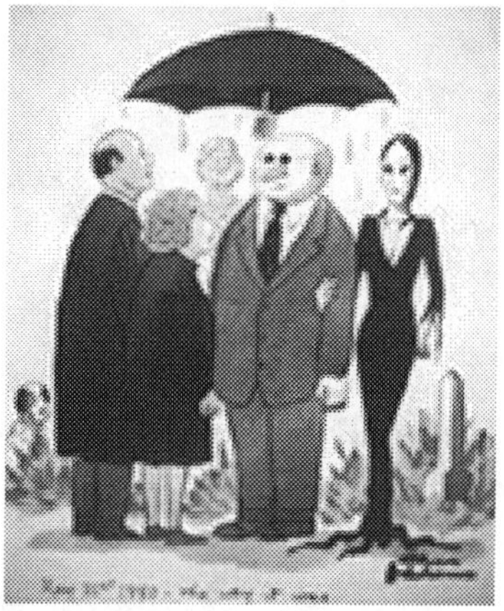

Dates of First Publication

Unless otherwise specified, the drawings were first published in *The New Yorker* magazine.

Page

3 June 4, 1984
4 July 26, 1952
5 January 3, 1942
6 August 10, 1940
7 May 20, 1939
8 September 30, 1985
9 August 14, 1965
10 Previously unpublished
11 January 22, 1938
12 Previously unpublished
13 October 10, 1964
14 Previously unpublished
15 1956, The McClure Newspaper Syndicate
16 Previously unpublished
17 December 31, 1979
18 February 15, 1982
19 Previously unpublished
20 November 27, 1937
21 July 12, 1952
22 October 29, 1979
23 Previously unpublished
24 Previously unpublished
25 1956, The McClure Newspaper Syndicate
29 November 14, 1942
30 March 9, 1957
31 October 3, 1955, The McClure Newspaper Syndicate
32 May 24, 1947
33 December 24, 1979
34 October 26, 1987
35 August 4, 1956, The McClure Newspaper Syndicate
36 Previously unpublished
37 March 6, 1948
38 Previously unpublished

39 March 31, 1945
40 March 31, 1986
41 Previously unpublished
42 September 6, 1946
43 Previously unpublished
44 Previously unpublished
45 Previously unpublished
46 December 1, 1945
47 Previously unpublished
48 Previously unpublished
49 Previously unpublished
50 Previously unpublished
51 March 29, 1982
52 July 22, 1985
53 February 14, 1959
57 February 10, 1940
58 February 17, 1951
59 October 21, 1974
60 January 28, 1950
61 September 29, 1980
62 March 12, 1949
63 September 13, 1941
64 April 16, 1984
65 June 23, 1956, The McClure
      Newspaper Syndicate
66 June 20, 1942
67 March 5, 1960
68 Previously unpublished
69 October 27, 1980
70 September 5, 1959
71 October 26, 1981
72 Previously unpublished
73 August 28, 1948
74 July 3, 1978
75 Previously unpublished
76 Previously unpublished
77 February 20, 1971
78 January 5, 1987
79 November 12, 1956, The McClure
      Newspaper Syndicate
80 Previously unpublished

81 January 30, 1989
82 Previously unpublished
83 Previously unpublished
87 Previously unpublished
88 1956, The McClure Newspaper
      Syndicate
89 August 19, 1950
90 July 28, 1951
91 November 16, 1940
92 April 2, 1949
93 November 17, 1951
94 May 28, 1938
95 Previously unpublished
96 Previously unpublished
97 November 9, 1946
98 July 15, 1950
99 July 7, 1975
100 April 27, 1963
101 September 9, 1950
102 1950, *Monster Rally*
103 January 18, 1941
104 June 1, 1963
105 October 16, 1937
106 December 3, 1949
107 January 24, 1942
108 January 17, 1959
109 July 23, 1949
113 April 2, 1955
114 August 24, 1940
115 Previously unpublished
116 December 5, 1942
117 February 19, 1955, The McClure
      Newspaper Syndicate
118 May 17, 1941
119 May 14, 1949
120 February 25, 1956
121 Previously unpublished
122 January 15, 1938
123 April 25, 1942
124 May 1, 1989
125 January 7, 1961

126 Previously unpublished
127 September 17, 1956, The McClure Newspaper Syndicate
128 June 10, 1944
129 Previously unpublished
130 November 29, 1947
131 Previously unpublished
132 Previously unpublished
133 July 12, 1947
134 Previously unpublished
135 June 7, 1952
139 September 10, 1956, The McClure Newspaper Syndicate
140 Previously unpublished
141 March 27, 1978
142 May 26, 1956, The McClure Newspaper Syndicate
143 Previously unpublished
144 March 30, 1957
145 March 30, 1957
146 December 5, 1955, The McClure Newspaper Syndicate
147 Previously unpublished
148 January 19, 1952
149 June 26, 1948
150 Previously unpublished
151 October 30, 1948
152 May 25, 1987
153 September 7, 1955, The McClure Newspaper Syndicate
154 September 26, 1977
155 Previously unpublished
156 Previously unpublished
157 May 11, 1981
158 Previously unpublished
159 Previously unpublished
160 March 24, 1945
161 Previously unpublished
163 Previously unpublished*

(*Note: Addams painted this piece in color on the occasion of his wedding in 1980.)